THINKING EN ESPAÑOL

Thinking en español

Interviews with Critics of Chicana/o Literature

Jesús Rosales

Foreword by
Rolando Hinojosa-Smith

The University of
Arizona Press

Tucson

Para los que se me han ido: mis padres, Genoveva y Raúl; mi Tía Luz y Tío Chuy

Para los que siguen conmigo: Mi esposa, María, y mis hijos: Angélica, Daniel y Francisco

The University of Arizona Press
www.uapress.arizona.edu

Printed in the United States of America
19 18 17 16 15 14 6 5 4 3 2 1

Cover design by Leigh McDonald
Cover art: *Lalo* by Cici Segura Gonzalez

Publication of this book is made possible in part by the proceeds of a permanent endowment created with the assistance of a Challenge Grant from the National Endowment for the Humanities, a federal agency.

Library of Congress Cataloging-in-Publication Data

Rosales, Jesús, 1955–
Thinking en español : interviews with critics of Chicana/o literature / Jesús Rosales ; foreword by Rolando Hinojosa-Smith.
pages cm
Includes bibliographical references.
ISBN 978-0-8165-3118-9 (paperback)
1. American literature—Mexican American authors—History and criticism—Theory, etc. 2. American literature—Mexican American authors—History and criticism. 3. Critics—United States—Interviews. 4. Criticism—United States—History—19th century. 5. Criticism—United States—History—20th century. 6. Mexican Americans—Intellectual life. I. Title.
PS508.M4R68 20147
810.8'086872—dc23

2014007751

♾ This paper meets the requirements ofn ANSI/NISO Z39.48-1992 (Permanence of Paper).

Contents

Foreword

Interviews with Critics

First of all, this text is not only important but also essential, for it will leave a recorded history of twelve critics at various stages of their careers, their philosophy, their learning, and their commitment to identify, mark, and explain themselves clearly without the jargon that generally tends to exclude the reader. In short, these critics will explain, without explaining away, their reasons for valuing and their thinking about one more segment of this country's literature. The text, then, is not a settling of accounts; rather, it shows the critics at work as they explain and define what constitutes Chicano literature, its impact and its influence in a highly personal way.

A brief digression: The inclusion of Juan Bruce Novoa's views was curtailed by his untimely death. However, he has left us his literary stance via his own numerous articles and via the publication, with the University of Texas Press, of the very first interviews with Chicano writers, whose names the literary critics will refer to in this work.

It is always a pleasure to learn about the lives of the critics, many of whom I know, have worked with, and have read through the years. It comes as a happy surprise to learn of their backgrounds, the influences they have undergone in their academic careers, and how their views and opinions have influenced younger critics. As a result, this publication is of great value to the reader, who can take in how familial background, education, and social and political beliefs inform the many differences within each of the critics' viewpoints; this approach not only makes for highly interesting discoveries but also ensures the absence of lockstep opinions. As has been written, a life without contradictions and differences is a dull life indeed. Happily, that is not the case here.

This volume's interview with the recently deceased Luis Leal has been a happy choice, for it was he who, in the mid-1970s, in an essay on Chicano literature in the early days of Nicolás Kanellos's literary journal *Revista Chicano-Riqueña*, made his debut with his influential article, "Mexican American Literature: A Historical Perspective," that, in academic terms, legitimized Chicano literature. He was influential in bringing knowledge of Latin American literature into the academy through his direction of no less than forty doctoral theses during his long, productive, and illustrious career at the University of Illinois at Urbana-Champaign. That he later directed other theses at the University of California, Santa Barbara, and during his visiting professorship at Stanford is widely known and requires no further comment here. Such is the caliber of the critics chosen by Professor Jesús Rosales, the editor of this publication.

Dr. Rosales's inclusion of Drs. Rosaura Sánchez, Erlinda Gonzales-Berry, and María Herrera-Sobek was no accident. They were undoubtedly the earliest Chicana scholars to influence future generations of women scholars.

Hailing from a working-class background, Sánchez experienced racial discrimination as a child, as a teen, and during her doctoral studies at the University of Texas at Austin. As the reader will learn, Sánchez fought back and graduated, going on to teach at the University of California, San Diego. California's gain was the State of Texas's loss.

That racial slurs and mistreatment are harmful to one's psyche and well-being is common knowledge among minorities, and let it be understood that the group of critics gathered here faced it as well. Its mention and citing by the interviewees is a given.

The important matter to remember is that each critic, by whatever means, has overcome those difficult times between childhood and adulthood. This is no mean feat, and Erlinda Gonzales-Berry's New Mexican background has served her as a creative writer; coupled with a clear mind, these experiences, as the readers will see, have enabled her to write forcefully and to the point. Although she has been living for some decades in the Pacific Northwest, her New Mexico roots are not forgotten.

The Mexico-born María Herrera-Sobek underwent a different and at times a more difficult trajectory. First, she had to acculturate to life in the United States by learning English while retaining her Spanish. Second, she had to adopt English as the language of her profession and thus take steps to assimilate, without giving up her traditional lifestyle. Invited to innumerable foreign and domestic universities, Herrera-Sobek is an enviable ambassador of good will and sound scholarship. In addition to this enviable record, she has served as an administrator at the University of California, Santa Barbara, while maintaining her literary scholarship.

In this regard, she shares an affinity with yet another foreign-born Chicano, Professor Francisco Lomelí, born and raised in the State of Zacatecas. His publications, through the years, have contributed lasting scholarship to Chicano/a studies. He performed a great service when, on top of his teaching assignments and scholarly work, he served, ably and gladly, as Luis Leal's cicerone when the old soldier began to falter. His inclusion here is well earned.

Publication is always a risky business; the early *El Grito*, out of the University of California, Berkeley, served our literature well until its departure from the literary scene in 1974. Unfortunately, Justa Publications met the same fate, although it did manage to publish important works despite its brief life. At Indiana University Northwest, in Gary, Nicolás Kanellos founded *Revista Chicano-Riqueña* and maintained its high standards with little to no funding; the move to the University of Houston saw Dr. Kanellos bloom, and, in many ways, saw to it that Chicano literature not only survived but also flourished. *Revista Chicano-Riqueña* (later renamed *The Americas Review*) lasted for more than two decades and its impact led to the founding of Arte Público Press at Houston. Due, then, to Dr. Kanellos's drive and intellect, Arte Público is the oldest Latino/Latina publishing house in the United States. His tireless efforts to include a wide representation of the Houston community have bolstered the press and opened opportunities to up-and-coming young writers as well as writers of children's literature, thus broadening the press's scope. From a historical viewpoint, the University of Houston's

Recovering the U.S. Hispanic Literary Heritage Project has provided decades upon decades of publications from nationwide sources that present the history and literature of Spanish-speaking American citizens, which has been long neglected by majority presses.

Most of us lead interesting lives, some of us lead exciting ones, and still others seem to lead more than one: A first-class jai alai pelotero in his youth, Gary Francisco Keller went on to earn his doctorate at Columbia University and to teach at a number of universities in the East and Midwest before sinking his roots in Arizona, where he is a chaired professor at Arizona State University and the full-time publisher of Bilingual Review/Press. Editor, art critic, classroom professor, and highly esteemed scholar of Mexican history, with special reference to the Mexican Revolution of 1910, Keller has also proved his worth as a film critic. Tireless and productive, Keller was an early champion of Chicano literature and is highly respected for his unceasing production of high-quality criticism.

Another worthy contributor to this volume, and the first Chicano, in the early 1970s, to publish a scholarly article in a national journal, Felipe de Ortego y Gasca has the distinction of coining the term "Chicano Renaissance," and of being ridiculed for it by those who did not know of the existence of Chicano literature produced and published in New Mexico in the nineteenth century. His scholarship, beginning with his journalistic work and extending to his activities in the classroom, has achieved nationwide recognition.

Poet, scholar, and feminist are all worthy descriptors for Tey Diana Rebolledo, but none fully capture her tireless contributions to Chicano literature. Born to a Mexican mother and a professor father of Peruvian birth, Tey has guided young Chicana scholars since her earliest days, as a protester against the war in Vietnam, during which time she met and marched with César Chávez, to her first assignment as an assistant professor, at the University of Nevada, Reno. Her knowledge of Mexican literature and her scholarship have earned her high honors and she enjoys well-deserved praise among the Chicana scholars of her generation. Finally, her creative writing has a force that cannot be ignored.

When one speaks of highly motivated classroom teachers, Juan Rodríguez comes easily to mind. A professor at Texas Lutheran University in Seguin, Texas, Rodríguez has influenced young Chicanos and helped them achieve their undergraduate degrees, despite dire economic circumstances. A one-time publisher of *Relámpago Press* and a frequent invitee to national conferences, Rodríguez was also a protégé of the late Professor Joseph Sommers. He is to be celebrated for his efforts to maintain the vibrancy of Chicano literature.

Charles M. Tatum earned his doctorate in Hispanic literature from the University of New Mexico. His discovery, publication, and early work on New Mexico men and women writers in the nineteenth and twentieth centuries opened all manner of avenues of study for Chicano scholars. While he claims to have made scant contributions to Chicano literature, his scholarship came at a time when this literature was beginning to seek recognition and, in many ways, his efforts led to its inclusion in the annual Modern Language Association (MLA) conferences, an important step that led to the formation of an interest group in MLA programs. Despite his administrative duties, he continues to publish and to serve, under the guidance of Professor Nicolás Kanellos, as a member of the Recovery Project at the University of Houston.

Our last contributor, Tomás Ybarra-Frausto, hails from San Antonio, Texas, and his birthplace, New Braunfels, can be seen as his first contribution to Chicano studies, principally because the education and cultural life that he obtained during his formative years reflect the marked distinction between the Chicano and the Anglo communities in San Antonio. His contribution to this volume shows how, by maintaining Spanish as his primary language, Mexico and Mexican culture continued to influence his personal life and, later, his university life, as well as his service with the Rockefeller Foundation.

Interviews are arguably the best vehicle for self-revelation. They support the transmission of information that, at times unknowingly and quite naturally, allows the reader to garner personal and deep as well as candid revelations, which the interviewees offer during the course of the interview.

This is not new; to the contrary, it is the natural order of things. Little by little, the interviewees forgot the recording device and worked at remembering times and events in their lives. The length of the interviews allowed our contributors to display their knowledge and supported the closest thing to the truth in any conversation: long-hidden, long-forgotten memories and events came gushing out as easily as water through a sieve.

This is for the good of all. Why? Because interviews reveal the etymological source of the word by looking inward at one's life, self, opinions, values, and beliefs. Errors may appear now and again with regard to dates or places, but what remains are the memories. Now, these too may be erroneous, but this is not in an attempt to evade the truth. These are natural lapses that may be amended during the course of the interview, and often are.

Interviews, in many ways, bring us closer to the truth than an autobiography does. One speaks in real time; one is not writing and editing one's thoughts and recollections. What is said, is said, and recorded.

In many ways, then, interviews provide access to the *inner view* of oneself. Revelatory? Oh, yes, and to one's profit in learning what makes these important critics tick.

—Rolando Hinojosa-Smith

Acknowledgments

I would like to thank all the critics who contributed to this volume, for their generosity with their time and for making this project possible. A special thank you to Rolando Hinojosa-Smith for writing the foreword and for the unconditional support that he has given me throughout my academic career.

Thanks to my colleagues at Arizona State University for their support and to my dear friends, Professor Ignacio García (Brigham Young University), Professor Javier Villarreal (Texas A&M University, Corpus Christi), and Professor Juan Antonio González (University of Texas at Brownsville) for their encouraging ánimo para darle duro y echarle ganas a todo.

Thanks to Chicano literature for making the study of literature a joy to read and for giving it meaning and purpose in my academic world. Sin ella sería un vil caminante empedernido, caminando desorientado por este complejo y ambiguo mundo académico.

Most of all, I would like to thank mi compañera de vida, María, la que siempre me brinda apoyo, fe y optimismo.

THINKING EN ESPAÑOL

Introduction

Thinking en español

A FUNDAMENTAL TRUTH EMBODIED in Chicano literature is the undeniable influence that Mexican culture has had on its literary history. An important consideration is the role that Spanish plays in its linguistic representation and ethos. Unfortunately, in our time, the presence of Spanish in Chicano literature is ephemeral and illusive, hanging on to its identity "like a loose tooth"—to borrow a line from Lorna Dee Cervantes's poem, "Oaxaca, 1974."* But, regardless of how anemic its presence might seem, Spanish in Chicano literature has been and always will be el hogar or the confidential language of the Chicano. It is the first language most of these Chicanos learned, and even in the most extreme of cases, where Spanish ceases to exist in their private lives, a majority still owns a first or "last name that fights" them—to borrow once again from Cervantes's poem.

In the beginning—1848, the symbolic birth of the Chicanos and Chicanas—Spanish was the primary language spoken by Mexican Americans. Working-class corridistas were narrating tales of Mexican Americans' cultural concerns, which impacted their daily lives in the Southwest. Mission beatas and presidio soldiers were sharing their humble life experiences with hired historians who stored these

* This poem, included in Cervantes's *Emplumada*, deals with the protagonist's painful search for cultural ties with Mexico, specifically with her indigenous past.

testimonies in library archives for others to discover and read. Viejito and viejita storytellers captivated audiences with their oral stories of cu-cuis, brujas, and lloronas that served as moralizing or frightening tales for them to enjoy or fear. Los preparados or educated Mexican Americans, who for the most part were the patrones of the working class, published their poems, testimonies, and novels in newspapers or in publishing houses at the local and national levels. Some wrote in Spanish, others in English. Those who wrote in English were interested in attracting a diverse cultural public as a mechanism for negotiating their survival within the dominant culture. They chose to maintain Spanish as their private language and English as their public one, as evidenced by the late-nineteenth-century works of María Amparo Ruiz de Burton, who wrote two novels in English but drafted her personal letters to her Californio friends in Spanish.* Others, such as Juan N. Seguín and Miguel de Otero, both politicians, in Texas and New Mexico, respectively, also preferred to write in English in an effort to establish a strong economic and political presence among the European American settlers of the Southwest.† Spanish, however, was not completely obliterated, for the patrones needed it in order to perpetuate the ownership and economic control that they held over their peones. The mighty knew how to cleverly cross the cultural spaces of their ranchos and haciendas, step aboard a boat or a transcontinental train to regions outside the Southwest, and mingle comfortably within non-Mexican communities of Midwestern or Eastern cities and towns. They would also send their children to the Catholic holy grounds of Georgetown University, in

* The two novels are *Who Would Have Thought It?*, originally published in 1872 in Philadelphia, Pennsylvania, and later, in 1995, by Arte Público Press, in Houston, Texas, and *The Squatter and the Don*, originally published in 1885 in San Francisco, California, and later, in 1992, by Arte Público Press. The letters, under the title *Conflicts of Interest: The Letters of María Amparo Ruiz De Burton*, were published in book form by Arte Público Press in 2001. All three publications were edited by Rosaura Sánchez and Beatrice Pita. They also wrote an extensive scholarly introduction to both novels.

† Seguín, *Personal Memoirs* (1858); Otero, *My Life on the Frontier, 1864–1882* (1935), *The Real Billy the Kid: With New Light on the Lincoln County War* (1936), and *My Life on the Frontier, 1882–1897* (1939).

Washington, DC, and the University of Notre Dame, in Indiana. These Mexican Americans were truly bilingual, writing business contracts or political speeches in English while sitting at home with the family in the parlor chismeando en español or articulating at the dinner table the mandatory hay que darle gracias a Dios por estos alimentos que vamos a recibir.

As a result of the great number of Mexicans who crossed the U.S.-Mexico border in the first decades of the twentieth century, Spanish continued to hold a strong presence in the Southwest. But soon, the accommodation and interaction periods of Mexican Americans in the United States caused English to overpower Spanish as the dominant language of Mexican American authors such as María Cristina Mena, Mario Suárez, Fray Angélico Chávez, and José Antonio Villarreal, to name a few.

With the arrival of the Chicano movement, working-class Chicanos and Chicanas enrolled at colleges and universities and soon published their academic and creative work in grassroots and established literary journals. The cultural nationalism of the times positioned the Spanish language as a leading form of expression in Chicano literature. Chicano literature written in Spanish in the 1960s and 1970s enjoyed a period of growth and validation. Some authors won national prizes: Tomás Rivera's *. . . y no se lo tragó la tierra* and Rolando Hinojosa's *Estampas del Valle y otras obras*, awarded the Premio Quinto Sol; others international ones: Hinojosa's *Klail City y sus alrededores*, awarded the Premio Casa de las Américas in Cuba. But those glory days were relatively short-lived and were ultimately overshadowed by English, this time for good, as Chicano authors who had previously written in Spanish shifted to write in that language. But, as stated at the beginning of this section, one cannot ignore the influence of Mexican culture on the literary psyche of Chicano literature. Its presence resembles that of la llorona, the legendary Mexican mythical figure that could be anywhere and whose presence never ceases to exist in one's imagination. Like la llorona, Mexican culture will forever lurk in Chicano literature: in themes, in its cultural subtleties, in its use of Spanish (even if it's only a sprinkling of words). English is the mandatory language of choice of Chicanos; it has to be. But the language will never lay an embargo over those who think en español.

Chicano Literary Criticism: Emergence and Affirmation Period (1960s–1980s)

Studies of Chicano literary history, as researched by Luis Leal and other leading critics, concur that its literary background begins with the Hispanic period, which also covers pre-Columbian cultures prior to the Spaniards' arrival in Mexico and up to 1821, when Mexico gained its independence from Spain. The period that Leal identifies as the Mexican period covers the years 1821 to 1848, the year Mexico was defeated by the United States in the Mexican American War. With the arrival of Euro-American settlers to the land occupied by Mexicans came cultural encounters and influences that slowly led to a period of transition that, according to Leal, lasted from 1848 to 1910. This period was followed by a period of interaction, from 1910 to 1942, at which point the Chicano period, which continues to the present, began. It is important to emphasize, however, that Leal divides this period into two parts: 1942 to 1965 and 1965 to the present.*

Spanish was the language the Mexican American population used up to the Mexican period. After 1848, while most working-class Mexican Americans expressed themselves in Spanish, educated Mexican Americans chose to write their creative work either in Spanish, as in the case of Vicente Bernal, Eusebio Chacón, and Daniel Venegas,† or in English, as in the case of María Amparo Ruiz de Burton, Miguel de Otero, and Juan N. Seguín. From the interaction period up to the first part of the Chicano period, it can be concluded that even though Spanish was well represented in the early decades of the twentieth century, for the most part English dominated. This changed with the emergence of the cultural affirmation and nationalism of the Chicano movement of the 1960s and early 1970s.

As far as literary criticism is concerned, it is undeniable that literary critics across the country wrote literary reviews of works written

* These periods of Chicano literature are included in Luis Leal's "Periodización de la literatura chicana," in Leal's *Aztlán y México: Perfiles literarios e históricos*, 44–50.

† Bernal, *Las primicias* (1916); Chacón, *El hijo de la tempestad* y *Tras la tormenta la calma* (1892); and Venegas, *Las aventuras de don Chipote o cuando los pericos mamen* (1928).

by Mexican Americans prior to the Chicano movement. It must be pointed out that María Ruiz de Burton, María Cristina Mena, and Josephina Niggli, among other writers, lived for extended periods of time outside of the Southwest (Ruiz de Burton and Mena on the East Coast and Niggli in North Carolina). All three were very active in the social and cultural life of mainstream communities, and their work targeted that reading public. Others, like Jovita González, worked with respected historians from the University of Texas, and her work was well received by them. In Arizona, the short stories of Mario Suárez were published in the *Arizona Republic,* while in California José Antonio Villarreal's novel *Pocho* was published by Doubleday & Company, a renowned New York publishing house. Critics who read the aforementioned writers must have existed. If we were to read their reviews of these works, however, it is safe to say that they would not have considered this literature to be part of a specific, socially conscious, Chicano literary canon, given that the historical circumstances of both the writers and the critics had not yet been defined.

With this in mind, one can argue that Chicano literary criticism began in the 1960s, with the social activism of the Chicano movement. During this period, a growing number of Chicano students began to attend graduate programs at regional and national universities. Students who expressed an interest in Spanish-speaking literatures found a home in Spanish departments, where they found a cultural ambience that appealed to them, particularly in the use of the Spanish language. They felt a sense of belonging that was absent in many other academic programs, which presented themselves as hostile and uninviting. It is no coincidence that the majority of the founding fathers and mothers of Chicano literary criticism were Chicanos and Chicanas who made their homes in Spanish departments.

Américo Paredes's seminal article, "El folklore de los grupos de origen mexicano en Estados Unidos," published in 1964 and later republished in English, in 1979, as "The Folk Base of Mexican American literature,"* may be considered the beginning of Chicano literary

* Paredes's article in Spanish was published in Lima, Perú, in *Folklore Americano* 14:14. The English version, from which these quotes were taken, was published in Sommers and Ybarra-Frausto's *Modern Chicano Writers: A Collection of Critical Essays*, 4–17.

criticism, for it represented the core of the Chicano spirit and its yearning for identity and acceptance within the mainstream culture of the country. In this article, Paredes argues that by the end of the 1830s ethnic relations between Mexican and European settlers along the Texas border had intensified to the point of creating cultural conflict. Paredes describes this tension as "a blaze stirred up by the daily conflict between the quietism of the Mexican and the power, the aggressiveness, and the foreign culture of the Anglo-American" (7). From these encounters, concludes Paredes, emerges a new Mexican American folklore that forms the base of Chicano literature:

> The shock of cultures and people in a continuing situation of cultural conflict has given Mexican-American folklore the traits which distinguish it from other folklore, including that of Mexico. (12)

However, the first formal intent to establish a corpus of Chicano literary criticism came with José Armas and the publication of *De Colores: Journal of Chicano Expression and Thought: Chicano Literature and Criticism* (1977).* Donaldo W. Urioste and Francisco A. Lomelí, the editors of this issue of *De Colores*, consider that it "represents the first major effort by any journal—Chicano or otherwise—to compile articles strictly on literary criticism" (4). They also stress that even though Chicanos had written for decades, critics had refused to study Chicano literature because "they considered it to be political, cultural propaganda, overly regionalistic, [and] linguistically narrow" (4). In preparation for this issue, Urioste and Lomelí emphasized that one of their primary goals was to "*como chicanizar la crítica*," (4) for they believed that most critics trained at traditional schools did not know how "to interpret the new modes of expression

* José Armas served as managing editor of this journal. The quotes that follow are taken from the issue dedicated to Chicano criticism: *De Colores: Journal of Chicano Expression and Thought: Chicano Literature and Criticism*, vol. 3, no. 4, p. 4. In 1976, Lomelí and Urioste coedited a bibliography titled *Chicano Perspective in Literature: A Critical and Annotated Bibliography*, also published by Pajarito Publications.

inherent in Chicano literature" (4). In other words, "*chicanizar la crítica*" requires knowing

> how to promote the idea of dealing with our literature in its own terms in order to arrive at comprehending its merits and flaws. We feel that this concept will propagate further studies that can focus on tapping and deciphering elements unique to our literary expression. (4)

The editors also point out that the journal was innovative because it was aggressive in promoting an emerging Chicano literary tradition.

In an essay written for the 1977 issue of *De Colores*, "Role of Artist and Critic in the Literature of a Developing Pueblo," Armas, the journal's managing editor, highlights the cultural determinism of the Chicano movement. Chicano literature is important because, according to him:

> it is a serious reflection of the Pueblo. It is uncommercialized literature because the commercial publishers are not peddling it. It is uncompromised work of integrity that comes from the heart and experiences of a real people. Our literature is the affirmation of a community on the move. In talking about the materials that *De Colores* has published, I acknowledge that we are important not because we publish only great literature, but because we are recording a phenomena, the development of a pueblo at a crossroads. The literature of a people who are deciding its destiny and relationship with the rest of the world. (9)

With this emotional statement in mind, Armas offers five ways in which Chicanos can contribute to the development of Chicano literature: 1) understanding the Chicano status as an undeveloped pueblo within the dominant society that must look within itself to further its development; 2) using literature for the development of the pueblo (it should teach Chicano history and affirm its cultural values); 3) asserting social responsibility in the writing and criticism of Chicanos; 4) acknowledging that criticism must stem from some standard that must develop out of and be relevant to the Chicano experience and its literature; and 5) recognizing that the standard of criticism of Chicano literature must be consciously developed (9–10).

The publication of this issue of *De Colores* laid the foundation of a Chicano literary criticism that augmented the publication of a number of books that appeared in the 1970s and in the following decade, including *Modern Chicano Writers: A Collection of Critical Essays* (1979), *The Identification and Analysis of Chicano Literature* (1979), *De Colores: Journal of Chicano Expression and Thought Volume 5, Numbers 1 & 2: Contemporary Chicano Literary Criticism* (1980), *Beyond Stereotypes: The Critical Analysis of Chicana Literature* (1985), *International Studies in Honor of Tomás Rivera* (1985), *Aztlán y México: Perfiles literarios e históricos* (1985), *Contemporary Chicano Fiction* (1986), *Chicana Creativity and Criticism: Charting New Frontiers in American Literature* (1987), and *Pasó por aquí: Critical Essays on the New Mexican Literary Tradition 1542–1988* (1989), among others. All of these publications conveyed the spirit of the Chicano's urgency to recuperate a literary history that had been lost or ignored by the mainstream U.S. literary canon, and affirmed a Chicano and Chicana voice within the parameters of that canon.

Chicano Literary Criticism: Arrival and Maturation Period (1990s–Present)

It can be said that with the publication of Ramón Saldívar's *Chicano Narrative: Dialectics of Difference* (1990), Chicano literary criticism reached a higher level of maturity. An increasing number of authors continued to publish edited books of criticism, such as José David Saldívar's *The Dialectics of Our America: Genealogy, Cultural Critique, and Literary History* (1991), Genaro M. Padilla's *My History, Not Yours: The Formation of Mexican American Autobiography* (1993), Tey Diana Rebolledo's *Women Singing in the Snow: A Cultural Analysis of Chicana Literature* (1995), and Leticia M. Garza-Falcon's *Gente Decente: A Borderlands Response to the Rhetoric of Dominance* (1998), among many others. A number of books of criticism emphasized the work of individual authors, for example, *Rudolfo A. Anaya: Focus on Criticism* (1990), *Bandido: Oscar 'Zeta' Acosta and the Chicano Experience* (1995), *Miguel Méndez in Aztlán: Two Decades of Literary Produc-*

tion (1995), *Sabine R. Ulibarrí: Critical Essays* (1995), *Alejandro Morales: Fiction Past, Present, Future Perfect* (1996), *Critical Mappings of Arturo Islas's Fictions* (2008), and *Rebozos de Palabras: An Helena María Viramontes Reader* (2013).

Present Chicano literary criticism enjoys a deep sense of sophistication and now has become part of the intellectual class. This is no longer the humble language that voiced the social commitments of the Chicano movement of the 1960s and 1970s. Chicano literary criticism has entered an open arena of criticism that boasts a wide range of complexities and upper-class barrio logos. Chicano literary criticism has arrived and matured, but in the process it has negotiated part of its identity, for now it is housed under the same oversized umbrella that shelters other Latinos or Hispanics in the United States.

Efforts to globalize Chicano literary criticism have become mandatory and are trying desperately to keep pace with the ceaseless changes in our transnational realities. At the national level, the fact that Chicano literature is part of the American (U.S.) literary canon, and that it is written mostly in English, makes it logical and practical to compare it with other ethnic literatures of the country. Two examples that voice this transcultural comparison come to mind: José F. Aranda Jr.'s *When We Arrive: A New Literary History of Mexican America* (2003) and Marta E. Sánchez's *"Shakin' Up" Race and Gender: Intercultural Connections in Puerto Rican, African American, and Chicano Narratives and Culture (1965–1995)* (2005).

Aranda states that his study is an attempt to create a dialogue between Chicano studies and American literary history for the purpose of clarifying "the interrelationships between Chicano/a literature and mainstream literary discourse" (ix–x).* His goal is to foster "a diverse readership, with diverse needs and expectations" (x). Aranda explains the purpose of his work as follows:

> The critical aim of this book is not to deconstruct Anglo American Puritanism as much as it is to integrate Early American Studies with Chicano/a Studies. Only by revising the symbolic

* The following quotes are taken from Aranda's book *When We Arrive: A New Literary History of Mexican America*.

> content of American literary history can one hope to present questions of authorship, canon formation, and of revision. I seek to further José David Saldívar's argument (in *Border Matters*) to respatialize the field of American Studies by way of a knowledge base that is Mexican and Mexican American, and acutely conscious of the significance of the U.S./Mexican border to American culture, history, and politics since 1848. (xvi)

In an effort to reach this goal, Aranda divides his chapters among the works of Mexican American authors María Amparo Ruiz de Burton, María Cristina Mena, Daniel Venegas, Américo Paredes, Jovita Gonzáles, Luis Pérez, and José Antonio Villarreal. In chapter 5, "From Camelot to Barrio on a Hill: Contemporary Chicano/a Literature and the Puritan Crucible," Aranda compares American colonial literature and Chicano literature and discusses the "interrelationships" that exist between Cotton Mather and Pat Mora, Michael Wigglesworth and Lorna Dee Cervantes, and Edward Taylor and Gary Soto.

Sánchez's comparative study of Chicano literature studies the differences between Chicano literature and the literature of other ethnic groups in the United States, in this case, those of Puerto Ricans and African Americans. Furthermore, the book explores the relation that one has over the other, and most importantly, the relation it has with the American dominant culture. Sánchez identifies her comparative approach as "intercultural." According to her, this word

> signals a relatively recent rubric of social and literary analysis that posits cultures in contact. Rather than the most common label "multicultural" that characterizes contemporary discussions about racial and cultural diversity, I prefer "intercultural" to describe the approach I take to the three core literary texts and the writings of the intellectuals who initiated controversial discussions about the groups. While multi- suggests a "plural" array of cultures, inter- emphasizes the dimensions of cultural contact I want to stress—that cultures are relational, that cultures are interdependent and interactive, and that cultures are neither discrete nor pure. . . . Better than "multicultural," "intercultural" bespeaks the way communities situate

> themselves and the ways they are situated by each other and by the dominant Anglo communities. It also highlights textual space as a contestatory site where readers negotiate meaning in the context of literatures and cultures other than their own. (7)*

Sánchez's book focuses on the years "1965 and 1995" and studies three works by Puerto Rican, African American, and Chicano writers: *Down These Mean Streets*, *Manchild in the Promised Land*, and *The Autobiography of a Brown Buffalo*, respectively. In a sense, this type of effort to incorporate a connection with other ethnic groups was not uncommon, as Chicanos actively participated in the efforts of other ethnic minorities in this country to win civil rights.

It is clear that Chicano literary criticism changes as a function of the unpredictable nature of its challenges. The globalization of Chicano literature will surely lead Chicano criticism to reach heights that in the past seemed insurmountable. One wonders if the persistent use of Spanish in Chicano texts and criticism will become an impediment to this ambitious process.

Critics of Chicana/o Literature Interviewed for This Book

In the introduction to one of the early anthologies published on Chicano literature, *Literatura Chicana: Texto y contexto / Chicano Literature: Text and Context* (1972), the editors, Joseph Sommers, Tomás Ybarra-Frausto, and Antonia Castañeda Shular, in an effort to explore the validity of Chicano letters, questioned the lack of publications of Chicano literature by mainstream editorial houses. They came up with the following historical and sociological reasons for this lack:

> The scarcity of Chicano literature is primarily the result of an exclusionist and intolerant American society that has maintained

* M. Sánchez, *"Shakin' Up" Race and Gender: Intercultural Connections in Puerto Rican, African American, and Chicano Narratives and Culture (1965–1995)*, 7.

> a purist and static view of literature. The basis for what is literarily valid and thereby publishable has been the degree of conformity to pre-established literary, ideological and linguistic norms—norms which reflected the interests of the groups in power. . . .
>
> Another factor to consider in the treatment of Chicano literature is the unique historic circumstance of Chicanos with respect to Mexico. The Spanish-speaking population in this country was linguistically, culturally, and literarily bound first to Spain, then to Mexico. (xxv–xxvi)

This statement summarizes the Chicano ethos of the 1960s and 1970s. Chicano literature did, in fact, exist before the Chicano movement but was ignored and mapped out from the American literary tradition. The connection that the movement had with Spanish, Latin American, and Mexican culture made it appealing for new academic students of literature to enroll in Spanish departments across the country, where Chicanos were able to study Mexican culture and improve their Spanish language skills.

This book of interviews focuses on the critics who pioneered the academic study of Chicano literature. The goal is to highlight the lives of select critics of Chicano letters, specifically those who were trained in departments of Spanish and Portuguese at U.S. universities and whose Mexican, Latin American, and Spanish literary studies is a critical and compelling component of their academic formation. The only exception is Felipe de Ortego y Gasca, who studied in the Department of English at the University of New Mexico. However, he was also influenced by Spanish, Latin American, and Mexican literature and is considered a pioneer of Chicano literary history. All the critics wrote their PhD dissertations on Spanish, Latin American, or Chicano themes. In addition, they all played major roles in the formation of Chicano literature, both as scholars and teachers. As scholars, most of them wrote their literary criticism in English in order to survive the demands of tenure and university promotion policies. As teachers, those who taught in Spanish departments were able to read, speak, and *pensar en español.* Writing in English and lecturing in Spanish became a common academic pattern for many of them.

The interview questions were selected to highlight specific facts in the lives of the critics. It is important to connect their personal lives with their academic ones, for like the Chicano authors who emerged in the 1960s and 1970s, most share a working-class background. The questions delve into their personal lives and their academic influences and inspirations, in particular from the Spanish-speaking world, and examine their unique contributions to the growth of Chicano literature. The interviews emphasize the relation between the Spanish language and their academic worlds and seek the critics' opinions on its future survival in Chicano letters. Most of the interviews, originally conducted in Spanish (Kanellos being the exception), were translated into English by the author of this introduction. However, a select number of Spanish words or phrases are included in each interview to maintain un cachito of authenticity to the critics' Mexican and Chicano cultural use of the Spanish language. For the most part the questions are the same, but a certain flexibility is allowed to fit a given critic's personality and unique contributions to Chicano letters. For this reason, some interviews are shorter than others. Some critics also chose to elaborate on their responses more than others did. Hay que reconocer que a muchos de nosotros nos gusta hablar por los codos y otros, en cambio, decir que *en boca cerrada no entran moscas*.

More importantly, this book recognizes the valuable work that these critics have contributed to the formation and growth of Chicano literature, culture, and criticism. A number of books have featured the lives of Chicano and Chicana writers; for example, three volumes of the *Dictionary of Literary Biography: Chicano Writers* are dedicated to Chicano authors (volumes 82, 122, and 209), as are *Chicano Authors: Inquiry by Interview* (1980) by Juan Bruce Novoa and *Conversations with Contemporary Chicana and Chicano Writers* (2007) by Héctor A. Torres, to name a few. On the other hand, there has not yet been a book published on the critics who analyze the work of creative writers. Critics represent la otra cara de la misma moneda. On the one hand, there is the author or creator of the text, and, on the other, there is the critic, the analytical messenger who helps the creator become a household name, at least in academia. And in many cases, critics function as both creators and critics: la misma moneda.*

What follows is a brief introduction to each of the critics interviewed for this project. These introductions serve to highlight their life and their work, primarily the early works that impacted the development of Chicano literature in the 1960s and 1970s. Unfortunately, one significant critic who was invited to participate is not included in this book. Juan Bruce Novoa, who initially accepted the invitation, fell tragically ill and eventually passed away before the interview could be conducted. Bruce Novoa played an integral part in the development of Chicano literature through his numerous engaging literary articles, as well as through his books on Chicano poetry and interviews with leading Chicano authors of his time.† His work has made an indelible contribution to the study of Chicano literary criticism.

The Critics

Erlinda Gonzales-Berry

Erlinda Gonzales-Berry's deep New Mexican roots have played an important part in her interest in the study of Chicano literature from this region of the United States. In 1989 she edited *Pasó por aquí: Critical Essays on the New Mexican Literary Tradition, 1542–1988*, which explores the Hispanic literary tradition in New Mexico. The essays included in this book examine historical literary texts beginning with the Spanish colonial period, including Alvar Nuñez Cabeza de

* The following critics have published novels or collections of short stories: Erlinda Gonzales-Berry, *Paletitas de guayaba*; Rosaura Sánchez, *He Walked In and Sat Down and Other Stories* (2000) and *Lunar Braceros 2125–2148* (2009) (with Beatrice Pita); and Gary Keller, *Tales of El Huitlacoche* (1984) and *Zapata Rose in 1992 & Other Tales* (1992). The poetry of María Herrera-Sobek, Tey Diana Rebolledo, and Luis Leal, and the short stories of Luis Leal and Francisco A. Lomelí have been published in various journals and books.

† Bruce Novoa explores this and other themes in *Retrospace: Collected Essays on Chicano Literature* (Houston, TX: Arte Público Press, 1990).

Baca's *Relación* and Gaspar Pérez de Villagrá's epic poem, *La conquista de la Nueva Mexico*, and ending with essays dealing with several of the most important contemporary writers from New Mexico, including Sabine Ulibarrí and Rudolfo Anaya. Gonzales-Berry points out that the intent of the book is to introduce the work of New Mexican Hispanic writers to the general public and to provide a different interpretation of the historical and social events that determined the multicultural character of the region. Her own contribution to the collection, "Vicente Bernal and Felipe M. Chacón: Bridging Two Cultures," examines the discourse of resistance and assimilation, as well as the contradictions that pioneer Hispanic writers from this period faced in regard to their historical realities. Gonzales-Berry specifies: "On the one hand, they felt pressed to prove that they were morally and intellectually fit to join the new order. On the other, there was the tug of the old ways and the desire to preserve tradition" (197). Their writing, she concludes, "bears a stamp of ambivalence with which they sought to bridge two disparate realities" (197).

The theme of literary recuperation that is associated with *Pasó por aquí* and her essay on the literary works of Vicente Bernal and Felipe M. Chacón offers insight into Gonzales-Berry's overall literary concerns, both as a literary critic and as a fiction writer. Her concern for recuperating and claiming a New Mexico literary past can be traced back to her years as a graduate student at the University of New Mexico. Like many Chicanas and Chicanos of the time, Gonzales-Berry initiated her literary academic career by exploring themes related to Latin American or Spanish writers in her dissertation. But once she was introduced to the emerging field of Chicano literature, she soon changed course and eventually wrote her doctoral dissertation on that innovative subject. The result, "Chicano Literature in Spanish: Roots and Content" (1978), traces the stages of development of the Chicano literary past and the important place that Chicano literature written in Spanish holds within that tradition. In her thesis, Gonzales-Berry outlines the five historical periods as presented by Luis Leal but focuses on the "Chicano Period," a literary period in which she feels Chicano literature emerged and claimed its identity within American literature. The development of this literature, according to the author, occurred in two stages: the first deals with self-analysis, which entails the rediscovery of one's history and the celebration of that historical background and identity; and the second deals with social protest as represented through *chicanismo*, or social change "through the assertion of the values and virtues of one's own culture" (15). These two stages, self-analysis—the rediscovery and celebration of one's history and identity—and social protest, are summarized through the study of Chicano texts written in Spanish and their direct connection to Mexican, Spanish, and Latin American literature.

Gonzales-Berry believes that Chicano literature written in Spanish is part of the Hispanic American literary tradition: the literature pertinent to Mexico, Spain, and the Latin American Spanish-speaking countries, including the Caribbean. She justifies this disputable literary bridge by affirming Chicano literature's binary nature: "while it [Chicano literature] certainly is a product of the Chicano experience in the United States, it not only has its roots in the Hispanic tradition, but is also a conscious attempt to create a spiritual bond with that tradition and as such becomes an offshoot of it" (18). For the Chicano writers who write in Spanish, their literature is a manifestation of their efforts to self-discover and self-define. By returning to the language of their cultural past, they become "cultural guerrillas" (29), trying to save Spanish from their "stammering stage and clothing it in opulent richness" (29). In sum, Chicanos' use of the Spanish language becomes an act of defiance against mainstream culture.

The social concerns voiced in Gonzales-Berry's initial literary projects remain an integral component of her academic work up to the present time. Her latest publication, *Mexicanos in Oregon: Their Stories, Their Lives* (2010), is an example of her continued commitment to resurrecting those voices from the present that are vulnerable to an uncertain future. That same commitment is evident in her creative work as well. Gonzales-Berry's novel, *Paletitas de guayaba* (1991), deals with the themes mentioned above and is written in Spanish. The Chicano authors that she studied in her dissertation—Rolando Hinojosa, Miguel Méndez, Sabine Ulibarrí, Tomás Rivera, Alejandro Morales, and Sergio Elizondo—undoubtedly inspired her to write the novel. *Paletitas de guayaba* is the story of Marina, a Chicana who travels to Mexico and discovers her Chicanidad (her Mexican American social consciousness). Her journey is a regreso a la semilla, an undeviating journey to her Mexican past, not to recover her mexicanidad, for she always felt very mexicana, but her Chicana identity, which existed while she lived in her home country but somehow had lay dormant or unchallenged in her daily life in the United States.

On a personal level, Gonzales-Berry has deep cultural ties with Mexico and the Spanish-speaking world. Like Marina, Gonzales-Berry also lived in Mexico as a "nueva mexicana," a Chicana that relates intimately with Mexico from a Mexican point of view. In addition, Gonzales-Berry has devoted time to serving many Spanish-speaking communities in the Southwest, including in New Mexico, California (where she worked as a high school teacher), and Oregon (where she currently resides). This lifelong commitment to Mexican and Chicano culture identifies Gonzales-Berry as a true New Mexican *de hueso colorado*, a unique and extraordinary individual who is able to maximize and honor both her chicanidad y mexicanidad with grace and undaunted naturalidad.

María Herrera-Sobek

María Herrera-Sobek was born in a small pueblo in the state of Coahuila, Mexico, and her journey to the United States exemplifies those taken by an endless number of unassuming mexicanas and mexicanos who emigrate to this country in search of a better life for themselves and their children. As a child, Herrera-Sobek lived in South Texas and later moved to Arizona, where she eventually attended college and received a BA degree in chemistry from Arizona State University. Her dedication and terquedad para triunfar led Herrera-Sobek to pursue a PhD in Spanish at the University of California, Los Angeles, where she specialized in Latin American literature. There, she chose to write her dissertation not on an obscure or forgotten author resuscitated from a library shelf but on one of the most celebrated and studied writers from the Spanish-speaking world, Gabriel García Márquez! A bold and daring challenge made to academia by a determined Chicana!

Soon after Herrera-Sobek began her university teaching career, she shifted her literary interest from Latin American literature to Chicano literature. Her awareness of the historical significance of the growth in this literature led her to examine its strengths and its weaknesses, its limitations and potentials. Along with other pioneering Chicano literary critics of the time, she helped to develop and promote it.

Herrera-Sobek is considered a leading critic of Chicano oral history, specifically of the corrido. Her first book, *The Bracero Experience: Elitelore versus Folklore*, can be read as a testimony to her life as a young, working-class Chicana in the Southwest. Her study of the bracero experience acknowledges the contribution these workers made to this country and presents them as hardworking men and women characterized by integrity and optimism. *The Bracero Experience* compares how the braceros are presented in the literature of elite Mexican authors with how the bracero presents himself through personal testimonies and folksongs. In general, the elite sees the bracero as "unpleasant, traumatic, and degrading" (74), while the bracero paints a different picture:

> The bracero . . . saw himself as a man conscious of what he was doing, aware of the dangers and sufferings that awaited him, but imbued with ambition nevertheless, going about life with an adventurous, inquisitive, conquering spirit. No matter what lay ahead of him in this strange, alien country known as the United States of America, he knew he could survive with less exploitation than in Mexico. (74)

This remark serves as a testament to the sixteen bracero men Herrera-Sobek interviewed for her study in 1969, all from Huecorio, Michoacán, Mexico, and to the men she knew from her personal life, including her own grandfather.

Herrera-Sobek's theoretical work on feminism and feminist theory is also important and innovative. She was the first scholar to organize a course on Chicana literature while she was teaching at the University of California, Irvine. The course led her to organize the first congress on Chicana literature, which resulted in the 1985 publication of *Beyond Stereotypes: The Critical Analysis of Chicana Literature*. In 1988, María Herrera-Sobek and Helena María Viramontes edited *Chicana Creativity and Criticism: Charting New Frontiers in American Literature*, the product of the second major conference on

Mexican American Woman Literature held at the University of California, Irvine, in 1987.

In *Beyond Stereotypes*, Herrera-Sobek expresses the need to break away from traditional female stereotypes, specifically Mexican iconic images like la Malinche, Sor Juana, and Josefa Ortíz de Domínguez. This required a reexamination and reevaluation of the Chicana from a woman's point of view. As Herrera-Sobek points out, the idea was "to formulate, to conceptualize, to freeze in a moment of poetic intensity a new vision, a new perspective, a new definition of what the Chicana perceives herself to be" (20).* Herrera-Sobek believes that in spite of all the stereotypes that exist of Chicanas, a new Chicana voice is emerging to challenge and destroy them. Nevertheless, there is still much work to be done and the voices of women will be an important part of this process. She argues that it is imperative for the Chicana to "explore the intricacies of her womanhood, her intimate self, and her soul and provide the world with a true image of who she is" (24).

Beginning with its rebirth in 1960s, Chicano literature, according to Herrera-Sobek, has always had a promising future. At the time, she felt that there were two prevailing currents of thought in the study of Chicano literature: a European, American, and feminist discourse, on the one hand, and a discourse that "argues for an emancipation from 'White' literary theoreticians in search for an authentic Chicano Critical course" (34), on the other.† In an article she wrote for *Chicana Creativity*, "The Politics of Rape: Sexual Transgression in Chicana Fiction," Herrera-Sobek comments that her analysis of the work of Cherríe Moraga (*Giving Up the Ghost*), Sylvia Lizárraga ("Silver Lake"), and Sandra Cisneros ("Red Clowns") provides an excellent example of the new perspectives that Chicanas are proving in their analysis of Chicano literature.

Herrera-Sobek's interest in folklore and feminism/literary theory continues to be an integral part of her career, as attested by her celebrated book, *The Mexican Corrido: A Feminist Analysis* (1990), a topic she continues to examine with an emphasis on Mexican *narco*

* The quotes are from Herrera-Sobek's introduction to *Beyond Stereotypes*.

† Herrera-Sobek, "The Politics of Rape: Sexual Transgression in Chicana Fiction," 34.

corridos, and her current projects on feminist theory. These interests operate at the personal level for Herrera-Sobek, who is also an accomplished poet, sharing philosophical themes that explore the personal:

Solitaria*	**Alone**
Solitaria	Alone
como hormiga	like an ant
que busca ciegamente	that blindly searches
su destino	its destiny
así voy	I move along
con pasos	walking
lentos	slowly
titubeantes	tentatively
en esta	in this
esfera milenaria	millenial sphere
que gira velozmente	that spins rapidly
en la oscuridad	in the darkness
de la eterna noche	of the eternal night
sin esperanza	without hope
de algún día	of someday
descifrar	deciphering
el origen	the beginning
y el final	and the end
de esta jornada	of this journey

as well as the social:

Fronteras†	**Borders**
Fronteras	Borders
que se lleva el viento	that the wind takes away
bailan	dance
en el reflejo alucinante	in the hallucinating reflection
de nubes pasajeras	of transient clouds

* Herrera-Sobek, "Solitaria," 9. The English translation is mine.

† Herrera-Sobek, "Fronteras," 90. The English translation is mine.

que cruzan por el cielo	that cross through the sky
libres	unrestrained
se deslizan	they glide
Norte—Sur	North—South
Sur—Norte	South—North
la línea divisora	the division line
inexistente	nonexistent

Like other Chicana/o critics of her generation, Herrera-Sobek has become an inspiring spokesperson for Chicano and Chicana letters. She has tirelessly presented at numerous national and international conferences in Mexico, Spain and other European countries (e.g., France, Germany, Hungary, Yugoslavia, Norway, Northern Ireland, Holland, Austria), Latin American countries (e.g., Uruguay, Venezuela), as well as Cuba, Puerto Rico, Canada, Russia, and Turkey. Herrera-Sobek has indeed achieved a special celebrity status among academics that study Chicano literature and culture, but it is refreshing to see that Herrera-Sobek's stellar academic reputation has not consumed the humility que siente for the common man or woman that defines her work.

Nicolás Kanellos

Nicolás Kanellos was born in New York City to a Puerto Rican mother and a Greek immigrant father. As a child Kanellos traveled frequently between the United States and Puerto Rico, providing him with the challenging opportunity to live the positive and negative experiences of a multicultural world: positive in terms of reaping the benefits of living within several cultures and negative in terms of living firsthand America's lack of acceptance of its minority populations. It was the negative experiences that impacted and shaped Kanellos's academic life. He participated in the Chicano movement of the 1960s and 1970s while a graduate student at the University of Texas and made it his lifetime goal to reconstruct and cement Hispanic/Latino culture as an integral component of the U.S. American experience.

As a result of the lack of literary representation for Chicanos and Puerto Ricans in the United States, as well as of the cultural subtleties that connected these two cultures—as far as social lazos are concerned—Kanellos and Luis Dávila founded in Indiana in 1973 *Revista Chicano-Riqueña*, a pioneer literary journal that served the Hispanic/Latino community for more than twenty years. The goal of this journal was to provide, as stated by its editors, a forum for Chicanos and Riqueños (i.e., all Latinos) to strengthen their cultural ties and to share their creative and academic work, in both English and Spanish. In addition to these goals, *Revista Chicano-Riqueña* also provided material for bilingual education programs and the surging ethnic studies programs at universities across the country that, at the time, was very limited. These materials included special issues and anthologies that featured theater, literature, and la mujer, from the Chicanos and Riqueños experience.

The success of the journal and the ability it offered him to organize special issues and anthologies (in essence, books) encouraged Kanellos to found Arte Público Press in 1979, the oldest and most respected publishing house of Hispanic/Latino literature in the United States. The Press's first published book, Tato Laviera's *La Carreta Made a U-Turn*, was of key importance for the launching of Arte Público: the book won the American Book Award and instantly put the Press in the national literary public eye. Arte Público Press published the works of Chicana and Chicano writers such as Rolando Hinojosa, Sandra Cisneros, Ana Castillo, Helena María Viramontes, and many others who, at the time, were not well known at the national level. In the 1990s Arte Público decided to publish children's picture books as well as young adult novels and anthologies, in both English and Spanish, under the newly founded Piñata Books. Today, Arte Público Press enjoys its position as the leading publishing house and promoter of Hispano/Latino literature in the United States.

Kanellos has published numerous books, and the small number highlighted here will serve as only a sample of his important contribution to Hispanic/Latino and Chicano literature.

Kanellos's passion for theater and for the preservation of the Hispanic Latino literary legacy is embodied in his book, *A History of Hispanic Theater in the United States: Origins to 1940* (1990), the first study to trace the past of Hispanic theater, in particular theater production in Los Angeles, San Antonio, New York, and Tampa. The purpose of this work, according to Kanellos, was to provide a book that would serve as a point of departure for the study of Hispanic theater in this country and of Hispanic contributions to this genre, which has been ignored by mainstream American literature. Kanellos comments:

> The Hispanic tradition in the United States is not one that can be characterized exclusively by social dysfunction, poverty, crime, and illiteracy, as the media would often have us believe. Rather, if we focus on theater, we can draw alternative characterizations: the ability to create art under the most trying of circumstances, social and cultural cohesiveness and national pride in the face of racial and class pressures, cultural continuity and adaptability in a foreign land. All of these can be accounted for in the trajectory of Hispanic theatrical development. (xiv–xv)

Kanellos unquestionably believes that the theater is the most popular and relevant artistic form to the Hispanic/Latino communities in this country. The book's landmark contribution did not go unnoticed, for it was the recipient of three book awards, including one from the Southwest Council of Latin American Studies.

Of equal significance to the Hispanic/Latino literary history is Kanellos's *Hispanic Periodicals in the United States, Origins to 1960: A Brief History and Comprehensive Bibliography*, which he edited with Helvetia Martell. He states that the general purpose of the book was to understand three key manifestations of periodical publication that in turn reflect the essential qualities of the Hispanic/Latino culture in this country: exile, immigration, and nativism. These manifestations, says Kanellos:

> are to be understood as operating simultaneously in a dynamic environment of mutual influence and interrelationship, as exiles, immigrants and Hispanic citizens of the United States often live in the same area, work in the same factories or fields and send their children to the same schools. Furthermore, both Hispanic exile and immigrant communities, in time, evolve into native communities, that is, a national ethnic minority that we

> call Hispanic or Latino today. Hispanic publications reflect these processes and dynamic relationships. (114–115)

Kanellos believes that periodicals will adapt to twenty-first-century technological representations. Furthermore, with the growth of the Spanish-speaking population in this country and its economic and political development, Spanish-language written representation will continue to flourish.

Kanellos's interest in recovering, preserving, and promoting the Hispanic/Latino literary legacy is exemplified by his editing of and contributions to literary anthologies. These anthologies include *Hispanic American Literature* (1995), *The Hispanic Literary Companion* (1996), *Noche Buena: Hispanic American Christmas Stories* (2000), *En otra voz: Antología de la literatura hispana de los Estados Unidos* (2002); *Herencia: The Anthology of Hispanic Literature of the United States* (2003) and *Encyclopedia of Latino Literature* (2008), in which he authored one-third of the entries. But perhaps Kanellos's most enduring legacy is his active endeavor, as director of the nationally and internationally recognized research program Recovering the U.S. Hispanic Literary Heritage Project, to identify, preserve, study, and make accessible documents written by Hispanics/Latinos in the United States from the colonial period to 1960. Kanellos's ambitious goals for such literary recuperation include, as he points out:

> to compile the master bibliography of all works written and published (some 18,000 entries to date); to locate, preserve, index, and digitize portions of all the newspapers published by Hispanics (some 1,700 located to date); to examine, index, and create access to important archives containing Hispanic materials; to fund scholars to research and write about works long forgotten; and to sponsor biannual international conferences on recovery. (30–31)

One of Kanellos's most celebrated Chicano literary findings is *Las aventuras de don Chipote o cuando los pericos mamen* (1928), by Daniel Venegas, one of the oldest Chicano novels written in Spanish and a text that has been invaluable to the study of immigrant literature and the culture of Chicanos and Latinos in border literature studies of the twentieth and twenty-first centuries.

In *Hispanic Immigrant Literature: El sueño del retorno* (2011), Kanellos offers a personal account of the ever present themes of his comprehensive academic work—exile, immigration, and nativism—to which he has devoted his life. The book was awarded the PEN Southwest Book Award for Non-Fiction in 2011.

Kanellos's scholarly achievements have earned him countless awards. These include the American Library Association's Denali Press Award (1996), the American Book Award–Publisher/Editor Category (1989), and the Hispanic Heritage Award for Literature (1986), presented at the White House. Most recently, Kanellos was awarded the Galardón Don Luis Leal, Asociación HispaUSA (2012), in Toledo, Spain, in honor of his lifetime research and his cultural and academic achievements.

Given all of these accomplishments, one can undoubtedly conclude that Nicolás Kanellos has reconstructed and shaped the literary landscape of Hispanic/Latino letters and culture and indeed deserves to be el mero, mero guardián de nuestro pasado literario.

Gary F. Keller

Gary F. Keller was born in California but lived and studied in Mexico City before returning to the United States to attend graduate school and resume permanent residence. Throughout his career, Keller has dedicated his academic research to the Hispanic cultures of the United States, in particular the Puerto Rican and Chicano communities. Keller's major contribution to these cultures, and specifically to Chicano literature, is his founding of Bilingual Review Press and *Bilingual Review/La Revista Bilingüe*. Founded in 1973, Bilingual Review Press publishes scholarly and creative works by Hispanic and Latin American scholars and writers. It also serves as the publisher of *Bilingual Review/La Revista Bilingüe*, an academic journal that focuses on Spanish-English bilingual studies and Hispanic literature. In 1984, Keller and Bilingual Review Press introduced the "Clásicos Chicanos / Chicano Classics" series with the publication of José Antonio Villarreal's *The Fifth Horseman*, a novel originally published in 1974. The purpose of the series, according to Keller, was to dignify the presence of Chicano literature and make it accessible for future generations of readers to enjoy:

> The Clásicos Chicanos / Chicano Classics series is intended to ensure the accessibility over the long term of deserving books of Chicano literature and culture that have become unavailable over the years or that are in imminent danger of becoming inaccessible. Each of the republished volumes in the series will carry with it a scholarly apparatus that includes an extended introduction contextualizing the work within Chicano literature and a bibliography of the existent works by and about the author. The series is designed to be a vehicle that will help in the recuperation of Raza literary history, maintain the instruments of our culture in our own hands, and permit the continued experience and enjoyment of our literature by present and future generations of readers and scholars. (no page number)*

With the "Clásicos Chicanos / Chicano Classics" series, Keller affirms the strong social sentiments initiated in the Chicano literary movement of the 1960s and 1970s. In featuring a series dedicated to Chicano, rather than Hispanic, literature—choosing to title it "Clásicos Chicanos" and not "Clásicos Hispanos / Latinos"—Keller expresses a deep sense of Chicano cultural nationalism and self-determinism. Also, by adding the words "Clásicos" to the series, and by including a scholarly introduction by Luis Leal, an internationally renowned scholar, Keller provided legitimacy to the series. In addition, Keller was careful in choosing José Antonio Villarreal's *The Fifth Horseman* as the text with which to open the series. Villarreal's novel focuses on the Mexican Revolution, a monumental event in Mexican history that would trigger a mass exodus of Mexican immigrants to the United States in the first decades of the twentieth century. This would become one of the most significant events in Chicano history, and what better way of introducing the series than by publishing a novel that glorifies this event and by asking Leal, the

* Keller, "About Clásicos Chicanos / Chicano Classics."

celebrated scholar of Mexican revolutionary narratives and unofficial dean of Chicano literature, to write the introductory essay. To date, Bilingual Review Press has published, besides Villarreal's novel, additional Chicano texts in the "Clásicos Chicanos / Chicano Classics" series: *The Road to Tamazunchale*, by Ron Arias; *The Devil in Texas / El Diablo en Texas*, by Aristeo Brito; *Peregrinos de Aztlán*, by Miguel Méndez; *Estampas del Valle*, by Rolando Hinojosa; *El condado de Belken: Klail City*, by Rolando Hinojosa; *Rain of Scorpions and Other Stories*, by Estela Portillo Trambley; *Barrio on the Edge / Caras viejas y vino nuevo*, by Alejandro Morales; and *Shaking Off the Dark*, by Tino Villanueva, and others.

Keller's interest in Chicano literature also extends to other fields of Chicano culture. In 1985 he edited *Chicano Cinema: Research, Reviews & Resources*, the first critical anthology of Chicano film. In the introductory essay of the anthology, "The Image of the Chicano in Mexican, United States, and Chicano Cinema: An Overview," Keller talks about the need for and existence of such cinema, calling it "a fresh body of water that renews a riverbed which over the years has ranged mostly from dry to stagnant" (13).* Relevant to this interest is Keller's passion for the iconic Mexican images of the *revolucionario* and the *adelitas* in Mexican films. For several years he has organized important international conferences at Arizona State University on this theme, resulting in the publication of *Good Bandits, Warrior Women, and Revolutionaries in Hispanic Culture* (2010) and in a projected second title, *Bandits and Revolutionaries in Literature, Folklore, and Film: The Good, the Bad, the Beautiful*, to be published in the near future.

Keller has also published books on Chicano art, including two beautiful volumes of *Contemporary Chicana and Chicano Art: Artists, Works, Culture, and Education* (2002). In his introductory essay to the first volume, "On Contemporary Chicana and Chicano Art: A Project Designed to Meet Las Alturas de las Circunstancias," Keller expresses his full awareness of the importance of Chicano Art and the purpose of this monumental publication:

* Keller, "The Image of the Chicano in Mexican, United States, and Chicano Cinema: An Overview."

> This project *Contemporary Chicana and Chicano Art: Artists, Works, Culture, and Education*, represents a concerted effort to showcase, inform, and animate our art in sufficient depth to make a valuable and lasting contribution to the field. It is a contribution that aspires to meet "las alturas de las circunstancias de hoy día del arte chicana y chicano," a contribution that aspires to reflect in depth (although far from definitively) the corresponding level of evolution, variety, vitality, and activity that Chicana and Chicano art has now attained. (17)*

Keller's statement summarizes the important contribution that Chicanos and Chicanas have made to the arts. It is through this contribution that Chicanos and Chicanas have achieved, he feels, multigenerational growth that should be considered and valued at the highest level.

It is clear that Keller's multicultural projects are intended to survive the test of time. The legendary Bilingual Review Press, the seminal *Chicano Cinema* anthology, the impressive art book projects, as well as his fiction and web-based poetry, make the versatile Keller a bold caballero who is always in the process of reinventing himself.

Luis Leal

Luis Leal was born on September 17, 1907, in Linares, Nuevo León, Mexico. At the age of nineteen, he left Linares to pursue his education at Northwestern University, in Evanston, Illinois. Leal completed his MA degree at the University of Chicago in 1941 but postponed his doctoral studies there due to the outbreak of World War II. Leal served in the U.S. Army in the Pacific, and after the war ended, he resumed his studies, receiving his PhD in 1950.

Leal's first teaching position was at the University of Mississippi. Later he worked at Emory University in Atlanta before accepting a tenure-track position at the University of Illinois at Urbana-Champaign, where he worked until his retirement in 1976. That year,

* Keller, "On Contemporary Chicana and Chicano Art: A Project Designed to Meet Las Alturas de las Circunstancias."

he accepted a visiting professor position at the University of California, Santa Barbara (UCSB), where he remained until his death in January 2010.

Leal's academic work on Mexican, Latin American, and Chicano literature is extraordinary. Throughout his long and prolific academic career, he wrote countless articles and books that were innovative and groundbreaking and had a tremendous impact on the literature and culture of the Spanish-speaking world. Leal's monumental research on Mexican literature led him to become a preeminent scholar of the Mexican short story. His landmark books on the subject include *Breve historia del cuento mexicano* (1957), *Antología del cuento mexicano* (1957), and *Bibliografía del cuento mexicano* (1958). Leal's other contributions to Mexican literature and culture include *México: Civilizaciones y culturas* (1955), *Mariano Azuela: Vida y obra* (1961), *Panorama de la literatura mexicana actual* (1968), and *Juan Rulfo* (1983). Along with his research on the Mexican short story, Leal studied the Latin American short story, publishing *Historia del cuento hispanoamericano* (1966), *El cuento hispanoamericano* (1967), and *Breve historia de la literatura hispanoamericana* (1971).

When Leal retired from the University of Illinois and accepted a visiting research position in the Department of Chicano Studies at the University of California, Santa Barbara, he would devote the rest of his academic career—more than thirty years—to the study and growth of Chicano literature and culture. Most scholars of Chicano literature consider Leal the rightful pioneer of Chicano literary criticism and the unofficial dean of Chicano literary history. His books on Chicano literature and culture include *Decade of Chicano Literature, 1970–1979: Critical Essays and Bibliography* (1982), *Aztlán y México: Perfiles literarios e históricos* (1985), *Corridos y canciones de Aztlán* (1986), and *No Longer Voiceless* (1995).

A Decade of Chicano Literature, coedited by Leal, Fernando de Necochea, Roberto Trujillo, and Francisco A. Lomelí, includes ten essays covering all literary genres of Chicano literature, and includes a comprehensive bibliography of Chicano literature from 1970 to 1979. Leal's contribution to this important decade in Chicano letters is a chapter titled "Journals," which offers a comprehensive summary of the Chicano journals that were published in the 1970s. Among the most important to appear in that prolific decade are *Aztlán: Chicano*

Journal of the Social Sciences and the Arts, which Leal believes "has served as a model for other Chicano journals dedicated to the publication of scholarly articles" (86); *De Colores: Journal of Chicano Expression and Thought*, *Revista Chicano-Riqueña*; and *La Palabra: Revista de Literatura Chicana*.* Leal ends his essay by stressing their importance to the development of Chicano literature:

> These journals have proven to be indispensable in encouraging and in recognizing Chicano writers and artists and in promoting the development of Chicano letters. A tradition in the publication of high caliber journals was established during the decade of the seventies, a tradition that helped Chicano literature reach a high aesthetic quality without, at the same time, abandoning the commitment to *la causa*. (92)

Leal's most celebrated book is *Aztlán y México: Perfiles literarios e históricos*, published in 1985. The book is divided into two parts: The first part, titled "Aztlán," includes eleven essays on Chicano literature and culture. The second, "Anáhuac," features twelve essays on Mexican literature and culture. "Aztlán" includes several seminal articles that have become essential to the study of Chicano literature and culture. For example, "En busca de Aztlán" and "The Problem of Identifying Chicano Literature" deal with Chicano identity; "Periodización de la literatura chicana," "Cuatro siglos de prosa aztlanense," and "El corrido de Aztlán" explore Chicano literary history; and "La narrativa de la Revolución mexicana y la novela chicana" examines the impact that Mexican literature has had on Chicano literature.

In the "Prefacio" to *Aztlán y México*, Leal emphasizes that Mexicans and Chicanos are, in effect, "dos aspectos de una misma cultura" (no page number), thus encouraging their unity and their mutual understanding:

* *Aztlán* was published in California, *De Colores* in New Mexico, *Revista Chicano Riqueña* in Indiana and later Texas (the name was later changed to *The Americas Review*), and *La Palabra* in Arizona. According to Leal, there were over one hundred and thirty journals and other periodicals that appeared in the 1970s.

> Aztlán y Anáhuac son símbolos míticos que unen al mexicano y al chicano tanto en el tiempo como en el espacio. De Aztlán sale el antiguo mexicano, funda Tenochtitlán en el Valle de Anáhuac, donde conquista, sacrifica y es conquistado.
>
> Siglos más tarde sus descendientes han de volver en busca de Aztlán, en busca del Paraíso perdido, en manos ahora de otros conquistadores. Aquí, en Aztlán, esos descendientes luchan contra los nuevos conquistadores para mantener la autonomía cultural. Para fundamentarla buscan las raíces perdidas en el antiguo Anáhuac. Allí encuentran sus símbolos y sus mitos. Y aunque sea verdad que a veces se da preferencia a formas externas apropiadas de la cultura dominante, en el fondo encontramos una corriente mitológica que nos une a todos, chicanos y mexicanos. (Prefacio, sin página)
>
> (*Aztlán and Anáhuac are mythical symbols that unite the Mexican and the Chicano in both space and time. The pre-Columbian Mexican leaves Aztlán, founds Tenochtitlán in the Anáhuac Valley, where he conquers, performs sacrifices, and is himself conquered.*
>
> *Centuries later his descendants returned in search of Aztlán, in search of the Lost Paradise, now in the hands of other conquerors. Here, in Aztlán, those descendants fight against the new conquerors to maintain their cultural autonomy. To reinforce it they search for their lost roots in the old Anáhuac. There they find their symbols and their myths. And even if it's true that at times preference is given to unfamiliar ways pertaining to the dominant culture, deep down we find a mythological current that unites us all, Chicanos and Mexicans.*) (My translation)

In 1996, Leal, with Víctor Fuentes, founded *Ventana Abierta: Revista Latina de Literatura, Arte y Cultura*, a literary journal published in Santa Barbara, California, that promotes the literature of U.S. Latinos who express themselves in Spanish. The journal has served as a source of inspiration for a new generation of Latino writers interested in using Spanish as their primary means of expression.

Leal's monumental academic work and his humanitarian concerns have been celebrated and recognized through numerous awards, including the National Humanities Medal in 1997, the most prestigious humanitarian award in the United States, and the Aguila Azteca Award in 1991, the highest honor awarded by the Mexican government. In addition, in 1998 Leal was elected to the North American Academy of the Spanish Language, and at UCSB Leal was honored with the establishment of the Luis Leal Endowed Chair in Chicano Studies.

Luis Leal was a tireless and prolific researcher who served—and will continue to serve—as an inspiration to the many students of literature and culture who directly or indirectly knew him. His humble and unassuming demeanor as a scholar, a professor, and as a común y corriente individual was truly remarkable. Luis Leal passed away in 2010, at the age of 102. His presence in this world truly embodied the espíritu inquebrantable of our Chicano literary history.

Francisco A. Lomelí

In describing his life as a young man in Mexico, Francisco A. Lomelí emphasizes the strong work ethic that his family instilled in him and the seriousness with which he took on his responsibilities, regardless of how small or insignificant they might have seemed. He took to heart all the tasks that were assigned to him, at home and at work, and always did his best to complete them with diligence and pride. Lomelí brought his strong Mexican work ethic to the United States when his family settled in San Diego, California, in the early 1960s. His energy and enthusiasm fitted well with the highly charged social exigencies of the time: the civil rights movement, the mandatory draft, the Vietnam War, and the Chicano movement, among other social concerns. His deep interest and concern for the dismal representation of Chicanas and Chicanos in higher education prompted him to get involved in student activities at San Diego State University. It was there, as a Spanish major, that Lomelí's transnational vision of bridging the literary achievements of different Spanish-speaking countries, including those of the Spanish-speaking communities in the United States, began to take root. While at San Diego State, Lomelí spent an academic year studying literature at the Universidad de Concepción, in Chile, and later at the Universidad de Cuyo, in Mendoza, Argentina, experiences that helped him define the social function and urgency of literature and would form his study of Chicano literature.

In 1974 Lomelí was accepted to the PhD program at the University of New Mexico. There, he faithfully continued his studies in Latin American literature and ultimately wrote his dissertation on Carlos Droguett, a Chilean novelist he had researched while in South America. By this time, however, Lomelí's literary interest and passion had shifted to the exciting and emerging field of Chicano literature.

While a graduate student at the University of New Mexico, Lomelí was involved in the academic changes that were beginning to take place in the Department of Spanish and Portuguese, where students were requesting courses in Chicano literature. These demands echoed those initiated in the English Department of the same institution that led Ortego y Gasca to organize the first course of Chicano literature in that department. The chair of the Spanish and Portuguese department approved the courses, and that decision led Lomelí and his graduate colleague, Donaldo W. Urioste, to research and organize one of the first Chicano bibliographies of the time, *Chicano Perspectives in Literature: A Critical and Annotated Bibliography*, published in 1976 by Pajarito Publications in Albuquerque.

In the Introduction to *Perspectives,* Lomelí and Urioste passionately explain the need for such a bibliography. They provide a brief history of Chicano literature and point out the historical dilemma that Chicanos have faced within American society for over a century. The literature of the 1960s—as opposed to the literature written by Chicanos prior to that decade—presented a distinct ideology that served "as elements with which to create a socio-political-artistic awareness" (11). The editors positioned Chicano literature as part of a world literature that comprised three cultural components: Mexican (mestizo: Indigenous and Spanish); Anglo-American; and "unofficial local realities" (11), which are best described as an eclectic combination of Mexican, Anglo-American, and Chicano influences. Wanting to include non-Chicano authors that were capable of portraying Chicano topics—even though Lomelí and Urioste believe that the uniqueness of the Chicano reality makes this very difficult to achieve—Lomelí and Urioste placed these authors in a category they define as "*literatura chicanesca* because it only appears to be Chicano" (12). They further explain this concept:

> It must be kept in mind that the perspective is from the outside looking in. This perspective loses the spontaneity of a natural outpouring of a people's subconscious through the writer's creativity; instead, it becomes a calculated object of study, which is valued from a relative distance, that is, not lived. (12)

The success of *Chicano Perspectives in Literature* led Lomelí and Urioste to edit an issue of *De Colores: Journal of Chicano Expression and Thought* dedicated to Chicano literature and criticism. This issue represented, as stated before, "the first major effort by any journal—Chicano or otherwise—to compile articles strictly on literary criticism" (4). In its editorial page the editors shared their vision of how to approach the critical analysis of Chicano literature: "One of our primary goals became *cómo chicanizar la crítica*, that is, how to promote the idea of dealing with our literature in its own terms in order to arrive at comprehending its merits and flaws" (4). This pioneering work is important for its inclusion of work by some of the leading critics of Chicano literature would impact the growth of Chicano letters in the decades to follow. This special issue includes articles by José Armas, "Role of Artist and Critic in the Literature of a Developing Pueblo"; Joseph Sommers, "Critical Approaches to Chicano Literature"; Francisco A. Lomelí and Donaldo W. Urioste, "El concepto del barrio en tres poetas chicanos: Abelardo, Alurista y Ricardo Sánchez"; Mario García, "Duality in Chicano Poetry"; Lauro Flores and Mark McCaffrey, "Miguel Méndez: El subjetivismo frente a la historia"; Gustavo V. Segade, "Peregrinos de Aztlán: Viaje y laberinto"; Juan Bruce-Novoa, "Miguel Méndez: Voices of Silence"; and Carlota Cárdenas de Dwyer, "First Chicano Literary Prize."

Lomelí's interest in recovering the Chicano literary tradition led him to participate in important work dealing with Chicano literary history and the development of Chicano letters, in particular that associated with the New Mexico literary tradition. Lomelí has published extensively on this subject and contributed two important articles in *Pasó por aquí*: "A Literary Portrait of Hispanic New Mexico: Dialectics of Perception," and "Eusebio Chacón: An Early Pioneer of the New Mexican Novel."* The latter analyzes *El hijo de la tempestad* and *Tras la tormenta la calma*, two short novels by Eusebio Chacón, who is considered one of the first Mexican American novelists from New Mexico.

Lomelí's editing of texts that introduced Chicano literature to the academic and general reading public is exceptional and impressive. Some of these essential texts include those he coedited, such as *Handbook of Hispanic Cultures in the United States: Literature and Art* (1994), with Nicolás Kanellos and Claudio Esteva-Fabregat; *Chicano Literature: A Reference Guide* (1985), with Juan A. Martínez; and the monumental *Chicano Writers: Dictionary of Literary Biography;* v. 82, v. 122 and v. 209 (1989, 1992, 1999), with Carl R. Shirley. These texts are excellent academic tools for introducing students to Chicano literature and its authors. They present Chicano literature in a comprehensive and approachable way that is also suitable for the general public.

Lomelí's tireless dedication to Chicano letters has led him, like many other Chicana and Chicano academics, to present his research at countless national and international conferences. What sets Lomelí apart from other scholars is his participation in academic appointments, such as his service several times as the director of the University of California's study abroad programs in Costa Rica and Chile, assignations that usually last for a minimum of two years per appointment. The daily encuentros and interactions with students, scholars, and local people from these countries that these appointments afford—a priceless opportunity to present a Chicano perspective on U.S. society to the world—make this Chicano a unique ambassador of Chicano literature.

Felipe de Ortego y Gasca

Felipe de Ortego y Gasca was born in Blue Island, Illinois, to migrant farm-working parents who, after years of traveling and working in the Midwest, decided to settle in that part of the country.

* This book of essays, edited by Erlinda Gonzales-Berry, is part of a series of books dealing with the development of New Mexican literature in New Mexico.

Tragically, Ortego y Gasca lost his parents at an early age and as a result was raised by relatives, living first in Chicago and later in Pittsburgh. Eventually, he lived with a relative in an African American neighborhood of East Pittsburgh. It was there that Ortego y Gasca discovered his love for music and learned to play the guitar.

In 1943 Ortego y Gasca joined the U.S. Marine Corps and participated heroically in World War II. He was one of the few Chicanos to fight in the War of the Pacific, in Iwo Jima and Okinawa, and was honorably discharged in 1946 as a platoon sergeant. On his return to the United States, he took advantage of the educational benefits offered to veterans who served in the war and enrolled at the University of Pittsburgh, where he undertook comparative studies in English, Spanish, and French, and took classes in Italian and Russian. Unfortunately, Ortego y Gasca did not finish the BA and for several years earned his living as a musician, touring with other performers through several Midwestern states, as well as New York and New Jersey. However, with the academic credits he earned at the University of Pittsburgh, he decided to return to education and obtained a language certificate that enabled him to teach several years at the high school level in a town near Pittsburgh.

Ortego y Gasca's quixotic spirit led him to leave his teaching position and return to military life, this time joining the Air Force, where he served as a second lieutenant. His superiors encouraged him to apply to flight school, and he eventually earned his pilot wings at the Goodfellow Air Force Base in San Angelo, Texas. Ortego y Gasca served in the Air Force for nine years and retired from military life in 1962, soon returning to work as a high school language teacher in El Paso, Texas. Motivated by the possibility of teaching at the college level, Ortego y Gasca studied for his MA at Texas Western, now known as the University of Texas at El Paso (UTEP), and his PhD at the University of New Mexico.

At the University of New Mexico, Ortego y Gasca enrolled in the Department of English, where he planned to write his doctoral dissertation on Geoffrey Chaucer, the English writer of the Middle Ages known as the father of English literature. His academic goal changed, however, when the director of the newly established program in Chicano studies asked him to organize a course on Mexican American literature. Ortego y Gasca accepted the request and desperately searched for reading material to be used for the course—a daunting challenge in the late 1960s. This experience profoundly impacted Ortego y Gasca's academic interests, and as a result he put in a request to change the topic of his thesis. His director accepted his request, and in 1971 Ortego y Gasca completed "Background of Mexican American Literature," the first dissertation written on Chicano literary history, in which he introduced the celebrated "Chicano Renaissance," a term that attested to the reinvention and "boom" in Chicano literature of the time.

"Background of Mexican American Literature" is a seminal work that establishes the roots of Chicano literature and its place in American literature. In his dissertation, which comprises an introduction and four chapters, Ortego y Gasca argues that the literature written by Mexican Americans in this country has tragically been ignored and neglected by the dominant culture. He asserted, "Mexican Americans (in the Southwest) are seen by Anglo Americans in a relationship resembling that of foster parents to a legally adopted child" (53).* Given this relationship, it became imperative to find the true parents of that "adopted child," a feat that could be accomplished only by the discovery or recovery of a Chicano literary past. Even though Ortego y Gasca recognizes that pre-Columbian literature should be considered as part of the roots of Mexican American literature, he doesn't explore the subject and instead initiates the Chicano's literary tradition, beginning with the Spanish conquest of the Southwest. Chapter 2, "The Beginning and the 19th Century," explores the Spanish colonial literary presence in the Southwest and the Mexican American literature that was written after 1848, highlighting works such as *History of California* by Mariano Vallejo, who he feels has a "desire to be fair to all the participants in the drama of California" (90), and Andrew Garcia's *Tough Trip Through Paradise*, a book about his exploits in Montana from 1878 to 1879, and whose experiences "indicate that Mexican Americans played significant roles in the development of the Northwest frontier" (93). Chapter 4, "Mid-Century and the Chicano Renaissance," is of particular interest because it uses the word "Renaissance" to define the nascent

* The quotes are taken from Ortego y Gasca's dissertation, 1971.

Chicano literary movement and thereby challenges the scope and parameters of the literary term, long associated with European literature. For Ortego y Gasca—who trained in English literature, had an interest in Chaucer, and had written his MA thesis on William Shakespeare's *Hamlet*—the word "Renaissance" was, in Chicano terms, a literary "alternative" (214) to mainstream American literature that, he argued, should also mark the social rebirth taking place in the Chicano literary world: "The Chicano Renaissance is but the manifestation of a people's coming of age. It has been long overdue, and in another country, like Milton's unsightly root, it bore a bright and golden flower" (241).

The impact of "Backgrounds of Mexican American Literature" on Chicano letters, as well as the new space that Chicano literature was beginning to occupy in the literature of the United States, led representatives of Simon & Schuster to ask Ortego y Gasca to edit what would become *We are Chicanos: An Anthology of Mexican-American Literature* (1973), one of the first anthologies of Chicano literature published by a major New York editorial house. In the introduction to the anthology, Ortego y Gasca characterizes the condition of Mexican American literature in this country, once again adding a touch of his English literary background to his analysis:

> Like the British roots in the new American soil, the Hispanic literary roots have yielded a vigorous and dynamic body of literature which unfortunately has been studied historically as part of a foreign enterprise rather that as part and parcel of our American heritage. The reason advanced has been that such works are not properly within the traditional Anglo-American definition of American literature. Linguistic chauvinism has been the principal reason for the exclusion of the Spanish-language literature of the United States from the corpus of American literature. . . .
>
> Heretofore, Mexican-Americans have been a marginal people in a sort of no-man's-land, who, like Hamlet crawling between heaven and earth, have been caught between the polarizing forces of their cultural-linguistic Hispanic heritage and their political-linguistic American context. (xvii–xx)

Ortego y Gasca goes on to assert that the Chicano literary past had been so neglected that of the millions of Mexican Americans living in the United States only a few were aware of its existence. He determined that, like black American writers, the Chicano writers are discriminated against and neglected but that, fortunately, the 1960s heralded "the renaissance of the Mexican-American" (xxii), and the 1970s bore the promise that "this renaissance will exert an ever-growing awareness in Mexican-Americans not only in terms of creative efforts in drama, fiction, and poetry, but in terms of seeking a more substantial literary identity in the ever-widening mainstream of American literature" (xxi). Ortego y Gasca intends *We are Chicanos* to help to fulfill that promise.

Ortego y Gasca worked at various universities before retiring in 1999 from Texas State University, Sul Ross, in Alpine, Texas. He has dedicated his professional life to accentuating the contributions of Chicanos in the fields of education and literature. Felipe de Ortego y Gasca's personal and academic life has placed him squarely on the world's stage, where he performs a diverse set of roles—from the romantic to the tragic—for a public eager to applaud the valiant and hecho en casa Chicano Renaissance Man.

Tey Diana Rebolledo

There is no doubt that Tey Diana Rebolledo's diverse racial background (her mother was Mexican, her father Peruvian) and the fact that she grew up in various cultural spaces (Mexico, the East Coast of the United States, New Mexico) formed her interest in Chicana subjectivity and literary history, essential themes that are continually present in her academic work. Equally important in her academic development is Rebolledo's mother, whom she describes as being very frank and straightforward, personal characteristics that contextualize Rebolledo's outspoken and open literary style, which her reading public welcomes.

As a graduate student at the University of Arizona, Rebolledo studied the works of Rosario Castellanos and other Mexican, Latin American, and Spanish writers. Rebolledo's literary orientation began to change, however, when she discovered Chicana literature at a poetry reading where Margarita Cota-Cárdenas, a fellow student, read her innovative and captivating poems. Cota-Cárdenas's themes of Chicana empowerment and her unique linguistic use of Spanglish opened up exciting new literary possibilities that stirred in Rebolledo a newfound interest in Chicana literature.

Rebolledo emphasizes the study of Chicana literature, in particular that of New Mexico women writers. For Rebolledo, it is imperative to present Chicanas as a focal point in the study of Chicano literature for they must recover their own literary heritage, which had been silenced by men. Rebolledo's numerous publications on the subject substantiate this effort: *Women's Tales from the New Mexico WPA: La diabla a pie* (2000); *Nuestras mujeres: Hispanas of New Mexico: Their Images and Their Lives, 1582–1992* (1992); *Las mujeres hablan: An Anthology of Nuevo Mexican Writers* (1988); and *Infinite Divisions: An Anthology of Chicana Literature* (1993).

Originally, *Infinite Divisions*, as Rebolledo and her coeditor Eliana S. Rivero point out, was intended to be a compilation of the intellectual and critical history of Chicana literature from the 1960s onward. They felt that starting earlier than the 1960s would make it difficult to find material to complete the project. However, as they initiated their research, Rebolledo and Rivero were pleasantly surprised to find that a wealth of literary material was available to them. They soon realized that they needed to publish as much material as possible, for fear of losing it forever.

Its extensive documentation of Chicana's literary and cultural history makes this anthology a vital part of the growth of Chicana and Chicano letters. It collects works by well-known authors from the twentieth century as well as the everyday voices of nineteenth-century community storytellers. In its introduction, the authors provide an overview of Chicana literary history. Of particular interest is the section, "The 1920–1950s: Flowering of a Literature of Resistance," in which the editors highlight the works of early-twentieth-century writers from New Mexico and Texas. Contrary to what others believe to be an exclusive and romanticized representation of Southwest literature, the editors present the works of Cleofas Jaramillo, Fabiola Cabeza de Baca Gilbert, Nina Otero-Warren, and Jovita Gonzalez as ones of resistance:

> These woman felt the need to document what they saw as a vanishing cultural heritage; their sense that their identity was being assimilated through history and cultural domination. . . . Although their writing presents the perspective of a landed society, they nevertheless cultivate the seeds of cultural resistance to Anglo hegemony. (17)

A section of the anthology, "The Chicano/Chicana Renaissance," is worth highlighting here because, as previously noted, Felipe de Ortego y Gasca was the first to use the term "Chicano Renaissance" to refer to the literary output of Chicanos in the 1960s. The editors of *Infinite Divisions* made a point of including women as part of this literary production and reconstruct the term to include a "Chicana Renaissance" in order to correct Chicanos' omission of women's participation in and contributions to Chicano literary history.

Rebolledo's *Women Singing in the Snow: A Cultural Analysis of Chicana Literature* opens up the space of Chicana literature by studying the literature of Chicanas who reside not only in New Mexico but in other parts of the country. The title of the book is a metaphor for the quest of survival of the Chicana voice:

> It could refer to the chain of women who never told their stories, or the symbolic hardships of women to write without a room of their own—women writing in the face of a cold, inhospitable, and unreceptive climate. Yet the image can also be seen as a metaphor for the triumph of women who manage, finally, to sing in spite of it all. (xix)

An example of Chicanas' particular way of telling their stories is the use of the Spanish language as a means of expressing a distinctive creative voice. In chapter 8, "The Problematics of Writing in Spanish," Rebolledo discusses the use of Spanish in Margarita Cota Cárdenas's *Puppet* and Erlinda Gonzales-Berry's *Paletitas de guayaba*, pointing out that for these two authors writing in Spanish becomes a political act of resistance. Rebolledo examines in these two works the author's concept of writing under the threat of being silenced. Rebolledo sees that in dealing with these issues both authors experience a "quintuple erasure: the English erasure of Spanish, the Anglo erasure of the Chicano, the Mexicano erasure of the Chicano, the patriarchal erasure of the female, and the Chicano erasure of the Chicana" (174). For this reason, the authors, Rebolledo believes, struggle to find "their own representational space" (174), a problem that must be addressed and solved.

Rebolledo's academic work demands Chicanas to look within themselves to find their own definitions of community while challenging the stifling literary limitations imposed on them by male writers. The Chicana's constant struggle for recognition and literary survival continues to be part of Rebolledo's critical undertaking in her later works. The title of her 2005 book, *The Chronicles of Panchita Villa and Other Guerrilleras: Essays on Chicana/Latina Literature and Criticism*, confirms that Rebolledo is on a mission to establish the Chicana's place within the Chicano literary canon. The title can be read as an encouragement to declare "guerilla" warfare against anyone who dares to deny this quest.

Juan Rodríguez

Juan Rodríguez's impact on the formation of Chicano literature in the 1960s and 1970s is immeasurable and merits due recognition and respect. For more than forty years he has served not only as a scholar and teacher but also as the modern day corridista or omniscient communicator of the common occurrences relevant to Chicano literature across the country.

Rodríguez has described his peregrinación through Aztlán as an "academic migrant worker"—a description that parallels his early life as a migrant farm worker—where, after receiving a BA and MA from Texas Tech University and doing doctoral work at the University of Iowa, he moved on to hold temporary faculty appointments at the University of Arizona, the University of California, San Diego, the University of California, Berkeley, the University of Washington, and the University of Texas at Austin until he finally settled in Seguín, Texas, where he has served, since 1981, as a professor of Spanish and as head of the Mexican American studies program at Texas Lutheran University. Throughout those years Rodríguez helped develop Chicano studies by founding or teaching seminal courses in Chicano literature and culture at those universities. His efforts can be described as those of a guerrillero literario leading a socially conscious effort to distinguish Chicano literature at the institutional level.

Rodríguez's social activism has been a constant throughout his academic life. At Texas Tech he began to support organizations that voiced concern over the underrepresentation of Chicano students at that university. At the University of Iowa he actively participated in student organizations that demanded social change at the university and in the community. His commitment to disseminate Chicano letters across the country led him to found *Carta Abierta*, a literary newsletter that aimed to educate and inform readers of the current trends in Chicano literature. Some years later, *El Toque: A Quick Chiclit Fix for Webones* replaced *Carta Abierta*. Different name, same message. In 1980 Rodríguez found Relámpago Press and also began to distribute Chicano books at presentations and conferences at universities or at community centers where Chicanos lived and worked.

Rodríguez's direct and no-nonsense analysis of creative works written by Chicanos and Chicanas has led a few of his critics to see him as el niño malcriado of Chicano literature, a harsh critic que no tiene pelos en la lengua. Many times Rodríguez's frankness can be interpreted as callous and inflexible. For example, while many Chicano critics might emphasize the social commitment (i.e., "resistance" to Anglo domination) of early twentieth-century writers like Cleofas Jaramillo or Fabiola Cabeza de Vaca, Rodríguez would describe their writing as picturesque and self-serving for, as he writes, "All of them actually represented a step backward in the development of Chicano prose for they returned to the quaint presentation of the Mexican and the Mexican way of life" (70).* In other words, he emphasizes that the community that these writers actually represented wanted to save and preserve the welfare of the gente de razón (those powerful hacendados hispanos who were afraid of losing their wealth and power to the Anglos and who did not represent the majority of Chicanos or Chicanas). In another example, Rodríguez defends himself against accusations of being a sexist for using the word

* Rodríguez, "Notes on the Evolution of Chicano Prose Fiction."

"ruca" (the caló or vernacular name for female) by saying that his accusers misinterpret his choice of words because they do not speak Spanish or understand its cultural connotations well enough to make a fair assessment of what he is trying to communicate with his choice of words.

Rodríguez wrote several key articles on Chicano literary topics including "Notes on the Evolution of Chicano Prose Fiction," published in *Modern Chicano Writers*, and "El desarrollo del cuento chicano: Del folklore al tenebroso mundo del yo" and "La búsqueda de identidad y sus motivos en la literature chicana," both included in *The Identification and Analysis of Chicano Literature*. In those articles Rodríguez provides a brief and thoughtful summary of the development of the Chicano short story, the focus of his doctoral dissertation at the University of Iowa. Unfortunately, his doctoral committee did not approve of his topic choice and Rodríguez, unwilling to change it, decided not to complete the degree.

One important contribution that Rodríguez made to Chicano literary history is his research of the short stories by Mexican writers who settled in the San Francisco Bay area as a result of the Mexican Revolution in the early decades of the twentieth century. The short stories of Jorge Ulica, compiled by Rodríguez in *Crónicas diabólicas* (1982), is an excellent example of the social life of the Mexican and Mexican American in California at the turn of the century. A number of these stories deal with the Spanish language and the pocho (supposedly a Chicano traitor to the Mexican culture). These stories undoubtedly influenced Rodríguez's well-documented article on the short story (mentioned above), which emphasizes the "tenebroso mundo del yo," an existential concern present in many contemporary Chicano texts.

Rodríguez continues to be an active participant in the Chicano literary world and is particularly involved with those writers who reside in Texas. Rodríguez's literary followers extend beyond his generation. For those of his generation, he is an example of the 1960s and 1970s Chicano who remained forever faithful to the ideals of the Chicano movement. Rodríguez is well respected for his intelligence, his integrity, and his dedication to Chicano letters. For the new generation of critics of Chicano literature, Rodríguez is a human treasure living in a casa de piedra on the periphery of the Guadalupe

River in Seguín, Texas, waiting patiently to be discovered by a new wave of Chicano scholars.

Rosaura Sánchez

Rosaura Sánchez is the product of a working-class family and at an early age was exposed to economic hardships and deprivations. Sánchez's tough character and unbreakable spirit led her to place among the top students in her high school, allowing her to leave San Angelo, Texas—her place of birth—and enter the challenging academic world of the University of Texas at Austin (the flagship institution). Eager to experience and explore the world outside of Texas but aware of the financial limitations that would impede her from participating in the study abroad programs the university offered, Sánchez decided to join the Peace Corps, serving the indigenous communities in Ecuador for several years. Participating in the Peace Corps would be a life-changing experience for Sánchez, who began to question the practicality of her career choice (the study of Spanish and Latin American literature), asking herself why she had not decided to study medicine or another profession that could help people in a more practical way. On her return to the United States, Sánchez continued her studies in literature and linguistics with the idea of finding a practical application of her research and academic goals.

Deeply sensitive and concerned for the fate of the working class, Sánchez's immediate challenge as a scholar was to make her research both academically stimulating for the scholar of literature and accessible and meaningful for the common reader. It seems that Sánchez met these challenges through her choice of research interests and her personal creative work. This combination unquestionably mirrors her working-class objectives. Clearly, Sánchez's research interests reflect her desire to serve her Chicano community by analyzing and theorizing cultural themes that enhance the potential social solutions needed to better understand that community. Those topics include Chicano bilingualism, oral history, and the recovery of a Chicano literary past. In her fiction, she explores working-class aspirations and contradictions.

Sánchez's study of Chicano bilingualism resulted in the publication of *Chicano Discourse: Socio-Historic Perspectives* (1983). In this study,

Sánchez alleges that the study of Chicano bilingualism—the Chicano community's patterns of communication in Spanish and English—is an examination of language that "in terms of content and social constraints allow us to go beyond form and grammar in examining the social and ideological message implicit and explicit in the bilingual verbal interaction of Chicanos" (vii). In chapter 4, "The Spanish of Chicanos," Sánchez uses an analysis of the linguistic status of Chicano Spanish to demonstrate that the Spanish variants spoken in the Southwest are authentic, for they share common features with the Spanish spoken in Spain and Latin American Spanish-speaking countries and are not unique to the Spanish spoken in the Southwest. This connection is important for the Spanish-speaking Chicano or Chicana because it legitimizes their Spanish and weakens the argument that they are machacándolo through the violation of Spanish linguistic rules and subjective beauty. On the contrary, Chicano Spanish is acceptable and belongs to the extended family of Spanish variants spoken around the world. Moreover, according to Sánchez, Chicano Spanish is legitimate because "all variants occurring within Chicano Spanish can be explained within the rules of Spanish grammar and are not the result of English interference or convergence" (99).

One of Sánchez's major contributions to Chicano literature is her collaborative work with the Recovering the U.S. Hispanic Literary Heritage Project, where she served on the Board of Editorial Advisors. As a scholar Sánchez has contributed to several important projects dealing with the literary output of María Amparo Ruiz de Burton, considered one of the earliest Chicana novelists. Sánchez, along with Beatrice Pita, has coedited and written in-depth studies of Ruiz de Burton's two novels: *Who Would Have Thought It?* (1872) and *The Squatter and the Don* (1885). In addition, Sánchez and Pita wrote an extensive introduction to Burton's personal life and correspondence in *Conflicts of Interest: The Letters of María Amparo Ruiz de Burton* (2001). These contributions, along with Sánchez's *Telling Identities: The California Testimonios* (1995), are monumental in content and meaning and solidify Sánchez's and Pita's reputation as international authorities on the subject. Their work not only provides a view of a historical Chicana/o past but of a present and a future, as expressed in the following passage from their study of *The Squatter and the Don*:

> Here the past is not portrayed as a world to be restored, but what lies ahead is also the antithesis of progress and anything but a utopian vision of modernity, unless, of course, following the ethical argument on which the novel is premised, morality prevails and the social order is regenerated. (6)*

Sánchez has published two works of fiction, *He Walked In and Sat Down and Other Stories* (2000) and, in collaboration with Beatrice Pita, *Lunar Braceros 2125–2148* (2009). The seventeen stories that make up *He Walked In and Sat Down* were originally written in Spanish and deal with various aspects of the social life of the Chicano, specifically those dealing with social class issues, mostly of the working class and their conflict with identity, injustice, social commitment, and hope. *Lunar Braceros*, written in English, is a futuristic representation of similar social themes that face Chicanos in outer space. The fate of these Chicanos remains unclear for their oppression appears to continue by maintaining the translation of their "bracero" status into el más allá.

Rosaura Sánchez is one of the most respected Chicana scholars in academia, in part because she excels in meeting both the scholarly needs of her academic peers and the social needs of the common man or woman. Sánchez's intellectualism indisputably places her at the top of the coveted torre de marfíl, a place few scholars and poets are privileged to occupy. At the same time, she is also the avenger of the working class—the Chicana Fernández de Lizardi, la pensadora chicana—willing to put into practice her idealism for the benefit of improving the human condition.

Charles M. Tatum

Charles M. Tatum's strong ties to Mexico and to Mexican popular culture are reflected in his contribution to Mexican and Chicano literature and cultural studies. Tatum started his literary career specializing in Spanish and Latin American literature, writing his PhD dissertation on José Donoso, the Chilean novelist associated with

* Sánchez and Pita, introduction.

the Latin American literary "boom" of the 1960s and 1970s. This exposure to the political and social climate of Latin America in those decades and to the social and political activities surrounding the Chicano movement in the United States contributed to Tatum's shift in interest to Chicano literature.

Tatum was born in El Paso, Texas, but was raised in Parral, Chihuahua, Mexico. His love for Mexico never diminished for he always valued the simple and unassuming life that he felt he experienced in Parral, which he still considers "the capital of the world." It is no surprise that Tatum honored his love for Mexican popular culture by collaborating with Harold E. Hinds Jr. on several research projects that resulted in the publication of *Handbook of Latin American Popular Culture* (1985) and *Not Just for Children: The Mexican Comic Book in the Late 1960s and 1970s* (1992); in addition, they both cofounded and coedited the journal *Studies in Latin American Popular Culture.*

Not Just for Children is an important contribution to the history of the Mexican comic book. Nevertheless, the authors point out that their study suffers from certain limitations: They believe that their research findings are tentative and imperfect because an authoritative history of the comic had yet to be written when they started their project. Tatum and Hinds offer a valuable chronology of the history of the Mexican comic book, highlighting the 1930s through the mid-1950s as the period modern critics refer to as the Golden Age of the Mexican comic. Their study, however, focuses on the post-1950s era, specifically the 1960s and 1970s with the in-depth analysis of comics such as *La familia Burrón*, *Lágrimas, risas y amor*, *Los supermachos*, *Chanoc*, and the legendary Mexican superhero *Kalimán*, among others. The study explores the public's obsession with this type of literature and its association with media imperialism in México.

Tatum's contributions to Chicano literature began when he was a graduate student at the University of New Mexico. He says that in 1969, while he was teaching Spanish as a teaching assistant, a group of students asked permission to miss several days of class to attend the now historic National Chicano Youth Conference organized by Rodolfo "Corky" Gonzales in Denver, Colorado. Energized and highly motivated by the social and political ideals of the conference, the students returned to New Mexico eager to promote Chicano studies. They asked Tatum to organize a course in Chicano literature, which he enthusiastically agreed to do. From that point on Tatum's research interests changed completely, for after completing his dissertation on Donoso he concentrated his academic career on the study of Chicano literature.

Tatum's contribution to Chicano literature is invaluable. In 1982 Twayne Publishers published *Chicano Literature*, one of the first book-length studies of Chicano literary history. Research on that subject had existed before—including PhD dissertations written by Felipe de Ortego y Gasca ("Backgrounds of Mexican American Literature," 1971), Alba Irene Moesser ("La literatura mejicoamericana del suroeste de los Estados Unidos," 1971), and Alejandro Morales ("Visión panorámica de la literatura mexicoamericana hasta el boom de 1966," 1975)—but none of them had been published and made available to the general public. *Chicano Literature* offered the historical background to Chicano literature, starting with the history of Spanish culture in the Southwest represented by Alvar Nuñez Cabeza de Vaca's *Naufragios*. The book focuses on the twentieth century, especially the literature of the Chicano movement of the 1960s (of the seven chapters that make up this study only two deal with literary periods prior to the 1950s). The book touches on most of the genres of Chicano letters—poetry, novels, theater, and the short story—but excludes the essay. Tatum includes a section on Spanish-language newspapers and Spanish-language newspaper poetry from 1848 through the 1950s but excludes the important emergence of Chicano journals in the 1960s and 1970s.

Over the span of his academic career Tatum has edited three volumes of *New Chicana/Chicano Writings* (published in 1992 and 1993), coedited *En otra voz: Antología de la literatura hispana de los Estados Unidos* (2002), and contributed two volumes to the series "The Mexican American Experience," a project comprising texts designed to introduce Chicano studies to undergraduate students, including *Chicano Popular Culture: Que hable el pueblo* (2001) and *Chicano and Chicana Literature: Otra voz del pueblo* (2006).

Chicano and Chicana Literature is an introduction to Chicano literature and serves as a guide for teachers and readers interested in an overview of Chicano letters. Its seven chapters offer a historical and thematic overview of the origins and evolution of Chicano literature up to its current trends and themes in narrative, theater, and poetry.

An important component of this comprehensive narrative of Chicano literature is the first chapter, "Approaches to the Interpretation of Chicana/o Literature." This significant chapter provides an overview of theoretical approaches to Chicano literature, including Joseph Sommers's dialectical material approach; the critical approaches of the Saldívar brothers, Ramón and José, and sister Sonia; Rosaura Sánchez and Norma Alarcón; the feminist approaches of María Herrera-Sobek and Tey Diana Rebolledo; queer theory; postcolonial theory; cultural studies; and reception theory. The recent addition of a chapter on Chicano literary criticism demonstrates the growth and sophistication that Chicano literature has undergone since Tatum's 1982 publication of *Chicano Literature*. Tatum's dedication to popular culture continues to this day, as evidenced by his most recent publication, *Lowriders in Chicano Culture: From Low to Slow to Show* (2011), a book that studies how "lowriding" mirrors the unique social and political aspects of Chicano culture.

Throughout his academic career Tatum has shown great compassion and concern for the people he has served, both inside and outside of academia. He has demonstrated this dedication while serving for a number of years as Dean of Humanities and as the head of the Department of Spanish and Portuguese at the University of Arizona, working tirelessly to bring faculty and student diversity and equity to his institution. Tatum's ability to function as an administrator and as an educator—privileged positions from which to mentor and impact a student's mind—is to be celebrated and applauded. In the interview for this book project, he refers to his contribution to Chicano letters as simply doing "mi trabajito." This statement is misleading; in reality it should be interpreted as a modest description that only hints at Tatum's monumental lifetime accomplishments.

Tomás Ybarra-Frausto

Tomás Ybarra-Frausto was born in New Braunfels, Texas, in an area known as the Texas Hill Country, which includes the cities of San Antonio and Austin. What makes this area unique, as compared to other parts of Texas where a large number of Mexican Americans reside, is that it was settled by the Spanish, mestizo, and indigenous people from Mexico as well as people from Central Europe, primarily

German, Swiss, Austrian, Polish, and Czech. The presence of these settlers influenced the Texan culture in all aspects of life, including food, architecture, and music. For example, the accordion, the musical instrument German settlers in America introduced, is now deeply associated with Tejano (Mexican American Texan) music. This conglomeration of cultures influenced Ybarra-Frausto's early life, for he grew up learning not only Spanish and English but also German, for many of his childhood friends were German-speakers.

Ybarra-Frausto lived in a caring family environment with traditional values. Mexican culture was practiced and cherished both at home and in the barrio, or neighborhood, where he lived. When Ybarra-Frausto narrates stories of his youth, one senses that he yearns to recuperate the loss of innocence that today's modern world took away. Ybarra-Frausto's unconditional love for the traditions of his Mexican and Mexican American cultures led him to pursue a major in the humanities at the University of Texas at Austin and later at the University of Washington, in Seattle. It was in Washington that Ybarra-Frausto discovered Chicano literature, particularly its theater and poetry. In 1979, he received his PhD degree from the University of Washington with his dissertation, "Poetry and History: Three Contemporary Chicano Poets." It was also at this institution that Ybarra-Frausto met Joseph Sommers, an academic mentor who triggered his social consciousness and guided his academic life. With Sommers, Ybarra-Frausto collaborated on two important projects that contributed to the field of Chicano literature in the early and late 1970s: *Literatura Chicana: Texto y contexto / Chicano Literature: Text and Context* (1972) and *Modern Chicano Writers: A Collection of Critical Essays* (1979).

Literatura Chicana: Texto y contexto, coedited with Sommers and Antonia Castañeda Shular, is a pioneering and ambitious anthology of Chicano literature that can be identified as totalizadora for it is divided into four units or parts that as a whole cover a wide representation of various national literatures. The first part, "Analizando, satirizando, reclamando—La protesta social," presents social protest in a historical progression. For this reason, the anthology begins with selections from indigenous literatures from Mexico (*El libro de Chilam Balam*), continues with selections from Mexican literature (e.g., by Sor Juana Inés de la Cruz and Mariano Azuela), and ends with Chicano literature (*I Am Joaquín*, by Rodolfo "Corky" Gonzales). The second part, "Lo mero principal," includes literary representations of cultural myths like la llorona, traditional indigenous and Mexican food, humor, and barrio spaces that, according to the editors, embody "our conception of culture as a creation which has evolved along with changes in the people's material and spiritual condition" (xxi). The third part, "Dejando huellas . . . Caminos de la migración," deals with migration and includes selections of indigenous literature ("Crónica mexicayotl"), corridos from the Southwest ("El corrido de Kiansis"), and Mexican and Chicano authors from the twentieth century. The fourth part of the book, "Literatura de la raza—The Context of Chicano Literature," is unique because it includes only Mexican, Puerto Rican, and Hispanic American literature. For the editors, the purpose of including these three literary representations was "to place Chicano literature in a number of larger contexts" (xxii). They include Mexican literature because it serves as the antecedent to Chicano literature; Puerto Rican literature because there are "parallels and contrasts . . . in historical and cultural experience" (xxii) with the Chicano experience; and Hispanic American literature because Latin America offers an added context to Chicano literature. This context is presented in the following way:

> In their language, their themes, and their forms, Latin American poets and *cuentistas* often share the same preoccupations as Chicanos, often see reality in similar ways, often express themselves through images and symbols which strike echoes when we read Chicano poems or stories. For the language and many literary and historical antecedents, if not identical, are certainly close. (xxii)

Whether one agrees with the literary vision of the editors, this anthology was a groundbreaking, postmodernist approach to Chicano representation, one that at the time needed a viable literary corpus of texts for an emerging literature that was anxious to grow by any possible means.

Ybarra-Frausto enjoyed a successful academic career as a tenured professor at Stanford University, where he served as a mentor to many Chicanos and Chicanas that studied in the Department of Spanish and Portuguese at that institution. He also served at the Rockefeller Foundation, chairing the Smithsonian Council, as well as the Latino Oversight Committee, and encouraging communities from diverse backgrounds to better understand and value each other's art and culture. In 1998, Ybarra-Frausto was awarded the Joseph Henry Medal by the Smithsonian Center for Latino Initiatives for his exemplary contributions to the Foundation. As an academic, Ybarra-Frausto has contributed scholarly work to the field of Chicano theater and art, publishing extensively on the subject. One notable publication is *Arte Chicano: A Comprehensive Annotated Bibliography of Chicano Art, 1965–1981.*

In terms of Chicano popular culture, Ybarra-Frausto's lasting legacy perhaps lies in his landmark essay, "Rasquachismo: A Chicano Sensibility." The term "rasquache," which originally had a negative connotation in Mexico for its association with the impoverished or unrefined members of society, was reclaimed by the Chicano art movement to mean a particular art style or "sensibility." For Ybarra-Frausto "rasquache" was not an insulting term; on the contrary, he defines "rasquache" and "rasquachismo" as a unique Chicano sensibility that does not conform to a particular style or form. In relation to Chicano art and culture, Ybarra-Frausto defines "sensibility" as the understanding of a particular aesthetic code in a particular community that emerges from the experience of living in that particular communal space. The essence of rasquachismo is "hacer de tripas corazón," in other words, making do with what you have—make the most from the least—to create something useful and practical.

Ybarra-Frausto, now retired from Stanford University and the Rockefeller Foundation, has expressed a deep interest in mastering the skill of storytelling, not through the written word but through the spoken one. In essence, he is telling us that he wants to end his academic career the way he began it: through the oral tradition of his people. Ybarra-Frausto's current literary aspiration is to hacer de tripas corazón—to use whatever means possible, a little bit of the academic, a little bit of the popular, to someday contar a historical social masterpiece of his San Antonio community.

Conclusion

The main themes of the conversations with the twelve critics interviewed for this project can be summarized as follows: 1) Mexico plays an essential role in each critic's personal and academic background; this role is not indirect but deeply intimate, for all are uniquely bilingual and bicultural and received their formal literary education in Spanish graduate programs (Ortego y Gasca received his MA and PhD in English but also studied Spanish and Latin American literature in Spanish); 2) most are a product of the working class (all sympathize with the struggle of the working class) and share a sense of social consciousness and commitment that makes their contribution to Chicano literature one of urgency and communal responsibility; 3) all are pioneers in the development of Chicano literature and literary criticism and in the retrieval of its literary history; 4) all promote Chicano literature and culture at the local, regional, national, and international levels; 5) all belong to a first-generation group of scholars that serves as a source of inspiration for future generations of scholars of Chicano literature; 6) all leave a lasting legacy to Chicano literary history and criticism.

One hopes that future critics of Chicano letters—specifically those who are interested in Chicano literature written in Spanish—will validate the work of these pioneer scholars. This project aims to serve as an informational tool for the común y corriente reader who wants to understand, in the critic's own words (the voice of the storyteller, el cuentista), their personal contributions to Chicano letters.

I

Erlinda Gonzales-Berry

New Mexican *de hueso colorado*

IT MUST HAVE BEEN THE 1970S when I first met Erlinda Gonzales-Berry. No, I did not travel to New Mexico, and I did not have the opportunity to listen to her at a particular conference where she presented her research. I was aware of Erlinda when I was doing graduate work at Texas A & I University in South Texas and reading the works of such literary icons as Rolando Hinojosa, Tomás Rivera, and Felipe de Ortego y Gasca, among others, all at the height of the Chicano movement. As a student, I also read Erlinda's work and it definitely spoke to me, for I remember her as a critic/creative writer who spoke of an alienation and discrimination in her native New Mexico that was similar to the painful sentiments I faced in the South Texas border area.

As I ponder over thirty-five years in academia, I realize that I've had the opportunity to read, review, and teach about a scholar who has valiantly fought to bring awareness of the social realities of la raza in the United States. Her novel Paletitas de guayaba *is still a subject of research in the field of Chicano studies, and her pioneering work on New Mexico's literary tradition has left an indelible mark on Chicano literary history.*

It is my belief that Erlinda's work embodies the philosophical motto of don José Vasconcelos: Por mi raza hablará mi espíritu.

—Juan Antonio González

Erlinda Gonzales-Berry (1942–) was born in a rural region northeast of New Mexico, where her ancestors had lived since the last decades of the nineteenth century. She holds a doctoral degree from the University of New

Mexico and has taught at various institutions including Earlham College, in Richmond, Indiana, New Mexico State University, the University of New Mexico, and Oregon State University. Gonzales-Berry's interest in Chicano literary history, specifically that concerning her native New Mexico, led her to edit, Pasó por aquí: Critical Essays on the New Mexican Literary Tradition, 1542–1988, *a collection of essays dealing with the state's literary tradition. Erlinda Gonzales-Berry's commitment to Chicano literature has led her to expand her regional interests to the Mexicans and Chicanos who have immigrated to the Pacific Northwest. Gonzales-Berry is also the author of* Paletitas de guayaba, *a novel that has contributed significantly to Chicano literature written in Spanish.*

The interview with Erlinda was conducted through a number of e-mail correspondences from 2008 to 2012.

* * *

Erlinda, where were you born? Describe your childhood and the place where you grew up.

I was born in Roy, a small town in New Mexico. This place is located on the northeast part of the state, almost bordering with Texas and Oklahoma. My father had a ranchito that he had inherited from his parents in a place called Bueyeros. My great grandparents settled there in the 1880s and were granted government land through the Homestead Act. Before arriving in Bueyeros they had lived for several centuries in Jémez, and from there they moved to the northeast in search of pasture and water. My great grandparents from my father's side of the family owned large sheep herds. After the Santa Fe Trail was opened, thousands of saleas would be sent to the market in St. Louis, Missouri. In his ranchito my father and mother owned an orchard and several animals. That's how both my grandparents and my parents made their living. My parents always spoke of their ranchito as if it were their Garden of Eden. They worked hard and loved their life and freedom.

Describe your family life. What impact did your parents and your environment have on your early life?

I spent the first four years of my life in that ranchito and I remember very beautiful things from that pastoral lifestyle. But in 1946 a flood destroyed the atarque, the handmade dam that stored the water that we used for our personal needs, and we had to leave the rancho. We moved to Roy, a small town that was divided into two parts: the americanos (Anglos) who lived on one side of town and the mexicanada who lived on the other. My three sisters and I, like most Mexican children, attended a Catholic school run by nuns. With the exception of the nuns, we had limited interaction with the americanos. Therefore, I was raised in an environment that was distinctly Hispanic. Spanish was spoken at home with the grandparents and relatives. We were taught to respect our elders and to be gente. That meant to be nice, courteous, and respectful. Among our community an anciano would always be present to narrate stories from the past: of witches, of goblins, of bultos, and other fantastic things. I grew up in an environment rich in folklore, in traditional customs, in believing in the supernatural and the mystery of the world. This aspect of my upbringing has influenced my creative work very much. My mother was a teacher before marrying my father. At the age of seventeen she was offered her first job in a small isolated town in northern New Mexico. She worked as a teacher for the Mexican children that now we call "Hispanics." In those days the word "Mexican" was not stigmatized, at least not in our communities. In English, however, it was another matter. The word "Mexican" was never used. In that language we identified ourselves as Spanish or Spanish American. My mother did not get married until she was twenty-eight years old because as a young girl she had promised herself not to marry until all of her brothers had finished school. They were fatherless, and she took the responsibility of helping her mother raise the family. After marrying my father she stopped working to raise her five daughters. Since she was a teacher, my mother insisted that we learn English and I remember that she read and told us stories in English. By the time we entered school we were the only ones who were fluent in English. Of course, this skill gave us an advantage in our studies.

In 1948 my father signed a contract with the United States government to work in Mexico and help to eradicate the Aftosa (hoof and mouth disease). Therefore, we spent a year in Guadalajara, where I attended a bilingual school. In the afternoon, the classes were taught in Spanish and, of course, I was the dumb one because I didn't know how to read or write in Spanish. It didn't take long, however, for me to learn to read and write in my native tongue, and when we returned to the United States my formal Spanish was on the same level as my English. However, as we progressed with our formal education, my Spanish began to fall behind. Many years passed before I was able to recuperate it by studying it at the university.

In 1950 my mother returned to teaching. This time she taught at a small one-classroom rural school attended by twelve students. My oldest sister was already attending high school and lived with my grandmother in the town. My mother was my elementary school teacher of fifth to eighth grade and had a tremendous influence on my academic formation. Sometimes when I'm in the classroom I feel myself making the same body expressions as my mother did when she taught and that makes me remember her and feel nostalgic and happy at the same time. At home, my parents always stressed the importance of obtaining an education, and they instilled in us from an early age the need to attend a university. I believe that we were well prepared to function in two worlds: our cultural world and the world of the "American" culture.

When does your academic preparation begin?

My mother and my oldest sister always pushed me to excel in my studies and to be the "star" of the class. In junior high and high school, my parents had sent three of my sisters to boarding school in El Rito. At the school the young student population was all Mexican and many of the teachers also were Hispanics. In junior high and high school I graduated at the top of my class. I received a scholarship to attend the University of New Mexico. If I had competed against Anglo students I am not sure that things would have turned out that way. But in our school much was expected of us and we met the expectations. Sadly, this was not the case at the university. There, we found ourselves in uncharted territory. There was no one to help us or believe in us. Soon I ended up becoming a mediocre student. But I did graduate in four years after I selected the only career that we knew was possible for us: that of being a teacher. I left for California, where I lived for two years and worked as a high school teacher. Later I returned to New Mexico, got married, had a daughter, and at the same time continued teaching at the public schools.

But I was not happy. Something was missing, and that something was my need for intellectual stimulation. For that reason, I decided to return to the university and study Spanish at the graduate level.

When did you discover your interest for literature, in general, including U.S., Mexican, Spanish, and Latin American literature? What authors influenced your academic career?

Since my formal education was somewhat mediocre, I can't say that literature interested me. But when I started my Spanish graduate program I had to take literature courses due to the department's requirements. This led me to discover a world unknown to me. I felt that I had found what I was looking for. At the beginning it was the Spanish authors that I loved the most: Fray Luis de León, Alfonso "El Sabio," Miguel de Cervantes, Mariano José de Larra, Santa Teresa, Federico García Lorca, all the classic Spanish writers we were required to read. But when I started to take Latin American and Mexican literature *I knew I had arrived.* I was very interested in Octavio Paz. I remembered that in my doctoral exams I amazed my professors with my essay on Paz. But gradually, I became more interested in the "boom" authors. The Mexican "nueva onda" writers also influenced my academic formation. Unfortunately, in those days female authors were rarely studied. We studied only Sor Juana, Gabriela Mistral, Alfonsina Storni, the select few believed to merit academic attention. At the end of my studies I discovered Rosario Castellanos, and that led me directly to my interest in feminism.

When did your interest in Chicano literature begin? Which Chicano authors influenced your academic career?

In 1972 or 1973 I took a course outside of my regular program of studies. It was a course on Chicano literature taught by Ralph Flores. One of the novels we read was *Bless Me, Ultima.* When I read the novel it was like reading the stories of my own family on printed pages. I will never forget the joy of that experience. At the same time I was asked by the department to prepare a course on Chicana women. I will never forget how my colleague—who cotaught the course with me—and I found it difficult to find the appropriate reading material for the course. But luckily at that time Dorinda Moreno's book,

La mujer en pie de lucha, was published. This pioneer book was a literary anthology written by Chicanas. As a result of that experience, I decided that my doctoral thesis had to be on Chicano literature, specifically, its narrative forms. My committee accepted my proposal with the condition that I focus my study on authors that wrote in Spanish. Among those who interested me were Miguel Méndez, Aristeo Brito, Rolando Hinojosa, and Alejandro Morales, who by then had made names for themselves. And, even though he did not consider himself a "Chicano" author, I included Sabine Ulibarrí, who to me had a special meaning since he wrote about the life that I knew very well as a child. Without any doubt, these were the writers that had a major influence on my academic career. Among the women writers who were also influential I include Margarita Cota-Cárdenas and Ana Castillo.

How did you get involved in the Recovering the U.S. Hispanic Literary Heritage Project?

In 1987 I began to work on an anthology of articles dealing with New Mexican writers. It was published in 1990 under the title *Pasó por aquí: An Anthology of the New Mexican Literary Tradition*. On the basis of that publication I was invited to the first meeting of the so-called Recovery Project. This meeting took place in North Carolina. The following year the group met in Houston with other new members, and the rest is history. I feel very proud of having been part of this project from its initial stages, contributing my scholarship alongside don Luis Leal, Clara Lomas, Genaro Padilla, Chuck Tatum, Francisco Lomelí, and other scholars. Also, besides presenting my research at numerous conferences, I had the good fortune of working with an excellent group of collaborators—Nicolás Kanellos, Agnes Lugo, Kenya Dworkin, Chuck Tatum, José Fernández, and Alejandra Ballestra—on the two anthologies of the project: *Herencia* and *En otra voz*.

How and when does your creative writing begin?

In the mid-1980s Gustavo Sáinz was my colleague at the University of New Mexico. Gustavo led a literary workshop that everybody attended. As a result of that workshop, a creative impetus unleashed itself throughout our department, and I was inspired to try my hand at creative writing.

How does Paletitas de guayaba *come about? Why did you write it in Spanish knowing that you would have a limited audience here in the United States?*

Inspired by the colleagues who attended the Sáinz workshop, I wrote twenty pages of the novel and gave them to Gustavo to read. You can't imagine my surprise when he praised my work very highly, encouraging me to continue writing. If it hadn't been for his very positive feedback of my work, I doubt that I would have followed this literary path. Since everybody in the workshop wrote in Spanish, and since I was totally enveloped in a Spanish language environment, it was natural for me to write in that language. Also, my academic development at the graduate level was totally in Spanish, and I felt comfortable in that environment. I didn't think about the reading public. What interested me was putting into writing the voices that I heard inside of me.

What do you think of Chicano literature written in Spanish? Do you believe that it has a future?

Sabine Ulibarrí told me once that the writer who writes in Spanish in the United States does not have a future. To a certain degree I believe he's right. Look, I do believe that the Chicano literature written in Spanish is some of the best that has been written by Chicanos and Chicanas. Certainly it is one of the most experimental when you have in mind the works of Morales, Méndez, or Brito. However, outside of Spanish classes there is a limited reading public and few opportunities for authors to publish in Spanish. Nonetheless, I believe that we are going to see Mexican immigrants continue to come to this country at a young age. These newcomers will be fluent in Spanish, receive academic preparation, and produce creative writing in their native language. I have already seen this happen with some of my young students here in Oregon.

Being from New Mexico, as a Chicana, what differences exist between the Southwest (New Mexico) and the Northwest (Oregon), where you now work?

My New Mexican roots ran very, very deep, and I feel that everything is so different there. For example, I arrived in Oregon believing that everybody was a Chicano or Chicana. Very quickly my students made it clear to me that they were not Chicanos but mexicanos. Fortunately, the year that I spent as a child in Mexico and the fact that I studied—in-depth—Mexican literature, culture, and history allowed me to connect well with the student population and the environment that I found in Oregon. Soon I adjusted to them and it has been a great pleasure to be part of the Mexican environment that is found here. Of course, there is also a large Chicano and Chicana population that lives in this state. Personally, I feel that I have a lot in common with the Texas Mexicans who arrived and settled here in the 1950s and 1960s.

On what project are you currently working? Another novel?

My latest academic book was a collaborative project with Marcel Mendoza dealing with Mexican migration to Oregon. The book was published in 2010 and it's my last academic project. Over the past twenty years or so, I have been working on a narrative called *Rosebud.* It is based on my childhood and adolescence in Northern New Mexico. This work is written in English and I have not actively pursued a publisher. It's just been sitting in my computer for several years. I suppose I ought to send it out some time. A couple of years ago I retired from my academic position at Oregon State University (OSU) and founded a community support center for the Latino population here in Corvallis. Since then I have devoted my time completely to my work in the community. There is so much to do here that I don't have enough time to work as a writer or a literary critic. That type of work was something that I did at another time in my life. Now my passion to serve my community consumes me completely, and I don't have any energy left, or ganas, to write any intellectual work.

Any last thoughts concerning your role or function as a critic of Chicano literature? Also what do you think has been the major contribution of your work in relation to Chicano letters?

I believe that my doctoral dissertation and all the work that was published on Chicano writers that expressed themselves in Spanish have been my major contributions to the field of Chicano literature. Several articles on Chicana writers have made some impact, especially the work I did on Ana Castillo's *The Mixquiahuala Letters*. Of all that I've done, that has been my favorite piece of work. My contributions to the Recovery Project, headed by Nicolás Kanellos, and my participation in the *Herencia* and *En Otra Voz* anthologies have been very important. The anthology on the literature of New Mexico's Hispanic writers was an important contribution to the restoration of our literary/intellectual heritage. En fin, my contributions have been modest, but I hope that in the future I can be acknowledged as belonging to the initial efforts that helped establish the field of study that we call Chicano literature.

Selected Works

Gonzales-Berry, Erlinda. "Chicano Literature in Spanish: Roots and Content." PhD diss., University of New Mexico, 1978.

——, ed. *Pasó por aquí: Critical Essays on the New Mexican Literary Tradition, 1542–1988*. Albuquerque: University of New Mexico Press, 1989.

——. *Paletitas de guayaba*. Albuquerque, NM: El Norte Publications, 1991.

——. "*The* [Subversive] *Mixquiahuala Letters*: An Antidote for Self-Hate." In *Chicana (W)rites on Word and Film*, edited by María Herrera-Sobek and Helena María Viramontes, 115–24. Berkeley: Third Woman Press, 1995.

——. "Sensuality, Repression, and Death in Arturo Islas's *The Rain God*." In *Critical Mapping of Arturo Islas's Fictions*, edited by Frederick L. Aldama, 15–20. Tempe, AZ: Bilingual Press/Editorial Bilingüe, 2008.

——. *Mexicanos in Oregon: Their Stories, Their Lives*. Corvallis: Oregon State University, 2010.

Gonzales-Berry, Erlinda, and David Maciel, eds. *The Contested Homeland: A Chicano History of New Mexico*. Albuquerque: University of New Mexico Press, 2000.

Gonzales-Berry, Erlinda, and Charles M. Tatum, eds. *Recovering the U.S. Hispanic Literary Heritage*. Vol. 2. Houston, TX: Arte Público Press, 1996.

Gonzales-Berry, Erlinda, Tey Diana Rebolledo, and Teresa Márquez, eds. *Las mujeres hablan: An Anthology of Nuevo Mexicana Writers*. Albuquerque, NM: El Norte Publications, 1988.

Gonzales-Berry, Erlinda, Tey Diana Rebolledo, and Millie Santillanes, eds. *Nuestras mujeres: Hispanas of New Mexico: Their Images and Their Lives, 1582–1992*. Albuquerque, NM: El Norte Publications/Academia, 1992.

2

María Herrera-Sobek

Chicana Feminist Critical Theory

I DON'T RECALL EXACTLY when María Herrera-Sobek and I first met, but it must've been at a conference—perhaps MLA in Chicago in 1979? Or the National Association for Chicana and Chicano Studies (NACCS) conference in Ypsilanti, Michigan, in 1982? I do know that invariably, for over a quarter of a century, we have been meeting at conferences and enjoying each other's company. It was the 1980s when I recall hearing her speak at an MLA panel and, of course, I knew her publications. In the 1990s, we traveled to Paris for a conference on Chicano/a literature.

I was blessed to have had a chance to work more intimately with María at the University of California, Santa Barbara, at the end of the last century. During that year, as Acting Director of the Chicano Studies Research Center, I benefited from her experience at that institution. Whether writing, advising students, hosting international scholars, or preparing manuscripts, María is indefatigable. María has a well-deserved reputation as a prolific and distinguished scholar whose contributions to contemporary Chicana/o studies encompass three main areas: language and linguistics, folklore, and literature.

I cannot conceive of a Chicano/a literary world without María's writings. In more than twenty-five books (single authored or edited) and one hundred articles published in journals and collections, including an important article in PMLA *on Gloria Anzaldúa (2006), María has left her mark on Chicano/a studies.*

I am honored to call María my friend. It is also an honor to be part of a project that attests to the important role she has played in shaping the Chicano/a literary landscape.
—Norma Cantú

María Herrera-Sobek (1942–) was born in the state of Coahuila, Mexico, and grew up in South Texas near the U.S.-Mexico border. Herrera-Sobek's interest in literature led her to undertake her graduate work in California, where she received her MA in Latin American studies and PhD in Hispanic Languages and Literature from the University of California, Los Angeles (1975). Herrera-Sobek taught for twenty-one years (1975–1996) at the University of California, Irvine, before accepting a position as a professor of Chicana and Chicano studies and the Luis Leal Endowed Chair at the University of California, Santa Barbara (UCSB), in 1997. She currently holds the position of professor and is Associate Vice Chancellor for Diversity, Equity, and Academic Policy at UCSB. Her devotion and contributions to the study of Chicano literary studies, as a critic and as a creative writer, are impressive and admirable. Herrera-Sobek is a very productive scholar who is highly respected by her peers, at both the national and international levels.

This interview with María was conducted at her home in Goleta, California, in 2003 and continued in a number of e-mail correspondences from 2004 to 2013.

* * *

María, where were you born? Describe your childhood and the place where you grew up.

I was born in Mexico, in a small city called San Pedro de las Colonias, Coahuila. When I was a baby my maternal grandparents and my mother moved further north to La Frontera—the border—between the United States and Mexico. First they settled in Reynosa, Tamaulipas, but a few months later they crossed the border to El Valle del Río Grande (Rio Grande Valley). They were migrant workers and lived in different pueblitos in El Valle. Finally, they settled in Rio Hondo, Texas, a very small town of around 700 people. It was an agricultural place where cotton, carrots, tomatoes, chile, lettuce, onions, and other agricultural products were grown. We lived there for many years until I was about thirteen years old, when I graduated from the eighth grade. After that we moved to Arizona. We lived in another small pueblo called Gilbert, of some 2,000 people, that as of April 1, 2010, has increased to more than 208,457! My grandfather, again, worked as a farm worker. I attended Gilbert High School and after graduation went on to Arizona State University in Tempe, where I studied chemistry; then I went to the University of California, Los Angeles (UCLA), to continue with my academic studies. For my graduate work I changed my major from chemistry to Latin American studies because I was interested in learning about my culture, that is, the history, the culture, and all other aspects related to the Chicano/a population. While at UCLA I became involved in women's issues (the feminist movement), farm workers, and student social movements. I enrolled for my master's degree at UCLA and majored in Latin American studies and later went on for my PhD degree, which I received in Hispanic languages and literature, also from UCLA.

When you lived in Texas did you ever think that you were going to stay trapped in your family's migratory working cycle?

No. Never. I don't know why, but I always believed that I was different from the rest of my classmates and the people I knew. I had a very rare mentality; I was very precocious. Ever since I was about three or four years old and was surrounded by poverty and poor people I became acutely aware and conscious of the differences between poverty and wealth and knew that we were the poor ones, not the rich ones. I remember that I was very aware of this difference and that social inequality existed. Even then I felt deep in my heart that this state of affairs was not right. We were poor. My sister, who at the time was fourteen or fifteen years old, worked as a maid for a well-to-do family. One particular day she returned from cleaning one of those houses, the Benavides's family home—I still remember the last name of the family—over in Reynosa, Mexico, and spoke of the luxury and the wealth those people had. That made me question why we were so poor even though my grandparents worked very, very hard. That, I believe, is what awoke my social consciousness. Also, moving from one place to another in search of work as migrant workers in the United States, sometimes we went without eating;

that and sleeping on the floor, living in tecoruchos, all of that affirmed to me that we lived a life of poverty. The fact was that as a young girl I learned to read when I was very, very young––I was three or four years old––and this made me pay attention to the problems that existed around me. I read newspapers. The family asked me to read them the news. But basically, working as migrant workers for middle-class U.S. farmers and seeing the differences between our standard of living and theirs made me very conscious of social class structures and the horrible inequalities that existed. That motivated me to get educated so that I could someday help change society for the better and address the inequities that I experienced. Also, the extreme racism rampant in Texas at the time of my childhood made me aware of the social injustices we Mexican Americans suffered. In addition to all of the above, I loved school and learning. I adored going to school and doing well in class. It was very emotionally satisfying to me and I did very well in my classes. I was valedictorian both in the eighth grade and later on in high school.

When did you become interested in continuing a college education?

When my grandfather worked with the ranchers in Texas, one of the rancher's wives for whom my grandfather worked bought different types of popular ladies magazines, such as *Seventeen*, *The Saturday Evening Post*, *Vogue*, *Redbook*, *The Ladies Home Journal*, and so on. I would get the old issues and through them, I read about young girls who attended universities. I was around eight or nine years old when I began reading them. In the special issues of those ladies' magazines that came out in August, I read about how girls were planning to go to college and what they were supposed to wear in the fall. They featured, in glossy-colored pages, the most contemporary fashions and showed photographs of college campuses—mostly from Ivy League schools. Generally, these girls attended private schools for girls on the East Coast. When I became aware of their world, I decided that I would also attend a university just like these rich girls did. I would also read about scholarships that were available, so it didn't seem impossible to carry out my plans of going to college even though I was poor. I also read the Nancy Drew Mystery Stories series. The girls in her stories went to the university, including Nancy Drew herself, which for me was also a source of inspiration to continue my education. One of the ranchers for whom my grandfather worked thought that I was very smart and full of potential. He would ask me if I also was planning on attending a university. I would answer him yes, that I was going to go to college, just like his own daughters, Dorothy and Mary Ann, had done.

Did your family encourage you to continue your studies?

My grandparents, who loved me very much, spoiled me. They would pamper me, me consentían mucho because when my father died, my grandparents adopted me. So my maternal grandparents basically raised me as an only child. My mother was left a widow at a young age and already had three children; she was pregnant with me when my father died of an accident in a rodeo three months before I was born. For that reason, my grandparents adopted me. We were very poor, but whatever I asked for they would try to get it for me, depending on the economic circumstances. So when I told them that I loved school very much, they allowed me to get an education. They felt very proud of me. Me presumían con sus amigos. They always felt very proud that I was able to read and do math at an early age, at three or four years old. My grandparents were very supportive of my education even though they did not quite understand what I was doing at the universities I attended.

Did your grandparents move with you to Los Angeles?

No, I moved from Arizona to UCLA because UCLA was ranked very high. I chose UCLA over UC Berkeley and Stanford because I wanted to be closer to my grandparents and be able to visit them often, which I did.

Was there a particular professor at UCLA that influenced you in your academic career?

Yes, there were many professors at UCLA who were very kind to me and helped, mentored, and encouraged me greatly. Professor James

Wilkie, in particular, from the UCLA History Department and numerous professors from the Department of Spanish and Portuguese were very supportive, such as Professors Shirley Arora, Rubén Benítez, Stanley Robe, Eduardo Díaz, Carroll Johnson, John Crowe, and many others, as well. Professor Wilkie has been my mentor for many, many years and has always been very supportive. However, a professor from the Spanish and Portuguese Department asked me if I would be interested in studying for the doctorate in his department after my MA in Latin American studies. I told him that I liked anthropology and history and was interested in those fields, especially in the areas related to pre-Columbian culture, but that I also loved literature very much. He encouraged me to apply to the Spanish Department and I did. I was very happy with my decision since I absolutely loved literature: from Spanish Peninsular literature to Latin American literature. I loved all of my courses and took almost all the ones offered by the Spanish and Portuguese Department!

Was it at UCLA that you became interested in studying Chicano literature? What led you to acknowledge it?

No, my interest in Chicano literature came much later because at that time it wasn't offered in the Spanish and Portuguese Department at UCLA. For my doctorate degree I majored in Latin American literature. I began studying the incipient Chicano literature that was surfacing in small literary magazines, in ditto sheets, and so on. When I was offered positions to teach Chicano/a literature courses I researched, as much as possible, what was available. This was in 1972 and there was very little published in the major presses, but a lot was coming out of small presses and emerging Chicano journals.

My grandmother was a feminist and an advocate for women and human rights. Even though she did not have a formal education, my grandmother knew how to read and write and was also very militant. My grandfather leaned toward politics and my grandmother toward social justice. She was very religious and truly believed we were all God's children and all should be treated with respect and kindness. On the other hand, when I was a young girl there was a lot of discrimination in Texas. I attended a segregated school. This segregation and my grandparents' social consciousness awakened my consciousness of being a Chicana, of being Mexican. I felt that the dominant society abused and exploited us. My grandfather would work from 6 a.m. until 6 p.m. and would earn $3 a day in the 1950s. My mother earned 25 cents an hour washing dishes in a fancy restaurant in South Texas in the early 1970s! I grew up with that reality and with the motivation of someday being able to defend the rights of my people and fight for social justice. As a young girl, I heard that ranchers beat up Mexicans for no apparent reason; that they killed them by shooting them in the back. This would make me very angry, even as a child. I would hear these stories from grown-ups or would read about these atrocities in the newspapers.

When the Vietnam War began, I was opposed to it because I grew up very leftist and mistrusted U.S. politics given the United States' involvement in Mexican, Central, and South American politics. My grandfather nourished that mistrust in me. He never believed that any government was honest and to be trusted. He said that politicians were liars, that the U.S. government had stolen land from Mexico. However, I tried to balance these beliefs with what I was being taught at school: respect for democracy and patriotism. I lived in three types of realities. This double, triple consciousness was something I had to face.

Which Chicano authors influenced your academic career?

For the most part the authors from the late 1960s and early 1970s. I read and taught what are now Chicano classics: works by Tomás Rivera, Rolando Hinojosa-Smith, Rudolfo Anaya, Estela Portillo Trambley, Miguel Méndez, and the early Chicano male poets as well as works by Luis Valdez and the Teatro Campesino. Around 1975, I began to read Chicana writers in earnest. I had read Portillo Trambley, but now I included emerging Chicana writers like Alma Villanueva, Sandra Cisneros, Ana Castillo, Lorna Dee Cervantes, Lucha Corpi, and many others who began to make their entrance into the literary world. Because of that interest, in 1976 I introduced a course on Chicana writers at the University of California, Irvine.

When did you start your career as a critic of Chicano literature?

It is difficult to say, because how are we going to define Chicano literature? My MA thesis dealt with corridos. That study resulted in a book, *The Bracero Experience* (1979). If we look at the corrido as part of Chicano literature we find some of its origins there, and of course in the Spanish Colonial literature of the Southwest. Later, I published *The Mexican Corrido: A Feminist Analysis*. In 1976, I introduced a course on Chicana writers at the University of California, Irvine. I believe that it was the first university course in the nation to deal with this subject. In 1982, I also organized the first conference in the United States that focused on that subject. A book resulted from that conference, and in 1985 Bilingual Review Press published it under the title *Beyond Stereotypes: The Critical Analysis of Chicana Literature*.

What do you think distinguishes the literary critics of Chicano literature who study in Spanish graduate programs from those who study in English graduate programs at U.S. universities?

One of the aspects that highly distinguishes the critics of Chicano literature who have studied in Spanish programs from those who study in English departments is that for those in Spanish department doctoral programs the literary training is very broad, very extensive. The main difference I attribute this to is that, in general, English departments do not study Latin American literature or Spanish Peninsular literature. Students, and even professors in English departments, frequently do not know much about Latin American literature and much less Chicano literature or Spanish Peninsular literature. Students, therefore, who study in English departments tend to have a more limited perspective because they are not acquainted with Latin American, Spanish Peninsular, and Chicano/Latino literature. I believe that it is more difficult for them to understand Chicano literature. Of more concern is the fact that many critics who have a PhD in Chicano literature from English departments do not speak or read Spanish. So these students miss the whole world of Spanish Colonial literature of the South and Southwest written between the 1530s and 1848. They also miss much that was written in the nineteenth century, since much of it was written in

Spanish. These periods represent the origins of Chicano/a literature and are an integral part of this literature. On the other hand, Chicano/a critics trained in Spanish and Portuguese departments have a more extensive training because we are trained not only in Hispanic literatures but also in Anglo American and English literatures. One must remember that starting from grammar school up to the university level we are required to study Anglo American and English literatures. Our training in Spanish departments is VERY EXTENSIVE, VERY STRONG. I am very happy that I had that training.

For undergraduate students that are fluent in both Spanish and English, what do you think is the principal factor that leads them to choose a graduate Spanish program or a graduate English program?

Most likely what influences students to select a Spanish department or an English department is their fluency in language. If they are fluent in Spanish, and they have majored in Spanish as undergraduates, the student will probably lean toward doing graduate work in a Spanish department. The opposite is also true. If an undergraduate student majored in English they will veer toward an English department. However, today, with the establishment of Chicano/a studies in some universities, like UCSB and UCLA, as well as ethnic studies, students have more choices.

One speaks of Chicano literature as a working-class literature, a blue-collar literature. Do you believe that there are parallels between writers and critics, as far as this affirmation is concerned? In other words, does a working-class critic exist in Chicano literature?

Many of us who participate in this interview project come from the working class. And even though some Chicanos and Chicanas might not come from the working class, they are TREATED as if they did. I believe that this treatment and categorization, this general perception that all Chicanos/as are members of the working class, give us a certain philosophical vision of social justice and how we analyze a literary text. And it is possible that we analyze literature with that point of view in mind. My literary training was influenced by the New Criticism of the 1950s and later the poststructural criticism from the 1960s. The 1970s and 1980s brought new theoretical frameworks from which we could analyze our literature: feminist theory, postcolonial theory, deconstruction, new historicism, ecological criticism, reader-response theory, and others. When these new currents of criticism emerged—Marxist criticism, poststructuralism, deconstruction, reader-response theory, feminist criticism, semiotics, and other criticism and literary theories—we, Chicanos and Chicanas, absorbed them like sponges because they spoke directly to us and to our social class formation. We welcomed both Marxism and other new literary tendencies. Many of us were Marxist and feminist critics. As Chicanas we particularly welcomed feminist criticism. Our ties with the working class gave us a particular perspective of these new literary theories that emerged in the 1960s, 1970s, and 1980s. In particular, these literary currents focused not only on seeing and analyzing a closed text but also on seeing how that text was influenced by society and how it in turn influenced society.

And do you believe that this new generation of critics is going to continue with this tradition?

Yes, some critics will undoubtedly continue with this tradition. Others may not; maybe some already feel assimilated because they represent a new generation that emerged from the middle class and do not share the same working-class experiences that we lived in the second half of the twentieth century. The Chicano movement has produced a middle class whose children are going to function socially through another point of view. On the other hand, if the anger and oppressions against the Chicanos continue here in the United States, it is possible that another wave of Chicano and Chicana militants will arise. For example, the recent construction of the border wall between Mexico and the United States has been humiliating and depressing for us Chicanos/as. That is a social blow that the Mexican American, Chicano/a, Latino/a society has recently suffered. This humiliation is heartfelt. Even though I am a U.S. citizen, I feel this insult in my heart and it depresses me. I believe that many Chicanos/as and Mexican Americans feel the same way. Even though it might not directly affect us because we are citizens of this country—that is to say they are not going to deport us or deny us social services—it does affect us emotionally. I feel the force of a hand slapping me on the face when I read in the newspaper something written against Mexicans, against the undocumented and their children. I feel it physically. These social problems are going to stay with us for a long time.

Do you think that Chicana critics, because of those negative concepts connected to the Chicano, for example, being identified as "pochos" by Mexicans, feel uncomfortable when they participate in conferences alongside Mexican critics, or in fact, Latin American critics?

It is fair to say that there exists a tension between mexicanas and Chicanas. I don't know why this tension exists, but it does. What I have witnessed several times in Mexico is that the mexicanas feel uncomfortable with us Chicanas. There is a certain snobbism on their part toward us. On the one hand, I believe they admire us secretly because we speak English fluently and we function well within the Anglo American world. Also because we belong to the United States, the country that they secretly admire. But, on the other hand, they perceive us as second-class citizens and as inferior to them because of class and race. Chicanas are seen as indigenous people, and some in the Mexican middle and upper classes view us as such, in a contemptuous and racially discriminatory manner. In Mexico and in Latin America, one can still find clear racism against indigenous peoples. Also there is a lot of discrimination based on social class. We Chicanos/as identify with indigenous people due to the racism that we have suffered in the United States. The funny thing is that in Mexico it also bothers the elites if we, the Chicanos and Chicanas, identify ourselves as indigenous people! Then, it seems that they see us as a third race! I have noticed this on various occasions when I am in Mexico. They see us as an inferior third-world pueblo.

Do you believe that this is so because Chicano critics identify with the working class and want to give them a voice, while for many Mexican critics this might not be a priority?

It might be at the personal level. For example, I earn more money than university professors in Mexico, I am sure of that. I am paid extremely well at the university. University professors in Mexico/Latin America are middle class and so am I, but I identify myself with the working class. However, the middle class in Mexico sees us, all the Chicanos or Mexican Americans, as belonging to the working class. I believe that we in the United States have more of a sense of racial class, of dealing with racial issues because we have been strongly discriminated against due to our brown skin. Also, there exists that tension between Mexico and the United States as far as the power gap that exists between the two countries. This country is very powerful, the most powerful in the world, and the Mexicans find it very difficult to accept that we, the Chicanos and Chicanas, are part of that power.

As far as your role as a literary critic and creative writer, are you able to easily separate one from the other?

Well, sometimes it is difficult to write creative work such as poetry or narrative fiction when you are both a creative writer and a literary critic because being a literary critic takes a lot of my time from my creative activity and from writing poetry. I have found that to write poems I have to be relaxed and not distracted by other tasks such as writing books and scholarly articles. Generally, when my creativity emerges it's when I read something such as a novel or a book of poetry or see a movie and, of course, when I am not working on an article or book. When I travel I avoid the telephone and the computer. I have time to be alone and away from distractions, and this is when the creative juices start flowing. When I go to the ocean, that's when my poetry comes out. I do believe that in my case there exists a division between the creative process and the research process. Many times I do try to use poetic images to make my critical works more interesting. But to write poetry, I really need a process of introspection, of reflection, of thinking, of immersing myself deep in the inner crevices of my being. I need to take a break from research and its attendant critical function and let my mind develop the reality I feel, see, or think.

Can you say that in writing criticism you are able to use your creative voice but in writing poetry you cannot use your academic one?

I don't seem to be able to write poetry when I am immersed in writing my scholarly books and articles. I do not seem to be able to mix scholarly writing and poetry writing. It might be because the creative process that comes to me is similar to when one listens to a song and cannot get it out of one's mind. I think they call this getting an "earworm"! One might get tired of carrying the tune of that song that repeats itself over and over in one's mind, and even if one does not want to think about it, it's always there. That's how the poetic verses appear in my mind. If I am very busy with writing criticism or working on the computer I cannot seem to concentrate and allow that creative voice to come out.

Is it important for you to write in Spanish? In English? Or does it matter what language is used?

For me, it doesn't matter because, like I said, the poems come out of the most profound part of my being and they come out as if they were songs that begin to repeat themselves over and over in my mind. Those songs may come out in Spanish or English. Now, I believe that if I am reading poetry or a novel in English, then maybe my creativity might come out in that language. The same thing happens if I am reading in Spanish. When I am in Mexico my ideas come out in Spanish. The ambience has a lot to do with the language that one uses to express oneself.

Do you think that Chicano literature written in Spanish will survive?

I believe that it will survive because we are close to Mexico and Latin America and there is a constant transfusion of Mexicans, Latin Americans, and other Spanish-speaking people who bring the Spanish language to us and this will always be present. Our Latino pueblo is growing in great numbers in this country. I believe that as much as hegemonic society tries to destroy Spanish by passing laws or by peer disapproval, it will not be successful; our language will survive. The Spanish language is very beautiful and has a special place in the Latino heart.

What do you think of Chicano literature today? What are the most drastic changes that you have seen in Chicano literature in the last decades?

Personally, from the first moment I read it, I fell in love with Chicano literature. It was love at first sight. Chicano literature is fabulous, fascinating. I'm not saying it because I am a Chicana. Since I started to teach it at colleges and universities in California in the 1970s, I was immediately fascinated by it and so were my students, both Latinos and Anglos. I believed with all my heart then that it was a literature that was going to go very far, and I began to make it my own. At UC Irvine I had to gain respect for it. At that time some people in power in academia would denigrate it, would say that it was trash, that it wasn't useful, that it was going to rapidly disappear, and so forth. I knew that it wasn't going to be like that. I saw that our literature was political and contained fabulous aspects of creativity and singular structures and techniques. I felt that it offered strong and powerful messages, metaphors, and images. I had a lot of faith in it. I had read Carlos Fuentes, Gabriel García Márquez, all the fabulous writers from the Latin American "boom" of the 1960s, and when I read the work of Tomás Rivera, Rolando Hinojosa, Rudolfo Anaya, I saw its strength—strength as powerful as that of those Latin American authors cited above. For the above reasons I have made trips to Turkey, Spain, England, France, Germany, and other countries to promote Chicano literature. I know that the world is now acknowledging it. I believe that soon they are going to award us the Nobel Prize. I believe that it will happen in a few years. Hopefully, before I die. I'm seeing that our literature is becoming more international. In Turkey, Spain, and Germany they are reading Chicano literature and are falling in love with it. It fascinates them. For example, a Turkish girl who I know and who lives in Turkey read *Caramelo* and is now writing her dissertation on Sandra Cisneros. She says that she completely identifies with the girl in *Caramelo*, so there is a connection that exists between her reality and ours. We have a voice that speaks to the world.

As far as the changes in Chicano literature, some of the most salient came with the writings of Chicanas in the 1980s. Their voices were powerful and could not be denied. Since the 1980s women have taken a leadership role in publishing novels.

Our literature of course has evolved. We have had writers nominated for the Pulitzer Prize and some Latino writers have won it. It has also gained worldwide acceptance. In addition, *The Norton Anthology of Latino Literature*, of which I was an associate editor, was published in 2010 and has definitely put us on the map. Chicano literature has entered the mainstream canon and there is no stopping us.

I am also seeing some new genres being introduced such as "narrative journalism," which Luis Alberto Urrea has done so wonderfully in his book *The Devil's Highway: A True Story*. The memoir has also taken center stage. One continuity that I see is the topic of immigration. That still seems to be a popular topic, as seen in Reyna Grande's success in her memoir writings.

Tell us about your latest projects.

I have just completed the three-volume encyclopedia, *Celebrating Latino Folklore: An Encyclopedia of Cultural Traditions* (2012). This was a three-volume project of themes dealing with Latino folklore. It includes 320 essays—some are twenty to thirty pages long (5,000 words) and others are four or five pages long (1,000 words). It has taken me many years to finish this project, but the three volumes came out in July 2012.

Right now, I am also working on a book on aspects of nationalism and identity construction through the history and various representations of La Llorona, La Malinche, and La Virgen de Guadalupe. Another project that I'm working on deals with the environment and Chicano literature. The book is tentatively titled "Writing the Toxic Environment: Eco criticism and the Chicana/o Literary Imagination." I am very interested in the concern that Chicanos/as have for the environment.

Any last thoughts concerning your role or function as a critic of Chicano literature? Also what do you think has been the major impact of your work in relation to Chicano letters?

My contributions as a critic of Chicano/a literature and culture have been in four main areas: Chicana literary criticism and feminist theory, folklore and cultural studies, colonial literature of the Southwest, and, more recently, Chicana/o visual art. One major goal I have pursued has been to help firmly establish Chicano literary and cultural studies within mainstream academia. I have taken Chicano and Chicana authors from the early 1970s and applied European, as well as Chicano and Latin American, literary theories to their works at a time when this type of literature was being ignored; it was not considered serious or academic. My work in Europe, primarily in Germany, Spain, Turkey, and France, organizing and/or helping to organize conferences on Chicano literature, helped tremendously to establish our literature internationally as a literary field of study. Equally important, my work in the United States organizing conferences and panels at the Modern Language Association, the American Folklore Society, and conferences at the University of California, Irvine, where I had previously worked, helped to promote and establish Chicano literature in Europe and in the United States. I am also very active in the International Ballad Association based in Europe. I often present scholarly articles on the corrido via this organization throughout Europe. Another organization I am very active in is the International Association of Inter-American studies based in Germany.

My strongest contribution to Chicano literature has been in helping to establish Chicana literary studies, in other words, literary studies that deal with Chicana writers and the application of feminist theories in the Chicano/a literary world. It was at UC Irvine that I organized the first course on Chicana writers. It was also at UC Irvine that I organized a series of conferences on Chicana authors that resulted in the publication of several books: *Beyond Stereotypes: The Critical Analysis of Chicana Literature* (1985), *Chicana Creativity and Criticism: Charting New Frontiers in American Literature* (1988), and *Chicana (W)rites: On Word and Film* (1995). *Beyond Stereotypes*, I believe, was the first critical anthology on Chicana literature. The above were some of the first anthologies written on the works of Chicana authors.

Equally important has been my work on the Mexican/Chicano corrido. While don Américo Paredes is recognized as the founding "father" of Chicano studies and his work on the corrido is superb in introducing class and race to its study, my work, for example, *The Mexican Corrido: A Feminist Analysis*, as well as numerous scholarly articles, introduced gender to this field of study. Introducing feminist critical theory to the analysis and hermeneutics of the corrido is one of my major contributions to Chicano/a literary studies.

I also have helped establish the field of colonial literature of the U.S. Southwest. I have published numerous articles in this area and was the principal associate editor for *The Norton Anthology of Latino Literature* for this section of the book.

I am very pleased to see that Chicano/a literature and culture has been receiving more and more the respect that it deserves, both nationally and internationally. I am absolutely delighted to see the new writers and critics specializing in Chicano/a literature taking their place in the world of literary studies and making their superb national and international impact. The world is changing very rapidly, and transnational migrations are rapidly increasing. Our literature, with its immigrant experience and the depiction of third-world people living in first-world environments, with all the issues surrounding these experiences, strongly connect to present-day populations the world over: it speaks to both receiving countries and sending countries. The future looks very bright for Chicano/a literature and culture, indeed.

Selected Works

Herrera-Sobek, María. "The Function of Folklore in Gabriel García Márquez." PhD diss., University of California, Los Angeles, 1975.

——. *The Bracero Experience: Elitelore versus Folklore*. Los Angeles: UCLA Latin American Center Publications, University of California, Los Angeles, 1979.

——, ed. *Beyond Stereotypes: The Critical Analysis of Chicana Literature*. Binghamton, NY: Bilingual Press, 1985.

——. *The Mexican Corrido: A Feminist Analysis*. Bloomington: Indiana University Press, 1990.

——, ed. *Reconstructing a Chicano/a Literary Heritage: Hispanic Colonial Literature of the Southwest*. Tucson, AZ: University of Arizona Press, 1993.

——. *Northward Bound: The Mexican Immigrant Experience in Ballad and Song*. Bloomington: Indiana University Press, 1993.

——, ed. *Chicana Literary and Artistic Expressions: Culture and Society in Dialogue*. Santa Barbara: University of California, Santa Barbara, 2000.

——. *Chicano Folklore: A Handbook*. Westport, CT: Greenwood Press, 2006.

Herrera-Sobek, María, and David R. Maciel, eds. *Culture Across Borders: Mexican Immigration and Popular Culture*. Tucson: University of Arizona Press, 1998.

Herrera-Sobek, María, and Virgina Sánchez-Korrol, eds. *Recovering the U.S. Hispanic Literary Heritage*. Vol. 4. Houston: Arte Público Press, 2000.

Herrera-Sobek, María, and Helena María Viramontes, eds. *Chicana Creativity and Criticism: Charting New Frontiers in American Literature*.

Houston: Arte Público Press and Mexico/Chicano Program, University of California, Irvine, 1988.

——, eds. *Chicana (W)rites: On Word and Film*. Berkeley: Third Woman Press, 1995.

Herrera-Sobek, María, David R. Maciel, and Isidro I. Ortiz, eds. *Chicano Renaissance: Contemporary Cultural Trends*. Tucson: University of Arizona Press, 2000.

3

Nicolás Kanellos

El guardián de pasados literarios

NICOLÁS KANELLOS, simply put, is a rainmaker. He has helped facilitate the work of many emerging and established scholars for over forty years by founding Arte Público Press and the Recovering the U.S. Hispanic Literary Heritage Project. Although he is a world-class scholar, publisher, and professor, he did his greatest work as a mentor.

During the first semester of my MA program at the University of Houston I took his U.S. Hispanic Theater course. I learned a lot, but I was in over my head and barely passed. In my last semester I dared to take another course from Kanellos and did very well. He even congratulated me for my academic growth during those four semesters. I still remember the comments on the last page of my paper, "¡Te felicito . . . !" It was at that moment that I finally believed I could make it in academia. I don't know what he saw in me and other students who struggled, but he never gave up on us.

It was because of him that several of my classmates and I received our first publication experience working with the anthologies Herencia *and* En Otra Voz. *His lifelong commitment to U.S. Hispanic literature has benefited scholars and students alike. His legacy will not only be that he recovered significant texts but also that he uncovered the potential of future scholars to help build our field. Because of his work, our literature and those who study it thrive.*

—Spencer R. Herrera

Nicolás Kanellos (1945–) was born in New York City. Kanellos received his MA and PhD from the University of Texas at Austin, and worked at Indiana University Northwest, in Gary, Indiana, before joining the faculty of the University of Houston in 1980, where he presently serves as Brown Foundation Professor of Hispanic Studies. Kanellos is the founder of the highly acclaimed Revista Chicano-Riqueña *(later renamed* The Americas Review*) and Arte Público Press. He is the director of the Recovering the U.S. Hispanic Literary Heritage Project, author of* A History of Hispanic Theater in the United States: Origins to 1940 *(1990) and* Hispanic Immigrant Literature: El sueño del retorno *(2011), and editor of numerous books and anthologies dealing with Hispanic/Latino literature, including* Herencia: The Anthology of Hispanic Literature of the United States *(2002) and* En otra voz: Antología de la literatura hispana de los Estados Unidos *(2002). In 2008 Kanellos was elected to the Spanish American Royal Academy of Literature, Arts and Science.*

The interview with Nicolás was conducted through e-mail correspondences in 2013.

* * *

Nicolás, where were you born? Describe your childhood and the place where you grew up.

I was born in New York City and prior to my schooling went back and forth to Puerto Rico with my mother and later my brothers. And after starting school, I'd stay with my family in Puerto Rico during the summer. My mother was born in Arroyo, Puerto Rico, on the southern coast. She was a very intelligent woman and graduated valedictorian at her Catholic high school, where she learned clerical skills and English. Because of that, after she immigrated to the United States when she was about twenty-four, she was able to work as a secretary and a billing clerk and in other office jobs until she retired and went on social security. My father was the son of Greek immigrants and even went to a Greek school in New York. But his father abandoned him and his mother during the Depression, and he had no other family. For all intents and purposes, my mother's family of many sisters and brothers and cousins became his family. He finished high school—at night, I think—at a vocational high school specializing in textiles. But he never had a career, and he worked at all types of jobs, from loading cars onto ships, to assembly line worker, news stand clerk, postman, and toll collector on the New Jersey Turnpike, the latter of which he had the longest.

I mostly grew up as a street kid in New York City and Jersey City. I encountered a socially hostile environment and got into many fights. However, I was a good student and loved to read. In Jersey City, we lived in the warehouse district by Bay Street. There, I discovered what today I know are called "signatures," the sheets of 8–16–32–64 pages that are folded and sewn to make up a book; these were always thrown out in the garbage of one of the factories, and I made my own books out of them by folding and cutting them. In my adulthood, I later found out that that "factory" was a bindery for the American Book Company. Also my father bartered for books with the bindery workers and, thus, we were able to assemble an imperfect set of the Encyclopedia Americana and bound collections of the works of Steinbeck, Maugham, and Hemingway. I read all of these at a very young age. When I was about ten, I discovered what a library was and where it was. When I went there and a librarian tried to help me by asking what I would like to read, I didn't know what to answer. So I said what was familiar: Steinbeck! She frowned and said I was much too young for that.

From my early school years, I loved to sit and read newspapers, and I still remember my confusion and worry reading the *Daily News* and the *Daily Mirror* because of all the horrible things and distorted photo images they always printed about Puerto Ricans.

Also, me and my co-students were mostly poor, and one teacher always brought us a big shopping bag of gifts for Christmas and other occasions. She also gave us books. I remember the two books she gave me—to be my very own!—that I loved and read over and over again: *Black Beauty* and *Fifty Famous Stories*. I learned to read Spanish at the same time I learned to read English because the corner bodega had comic books in Spanish and I figured out the writing. And when I was in Puerto Rico in the summer, everything was written in Spanish, from the newspapers to books and signs.

One September, we had to report on what we did during the summer, and I wrote about flying down to and living in Puerto Rico. My teacher didn't believe we could afford tickets to fly—she probably had never flown herself—and she sent a letter home to my parents stating that I had lied. Actually, my aunt Aurea was married to a prosperous doctor and used to send me the ticket to Puerto Rico and I would stay with her; she and my uncle could not have children, and I was somewhat of a surrogate.

When I was a teenager, my family moved to a New Jersey suburb and I graduated high school from a college preparatory track, although my record was spotty. Thanks to this preparation and the role models I had in my aunts' husbands in Puerto Rico, I always knew I wanted to go to college, although I thought you could only be a doctor or a lawyer by going to college, for that's what Tío Federico and Tío Julio were. For years, I went around to the factories and warehouses to collect soda bottles in order to cash them in for two cents and five cents—a quart bottle—each in order to save money for college.

Thanks to this preparation, I was admitted to a college, and I continued to work part-time jobs and summer jobs during my studies. The soda bottle money went into my brother's and my bedroom set when we moved to the suburbs. My folks had no money for my college education; worse, they were broke from the hospital bills for my brother, who died of leukemia.

When does your academic preparation begin? When did you discover your interest for literature, in general, including U.S., Mexican, Spanish, and Latin American literature? What authors influenced your academic career?

I went to Fairleigh Dickinson University with a state scholarship based on economic need. Thanks to my jobs, scholarships, and taking a year off, I was able to go down to Mexico and study at the Universidad Nacional Autónoma de México (UNAM) for the 1965–1966 academic year. I decided on Mexico because I wanted to be free and not have to report to my Puerto Rican family, which would have been the case had I gone for a year to the University of Puerto Rico or the Interamericana. Mexico was a whole new world! I loved everything about it, and my fellow Mexican students accepted me as one of them. It was the type of acceptance and comradeship I had never experienced in New York or New Jersey but was similar to the love I felt from my cousins in Puerto Rico! At the UNAM, and on my own, I was able to go deep into Mexican literature, theater, history, and art. I think I was born then and there as a Latino who could bridge the Mexican and Puerto Rican and other Hispanic cultures and as a future intellectual.

At Fairleigh Dickinson, at first, I wanted to study to become a lawyer and fight for the rights of Puerto Ricans and other minorities—the civil rights movement was in full force and I became somewhat personally involved. I changed my mind about studying law because I was a good student in Spanish literature classes, and my professors encouraged me to become a Spanish teacher and go on to grad school; after all, I could make a living like them and command social respect as they did and continue learning. I also excelled in all of my American literature classes and in Italian. I also studied Italian literature at Rutgers.

I graduated cum laude in 1966 and went on to take a teaching assistantship at the University of Texas (UT). At UT, in addition to studying Spanish and Portuguese literatures, I became heavily involved in the Chicano movement: registering voters, taking voters to the polls, teaching people to poll watch, teaching volunteers to speak enough conversational Spanish to help with civil rights. I became a member of the Teatro Chicano de Austin, where I learned to act and where my singing and guitar playing came in handy. Let me add that one of the greatest influences on my life was that of my Aunt Providencia García, who was a pioneer in the Latin music publishing and recording business. It was she who gave me my first guitar, and it was she who modeled the cultural entrepreneurship and diplomacy that would serve me well as the founder and director of Arte Público Press.

In the graduate program at UT, I worked with scholars involved in classical Spanish theater, such as Stan Zimic, A. A. Parker, and Mildred Boyer, and eventually wrote my dissertation on the theater of Cervantes; it was impossible at that time to study anything Latino. But in the community, I got to do real theater and understand how the performance informed the literary text.

I hated grad school. I hated the department, and I had run-ins with a number of professors. Many of them, even the Spaniards and Latin Americans, were prejudiced against U.S. Latinos. A professor supervising the teaching assistants threatened to pull the ears from my head after I stood up to him! He was later placed on my dissertation committee without my permission. I would have never graduated had the Graduate School not forced the department to take the names off graduate exams and use a code for each student. It seems that the only students getting through were the lovers and relatives of the graduate school professors, at least that was said to have led to the Grad School intervention. Because of this anonymity, I ended up having the best exams in the department.

During this time, because of my fellow teatristas and students, such as corridista Rumel Fuentes, I sat in on don Américo Paredes's courses in the English Department and got to know him. We all revered him and, since he could sing and play the guitar and give us historical background on our songs and performances, it was a natural collaboration. We even went to a local bar and sang and played together.

Things were changing in the student make-up in the Spanish Department and in the culture in Texas. Because it was well known that I was in teatro, had put together a student literary magazine, and was an excellent teacher of accelerated Spanish, when I became All But Dissertation (ABD), the department asked me to prepare and teach the first courses on Chicano literature and Chicano theater. This I did with the help of don Américo. But I never got to teach the courses there because an opportunity came up for me to teach as an assistant professor at Indiana University Northwest, in Gary, Indiana. So I left Austin for Gary and taught those courses there, starting in 1972.

Besides my hate for the UT department, what propelled me to Gary was that Mexican Americans, Puerto Ricans, and other Latinos lived in the area, that the students were mainly steel workers, and that Chicago was accessible. In other words, it seemed to me to be very similar to Jersey City, and I felt I was called to help students from a similar background as mine.

At IUN, Luis Dávila, an assistant professor down in Indiana University Bloomington, and I founded *Revista Chicano-Riqueña*. In early 1973, we published our first issue of the literary magazine that would last some twenty-five years. I also founded a teatro, *El Teatro Desengaño del Pueblo*, and got involved with various civil rights and community action groups, including receiving training from Saul

Alinsky's institute. I worked with students and the community to write the first bilingual education laws for Indiana, created the bilingual education program at IUN, and created the Chicano-Riqueño Studies Department.

Describe your critical formation in graduate school.

Back when I was in grad school, there was hardly any theoretical training. We learned to analyze literary works via the New Criticism, and that was it. There were literally hundreds of literary works on the MA and PhD reading lists that we needed to know for the comprehensive exams, which also included a PhD qualification exam to be able to start doctoral courses. And we had to know and study the critical bibliography and historiography of the literature.

When does your interest in Chicano/U.S. Latino literature begin?

While I had always been aware of a creative tradition, of publications, newspapers, and books in Spanish in our Latino communities, in college and graduate school there was nothing in our textbooks, nothing in the libraries, and nothing on our reading lists. My interest in our literature intensified when I participated in the Chicano movement and in teatro. Luis Dávila and I founded *Revista Chicano-Riqueña* in part to create a publishing outlet for all the writers and artists we knew in the communities and in the civil rights movement.

What do you think distinguishes the literary critics of Chicano literature who study in Spanish graduate programs from those who study in English graduate programs at U.S. universities?

For the most part, scholars in Spanish have access to the literature of the whole Hispanic world. Today, they also have access to all the literature produced by Latinos in the United States from the colonial period to the present, more than 90 percent of which was written in Spanish. Many professors in English departments only have access to works in English because they do not speak or read Spanish, nor are they familiar with the literature written in Spanish for centuries in other countries. What is worse, many of these professors really only concentrate on the literary works created from the 1960s on, thus ignoring more than two centuries of Latino writing in North America.

One speaks of Chicano literature as a working-class literature, a blue-collar literature. Do you believe that there are parallels between writers and critics, as far as this affirmation is concerned? In other words, does a working-class critic exist in Chicano literature?

I would say that most of the first wave of Chicano/Latino literary critics—those attending college in the 1960s and grad school in the early 1970s—were from working-class backgrounds, as well. Today, I have met more and more Latino literary critics whose parents are professionals with a college education. When my generation started out, scholars in general did not even believe there was a Latino literature of the United States. I remember one MLA convention in the early 1970s where practically no one showed up for our panel, which was scheduled early on a Saturday morning or late night Saturday. What we did instead was form a circle with our chairs and talk to each other. Upon leaving the room after the session, a senior scholar in the corridor commented, "What, Chicano literary criticism before there is a Chicano literature?"

What do you think is the general attitude that mexicano writers and critics have of Chicano literature?

Lack of interest and concern.

Is it important for you to write in Spanish? In English? Or does it matter what language is used?

It is important for me to be able to write in both languages, to give lectures and presentations in both, in the United States and in Spanish-speaking countries. Our literature has always been transnational, has always crossed borders, and has always been articulated in more than one language.

What do you think of Chicano literature written in Spanish? Will it survive?

It has survived for more than two centuries without the help and/or intervention of the official institutions of American society. With the continued growth of the Latino population and with continued education, as well as the ubiquity and easy access of Spanish-language media, the prospects are excellent for its continuance and flourishing.

For undergraduate students that are fluent in both Spanish and English, what do you think is the principal factor that leads them to choose a graduate Spanish program or a graduate English program?

Job prospects.

What do you think of Chicano literature today? What are the most drastic changes that you have seen in Chicano literature in the last decades? Has it evolved or stayed the same?

There has been continued crossover to major publishers by Chicano authors, but still the editors making selections and the marketeers are not Latinos and tend to water down and disrespect our literature. I believe that the true Latino literature exists in the small, independent presses, which are also free to publish in Spanish.

Today, Latino literature has gone beyond the phase of proclaiming its existence and writing about identity and tradition to explore broader and more complex themes of a more general appeal, including the cultivation of formulaic genres, such as mystery/detective fiction and romance novels. There has also been a wholesale turn to children's literature over the last decade.

There is no real canon of Chicano or Latino literature, and there never will be one as long as forces outside our communities of writers and scholars are bent on exploitation; it is outsiders not working in our interest who make the publication and marketing decisions at large commercial houses and at literary agencies, as well as at government agencies and philanthropic foundations, and even at universities that just see our students as consumers and not potential creators and porters of knowledge and culture.

What led to the formation of Revista Chicano-Riqueña?

I had been working with students and community people to put together a mimeographed magazine of collected folklore and creative writing, called *La cadena de mi herencia.* Based on that mag and on one that students were putting together at Indiana University Bloomington, named *CACA*, a small grant was offered from Latin American studies at Indiana University Bloomington for me to start up a real magazine. I recruited my colleague Luis Dávila, an assistant professor down in Bloomington, as my coeditor, and we set about starting a national magazine in which all of those writers and artists from the civil rights movements could participate. Right from the beginning, we had the help of Tomás Rivera, Rolando Hinojosa, and Luis Leal, all pioneers in the literature, who helped by giving us material to publish and by promoting the magazine wherever they went. Also, one of my old professors in grad school, Theodore Andersson, was president of the American Association of Teachers of Spanish and Portuguese (AATSP) and arranged for free ads in *Hispania*, which brought in the first hundred or so subscriptions.

From the start, we decided that we wanted to bring together the various Latino communities and their writers and artists, as stated in the manifesto we published in our first issue.

Why does it later change to The Americas Review. *Why does it end?*

After a decade or so, we were getting steady funding from the National Endowment for the Arts, and one program in particular offered consultants. Our consultant studied our title and helped us decide that it was too limiting and that consumers, especially librarians, did not know what it meant. So we changed the title to broaden the appeal and marketing of the magazine.

I founded Arte Público Press in 1979, and by the mid-1980s our books were far outstripping the magazine in orders, usage, and impact. It is far more difficult to publish and maintain a magazine than to publish books. Running a magazine means maintaining a never-ending stream of correspondence; dealing with numerous writers, critics, book reviewers, for each issue; repeating every year the thankless task of getting people and institutions to renew their subscriptions; and so on. At its highest point, *Revista* had some five thousand subscribers and purchasers; by the late 1980s that had fallen to five hundred overwhelmingly institutional subscribers. The Arte Público books we published were now fulfilling the need we had satisfied previously with the magazine. So, after some twenty-five years of publishing, we closed *Revista* down. We offered various professors and writers around the country the opportunity to continue it, but no one was willing to put in the time and effort.

Tell us about Arte Público Press and the impact it has on Hispanos/Latinos and on the U.S. general public.

I don't believe this is a question for me to answer; I'm too closely identified with the press, and anything I say would smack of immodesty.

When did the Recovering the U.S. Hispanic Literary Heritage Project begin?

Recovering the U.S. Hispanic Literary Heritage Project was founded in 1992 by a group of leading scholars, librarians, and archivists from the United States, Mexico, and Puerto Rico to research, locate, preserve, and make accessible the written culture produced by Hispanics living in the United States from the colonial period to 1960. With a generous, ten-year funding from the Rockefeller Foundation, as well as with support from the Mellon, Ford, AT&T, Meadows, and Belo Foundations, the project was centered at the University of Houston and promptly set about funding scholars to conduct research. It has created a comprehensive project database, today numbering some 500,000 digitized items; microfilmed thousands of newspapers, documents, and books for preservation; compiled and published the first comprehensive bibliographic history of Hispanic periodicals for this time period; delivered online text databases of thousands of items plus some five hundred newspapers completely searchable through EBSCO and Readex; hosted nine bi-annual national conferences to date; published more than forty recovered volumes, plus nine volumes of selected conference papers; published two comprehensive anthologies and various other documents and books; and underwrote the microfilming of Hispanic collections from New York to Los Angeles. In 1999, the Recovery Project was selected as a grantee of the Save America's Treasures Program of the Interior Department to microfilm hundreds of U.S. Hispanic books printed on acid paper and make them electronically accessible. Books are now available on film through Inter-Library Loan and EBSCO, as well as through a microfilm distributor in Europe.

There are some five thousand scholars from around the country and the world affiliated with Recovery. The Recovery board includes the following members: José F. Aranda Jr. (Department of English, Rice University); Gabriela Baeza Ventura (Department of Hispanic Studies, University of Houston); Alejandra Balestra (College of Humanities and Social Sciences, George Mason University); Rose Marie Beebe (Department of Modern Languages and Literatures, Santa Clara University); Aviva Ben-Ur (Department of Judaic & Near Eastern Studies, University of Massachusetts, Amherst); Roberto Calderón (Department of History, University of North Texas); David Carrasco (Study of Latin America, Harvard Divinity School); Antonia Castañeda (Independent Scholar, Retired St. Mary's University); Kenya Dworkin y Méndez (Department of Modern Languages, Carnegie Mellon University); José B. Fernández (College of Arts and Sciences, University of Central Florida); Juan Flores (Department of Black & Puerto Rican Studies, Hunter College, CUNY); Erlinda Gonzales-Berry (Oregon State University); John M. Gonzales (Department of English, University of Texas at Arlington); José A. Gurpegui (Instituto Universitario de Investigación en Estudios Norteamericanos, Universidad de Alcalá); Kirsten S. Gruesz (Humanities Academic Services, University of California, Santa Cruz); Edwin Hernandez (Latino Studies, University of Notre Dame); Gilberto Hinojosa (University of the Incarnate Word); José M. Irizarry (Department of English, University of Puerto Rico); Donna M. Kabalen de Bichara (División de Humanidades y Ciencias Sociales, Tecnológico de Monterrey); Clara Lomas (Department of Romance Languages, The Colorado College); Francisco Lomelí (Department of Chicano/a Studies, University of California, Santa Barbara); Blanca López de Mariscal (Director of the PhD Program in Humanities, Tecnológico de Monterrey); Agnes Lugo-Ortiz (Department of Romance Languages and Literatures, University of Chicago); Hevetia Martell (Katy, Texas); Glenn Martínez (Department of Modern Languages, University of Texas-Pan American); Gabriel Meléndez (American Studies Department, University of New Mexico); Genaro Padilla (Office of Undergraduate Affairs, University of California, Berkeley); Yolanda Padilla (University of Pennsylvania); Raymund A. Paredes (Commissioner of Higher Education, State of Texas); Mónica Perales (Department of

History, University of Houston); Vanessa Y. Pérez Rosario (Department of Puerto Rican and Latino Studies, Brooklyn College of CUNY); Gerardo Poyo (Department of History, St. Mary's University); Marisol Ramos (Curator of the Latin American and Caribbean Collection, University of Connecticut); Raúl Ramos (Department of History, University of Houston); Bárbara O. Reyes (Department of History, University of New Mexico); Antonio Saborit (INAH Dirección de Estudios Históricos, México); Theresa Salazar (The Bancroft Collection of Western Americana, University of California, Berkeley); Rosaura Sánchez (Department of Literature, University of California, San Diego); Virginia Sánchez-Korrol (Department of Puerto Rican Studies, Brooklyn College of CUNY).

Describe your work on U.S. Hispanic/Latino literary history and your latest projects.

I consider myself a historian of Latino culture, with a special interest in literature, history, and publishing. Thus, I have written histories of Latino theater, Latino newspapers, and selected themes in Latino literature from the early 1800s to the present. Along those lines, I have also produced a number of reference works that are broad and all-inclusive, such as the *Hispanic American Almanac* and *The Handbook of Hispanic Cultures in the United States*, as well as more specialized volumes, such as *The Greenwood Encyclopedia of Latino Literature*. I have also developed a schema for Latino literature that helps make sense of the cultural interdependence of Latino native, immigrant, and exile experiences and communities, as described in some of my articles and in my book, *Hispanic Immigrant Literature: El sueño del retorno*.

I guess what I have tried to do—whether I have articulated it to myself or not—is to fill in the gaps of our cultural historiography and creative production in the United States.

My future goal is to produce a comprehensive history of Latino literature in the United States.

How did you discover Las aventuras de Don Chipote o cuando los pericos mamen?

When I was researching the history of Hispanic theater, which would later be published as a book, I compiled a list of the names of playwrights mentioned in Latino newspapers from coast to coast. Whenever I visited an archive or a library, I tried to find the writing of or biographical information about those playwrights. At the National Library of Mexico, I found Daniel Venegas's name listed in the card catalog as the author of a book. I ordered the book from the stacks and, after reading a good part of it and discovering its relevance to the history of Latinos, especially Chicanos, I had it photocopied with the idea that I would publish it with my introduction. It has since gone into six separate editions in Spanish and English and become a primary text for the study of immigrant literature.

Any last thoughts concerning your role or function as a critic of Chicano/U.S. Latino literature? Also what do you think has been the major impact of your work in relation to Chicano/U.S. Latino letters?

I really do not see myself as a critic but as a cultural historian, although I do write criticism of the works of such contemporary authors as Sandra Cisneros, Rolando Hinojosa, Tomás Rivera, Lucha Corpi, Tato Laviera, Victor Hernández Cruz, and others, and of such historical authors as José Alvarez de Toledo, Alirio Díaz Guerra, Elena Arizmendi, Teodoro Torres, and Daniel Venegas.

I leave the second question for others to answer.

Selected Works

Kanellos, Nicolás, ed. *Mexican American Theater: Then and Now*. Houston: Arte Público Press, 1983.

——, ed. *Biographical Dictionary of Hispanic Literature in the United States*. Westport, CT: Greenwood Press, 1989.

——. *A History of Hispanic Theatre in the United States: Origins to 1940*. Austin: University of Texas Press, 1990.

——, ed. *The Hispanic Almanac: From Columbus to Corporate America*. Detroit: Visible Ink Press, 1994.

——, ed. *The Hispanic Literary Companion*. Detroit: Visible Ink Press, 1996.

——, ed. *Noche Buena: Hispanic American Christmas Stories*. New York: Oxford University Press, 2000.

——, ed. *The Greenwood Encyclopedia of Latino Literature*. 3 vols. Westport, CT: Greenwood Press, 2008.

——. *Hispanic Immigrant Literature: El sueño del retorno*. Austin: University of Texas Press, 2011.

Kanellos, Nicolás, and Claudio Esteva Fabregat, eds. *Handbook of Hispanic Cultures in the United States.* 4 vols. Houston, TX, and Madrid, Spain: Arte Público Press and Instituto de Cooperación Iberoamericana, 1994.
Kanellos, Nicolás, and Helvetia Martell, eds. *Hispanic Periodicals in the United States, Origins to 1960: A Brief History and Comprehensive Bibliography.* Houston: Arte Público Press, 2000.
Kanellos, Nicolás, et al., eds. *En otra voz: Antología de la literatura hispana de los Estados Unidos.* Houston: Arte Público Press, 2002.
Kanellos, Nicolás, et al., eds. *Herencia: The Anthology of Hispanic Literature of the United States.* New York: Oxford University Press, 2003.

4

Gary F. Keller

The Bold Caballero of Bilingual Review Press

THE RELATIONSHIP BETWEEN CRITIC AND WRITER, though often depicted as contentious, is not the case with Professor Gary Keller. His work is positive in the very broadest sense, embracing many facets of literary scholarship. In his professional life he has helped set high standards for Chicano literature by his analysis, evaluation, and publishing. A writer himself, he has brought special insights to the works of others as teacher/advisor as well as publisher/editor of the enduring Bilingual Review *and Bilingual Review Press. He has encouraged new generations of writers, setting the highest standards for works published in the* Review *and at the Press and filling a unique and important role in broadening the audience for Chicano literature.*
—Nash Candelaria

Gary F. Keller (1943–) is a Regents' Professor and the director of the Hispanic Research Center at Arizona State University. He is a graduate of Columbia University, where he received his PhD in Hispanic Literature and Linguistics. In 1973 he founded The Bilingual Review/La Revista Bilingüe, *a journal that is known as a major resource for scholars and teachers interested in English-Spanish bilingualism. Keller also founded Bilingual Press, considered, with Arte Público Press, one of the leading publishers of Chicano and Hispanic literature in the United States. He has edited key publications dealing with Chicano culture, including* Chicano Cinema: Research, Reviews & Resources *(1985), the first Chicano film anthology of its kind, and* Contemporary Chicana and Chicano Art *(2002). In addition to being an important critic, editor, and publisher, Keller is also an accomplished poet and fiction writer.*

The interview with Gary was conducted at Arizona State University in 2008 and continued in a number of e-mail correspondences from 2008 to 2013.

* * *

Gary, where were you born? Describe your childhood and the place where you grew up.

I was born in National City, the naval base of San Diego, California, on the first day of January 1943. I spent the first nine, ten years of my life there. My father worked during World War II on a high security project. Despite not having attended college, he knew a lot about chemistry and about removing tin from cans. At the time, the Germans had succeeded in doing this procedure, which was very useful in the manufacturing and production of weapons. The North Americans were trying to duplicate the process and my father was associated with that effort. After I turned nine or ten, we crossed different border cities, arriving in El Paso from San Diego and Tijuana. Then my father settled in Mexico City, where I grew up. I finished elementary, high school, and university studies in the United Mexican States. I attended the University of the Americas; at that time it was located in Mexico City, now it's located in Cholula, close to Puebla. My father worked for General Electric. I wrote an extremely autobiographical short story called "The Man Who Invented the Automatic Jumping Bean" that talks about this period of my life and about my father.

Do you feel that growing up in Mexico helped you to become interested in Mexican culture and to understand the differences that exist between Mexicans and Chicanos?

Yes, but years later, because the term "Chicano" had another meaning at that time. "No seas chicano" or "Don't be Chicano" was like saying don't be ignorant or naïve. I did not participate in the Chicano movement, nor did I understand it until after I attended Columbia University. I knew about it through Francisco Jiménez, who now teaches at Santa Clara University in California. He was a colleague and classmate of mine at Columbia. He got involved in the movement before I did. He wrote short stories for *Quinto Sol* and in *El Espejo*, the first Chicano literary anthology.

Why did you choose Columbia University to pursue your PhD degree?

My mother lived in New York at that time. She traveled everywhere. She was an archeologist and attended the University of the Americas in Mexico City. She graduated from that institution when I graduated from high school. I use to write her class notes and that gave me the opportunity to read academic books. Besides, I did it because my mother paid me a certain amount of money per page to write them, so I wrote many pages. In 1973, when I graduated from the University of the Americas, I decided to go to New York to work and attend graduate school. Another reason I went there was because I had experienced a painful love relationship and so decided to leave Mexico. At that time I felt I did not have any options because I did not understand anything about graduate schools. I didn't understand that one could apply for financial aid and not have to work all the time to pay for one's undergraduate studies like I did.

At Columbia, did you enroll in the Spanish program?

I arrived at Columbia in the summer of 1963. I had graduated in May and by July I was in New York. I quickly found a job, in the Department of Parks and Recreation of the City of New York. I soon filled out an application for admissions at Columbia University and since I did not ask for financial aid, nor did I know how to ask for it, they were very happy to accept me. When I arrived at Columbia I took a course on religion. I was interested in religion and philosophy. I majored in those subjects at the University of the Americas.

Did you become interested in Spanish and Latin American literature at Columbia?

Yes. At Columbia I studied Spanish Peninsular and Latin American literature and took many courses in other departments. I was very interested in the bohemian movement. I was, more or less, a bohemian. At that time I took courses on India. I took courses on philosophy. However, most of my professors taught Latin American courses. Andrés Iduarte, who was exiled from Mexico, was the head of the National Institute of Fine Arts in Mexico at the time of the Frida Kahlo mess (he allowed the Soviet flag to drape Kahlo's coffin). After that problem, in which things did not turn out very well for him, he went to New York to be a professor at Columbia University. I took many courses with him and also with Gonzalo Sobejano, who had arrived as a young professor from Germany the same year that I enrolled at Columbia.

What was the topic of your doctoral dissertation?

My doctoral dissertation was on Gregorio Marañón, a Spanish Peninsular medical doctor. Gonzalo Sobejano helped me a lot with it. In the past, one had to do a master's thesis that now would be considered a doctoral thesis, two to three hundred pages long. I wrote my MA thesis on another Spaniard, Ramón Pérez de Ayala; therefore, I was trained in Spanish Peninsular and Latin American literature. As a graduate student I had already written essays on other topics, on *Los de abajo*, for example, a work that was published in *Cuadernos Hispanoamericanos*, but I didn't really get into the chicanada until probably after the All But Dissertation (ABD) status, and after I received my doctorate. Mainly, I did linguistics. First, I went from literature to linguistics, then, from linguistics to ethnic studies. Around 1971, I was teaching at the City College of New York and the school asked me to establish a graduate linguistics program, which I did very willingly. That led me to read Chicano and Puerto Rican literature because I became very interested in bilingualism and the intercalation from English to Spanish, the so-called code switching. I did Chicano studies, with an eye on linguistics and bilingualism.

What were your first academic appointments or jobs?

While I was a graduate student I had two or three jobs. I had the job at the Department of Parks and Recreation, which I kept until I left New York, and I had two university jobs: I taught every advanced course at Our Lady of Good Counsel College and I taught at Pace University. The job at Our Lady of Good Counsel College was magnificent for me. I began to work there in 1977 because I had obtained my masters that year. The nuns taught all the basic courses and I taught all the advanced courses, about which I knew absolutely nothing. But I stayed. I would be one step ahead of the students. I was a week ahead of them, but I learned everything about everything because the school used the quarter system and I taught three different advanced literature courses every ten weeks. With the doctorate still unfinished, I was offered a position as an instructor at Columbia University. With the doctoral degree almost in hand, I obtained the position of assistant professor at City College of New York. In 1975 I worked for York College of the City University of New York.

How did the journal Bilingual Review *begin?*

Bilingual Review was founded by a group of students and very young professors who were passionate about the subject of bilingualism and bilingual education. The experts on the subject were Eduardo Rivera, who was an English professor in the City College of New York, and myself. Working with us were some bilingual education experts, including Hernán Lafontaine, then the head of bilingual education in New York City, some excellent undergraduate students, and some students who were beginning their graduate studies. One student I remember is Diana Vélez, now a professor at the University of Iowa. She was one of my students. We dedicated the first issue of the journal not to bilingual education but to bilingualism. From the start we published articles on ethnic studies and some creative writing pieces. In 1976, in the bicentennial year of the declaration of independence of the United States, we began to publish books. The first one was *Bilingualism in the Bicentennial and Beyond*. After a year or two, besides publishing books on research, we published poetry, short stories, and novels. Among the first novels were Ana Castillo's *The Mixquiahuala Letters* and Alma Villanueva's *The Ultraviolet Sky*. We also started a series called "Clásicos Chicanos/Chicano Classics," and under that series we published works such as José Antonio Villarreal's *The Fifth Horseman*, Miguel Méndez's *Peregrinos de Aztlán*, and Ron Arias's *The Road to Tamazunchale*. It gives me great satisfaction to say that we were one of the first presses to publish Chicano and

Latino texts in this country. I am very pleased that teachers and academics can rely on us when ordering books for their courses or scholarly research.

Have you observed any changes in the interests of the writers of today from those who you published in the past?

Yes. I believe that the two most important ones had to do with the transformation of the author and, hence, of his or her writing. When we started *Bilingual Review*, the literary movement was completely integrated within the civil rights movement. The Chicano movement and the Chicano literary movement were inseparable. The political and creative components of El Teatro Campesino are an example of that. But with time, a group of professional writers emerged from academic and creative writing programs from universities across the United States. The greatest change among the majority of current authors is that they are university educated. All Chicano movement writers, without exception, wrote poetry, theater, novels, and short stories that dealt with social justice. Today's authors, on the other hand, write literature dealing with themes of interioridad or inner self, of psychological development and of problems or relations between men and women and less on social protest. One issue that should be stressed is the relation that exists between the individual and the Chicano, Mexican, and North American communities. Another thing that should be mentioned is the presence of emerging women's voices that are now dominating Chicano literature. We were one of the first editorial presses to publish Chicana and Puertorriqueña writers, including a research book called *Theory of Practice of Feminist Literary Criticism*, edited by Gabriela Mora and Karen Van Hooft.

Will there be more transformations in the future?

Well, I am not someone that makes predictions about the future, but let me say something about the future of technology. Bilingual Review Press is now publishing electronic books in DVD form. We have publications in the form of websites. This tendency is going to increase because technology is so generous, above all, with the visual element and with the search of narratives. For example, if one wants to look up the word "tiznada," a word that I studied in *Los de abajo*, one can search for it and find it easily in the electronic publication. It is also very easy to renew a bibliography or modify a text. With books one cannot do that; it is almost impossible to do. One has to make an edition and when that edition is finished, that's it, it's done. We are putting the bibliographies of some of our books on our website because there they can be changed, modified, and extended through the years. That is what we are doing with the hardcopy books dealing with art and cinema.

Going back to Bilingual Review Press publications, have you considered publishing books written solely in Spanish?

In the past we have published a good number of books in Spanish. Miguel Méndez, for example, writes solely in Spanish. Aristeo Brito wrote *El diablo en Tejas* in Spanish, but I believe that that tendency is decreasing quite a bit. On the other hand, it is compensated for because the major editorial houses now publish Spanish editions of the most popular and important Chicano literary works. We do the same. The book that we have sold the most copies of is Elva Treviño Hart's *Barefoot Heart*. We have published six, seven different editions of ten, fifteen thousand copies of that book. We have a version in Spanish that we finished publishing a year or two ago that is called *Corazón descalzo*.

Do you believe that Chicano literature written in Spanish is losing ground or strength?

It is difficult to tell. We don't know, but I will say this. In the 1960s and 1970s the majority of the writers who wrote in Spanish, such as Miguel Méndez, Tomás Rivera, and Aristeo Brito, were raised in la mexicanidad, within a Spanish-speaking language environment. Even though they were born in the United States, they were segregated and lived in Spanish-speaking communities. For example, Rolando Hinojosa and Tomás Rivera lived in The Valley of South Texas. But at that time there was also a large Chicano population that did not command Spanish well enough to write in Spanish. The Chicano population spoke Spanish well, but in very few instances could they write fluently in that language. That has not changed. On the other hand, Chicano literature has now been internationalized. It is published in Spain and in Mexico.

What do you think of the critics of Chicano literature who are academically trained in Spanish graduate programs versus those trained in graduate English ones? Are there major differences between these two groups?

Well, I am not an expert in this, but I do have some observations that have made an impression on me when I have spoken with writers and attended conferences, such as the Modern Language Association (MLA) conference and the National Association for Chicana and Chicano Studies (NACCS) conference. The critics of Chicano literature trained in Spanish departments obviously are interested, more than those in English departments, in literary works written in Spanish. What is apparent is that the relation between Chicano literature and Latin American authors like the "boom" writers—Gabriel García Márquez, Mario Vargas Llosa, and Carlos Fuentes—is evident. But critics trained in English departments also know them. Many might not speak or read Spanish well, but many do. I believe that the relationship that exists between Chicano writers and Mexican and Latin American writers is more noticeable. Now, what fascinates me more is bilingualism and the intercalation of codes. I believe that there exist differences of perspective in regard to this. The critics that are trained in departments of Hispanic literature tend to think of so-called Spanglish as pertaining to the vernacular of Spanish, but the North Americans might see it as a form of English with words or phrases made up or derived from Spanish. It would be very interesting to examine this in a conference to see what critics trained in English literature versus those trained in Hispanic literature think of creative writing and bilingualism.

Tell us about the Hispanic Research Center at Arizona State University.

The Hispanic Research Center is already celebrating its third decade of existence with great success. Our largest programs are in the sciences and engineering, where we help minority students, the majority of them Spanish-speakers. In addition, we also help African Americans and Native Americans obtain their undergraduate or graduate degrees, primarily doctorates, in engineering, science, or mathematics. The federal government has helped us a lot, especially the National Science Foundation, the Department of Energy, and the Department of Education. Since 1986 we have received, maybe, thirty to thirty-five million dollars for those programs. Another very important part of the Hispanic Research Center is the division of publications and products that include the journal *Bilingual Review,* the Editorial Bilingüe, and the group that makes digital initiatives and produces websites and DVDs. The money there is not as abundant as it is for the sciences. Almost every year we are awarded one, probably two, different grants from the National Endowment for the Arts, the Arizona Commission for the Arts, and the Lila Wallace-Reader's Digest Foundation. We have received a good amount of external money to fund our projects. Now, as to the manner in which the Hispanic Research Center is constructed, we have maybe forty or fifty individuals that work for the Center, including students, and 85 to 90 percent of their funding is obtained from outside sources, generally from outside of Arizona. Therefore, the support that we receive from Arizona State University (ASU) or from the government of the state of Arizona—and I'm not saying that it's minimal, because it's extremely important—does not even reach 20 percent of what we need. All the work we do with the editorial, all that we publish, we have to fund from outside sources and from our book sales. We secure a number of funds; we like that, we are opportunists. We are looking at the things that are occurring in the world and we make products that truly help and that are necessary. We don't publish anything, in hard copy or electronically, that is based on vanity; for example, we won't publish a professor's personal project.

How are these new DVDs and websites published?

Let me emphasize that this type of work is a product of group collaboration. We all work together to create everything. We have experts for everything that is needed. We have people that know how to do graphic design. We also have people that know about computer programming and software. Others are able to digitalize manuscripts and are experts in electronic bibliographies and in the visual elements: photography, flyers, or artwork. Sometimes we publish sculptures in electronic form and have experts that are able to present the sculpture in 360 degrees. On our website we have Luis Jiménez's sculpture—located in our university museum—and see through the four sides of his *Southwest Pieta*. That is very beautiful. For me it is very pleasant to be able to remove oneself from solipsism—a dangerous tendency for humans who work alone—and instead emphasize group collaboration where all people have something to say and whose collective voice is heard.

Tell us about your interest in Chicano cinema.

My interest in the Chicano in U.S. and Mexican cinema is part of the second stage of my professional life; I like to say that I reinvent myself professionally every fifteen to eighteen years. In the 1980s I grew an interest in Mexican and Chicano cinema, and I published articles and books on the subject, including *Chicano Cinema: Research, Reviews & Resources*, the first anthology on Chicano film. The recent conferences that I organized at Arizona State on Mexican and Chicano cinema were the result of my deep interest in el bueno y generoso Mexican and Chicano social bandit that many would identify as a mere outlaw. These social bandits are an important part of a popular folk literary tradition that includes Don Quijote and Joaquín Murrieta, to give some examples. Two books resulted from these conferences: *The Bold Caballeros and Noble Bandidas*, published in 2010, a second one to be published in the near future. In the conferences I emphasize the Mexican Revolution in part to highlight revolutionaries like Pancho Villa, Emiliano Zapata, and the adelitas, and also to recognize the centennial celebration of this conflict. Maybe in 2016, with the centennial of the incursion of Pancho Villa into Columbus, New Mexico, I will organize a conference around this theme and maybe another book will result from it.

On what project are you currently working?

Well, I write once in a while. But I have to fulfill my obligations to our employees and to the students; we have graduated thousands of students in the sciences, and that comes first. But I like to write. Some of my work has certain recognition. Perhaps the best known is my short story "The Man Who Invented the Automatic Jumping Bean"; that has been republished in different books. It won the Pushcart Prize. The novelist Ann Tyler nominated it for that prize. Another work worth mentioning is *Zapata Rose*, a novella—with a double "l"—written in English, in 1992. It was reedited under the title *Zapata Vive*.

Recently, I read a poem by Wallace Stevens, a North American poet, called "Thirteen Ways of Looking at a Blackbird" that inspired me to write the poem "Thirteen ways to Capture Our Quetzal in Good Faith." The beauty of this is that to read it, you have to do it in electronic form because with each one of the "Thirteen Ways" I include a photograph, or a portrait, that visually complements the text. The poem is found in our website "Latino poetry on line," sponsored by The National Endowment for the Arts.

In addition, I am writing a long essay about la frontera and how it's presented in U.S., Mexican, Chicano, and alter cinema, a cinema that mixes lo mexicano with lo chicano, or lo europeo with lo norteamericano. My point of departure is 1911 and I end it in the present with whatever new movie comes out. The article was requested by a professor from the University of Bordeaux and will be published in a year or two in France. I am also working on a long-term project on San Francis of Assisi and the Franciscan's journeys to America. In this paper I include the Virgin of Guadalupe because the Franciscans were the first religious order to become aware of the apparition of the Virgin of Guadalupe through San Juan Diego. They were the first to accept the miracle, the vision, and the epiphany of this saint.

Any last comments that you would like to share?

I believe that this project of interviews is valuable and overdue. Some of our literary critics have passed away and many of us are getting old, so it is a responsible thing to recover one's tradition, culture, and historical past. I hope that this project fulfills this noble and generous mission as well.

Selected Works

Keller, Gary. *Tales of El Huitlacoche*. Colorado Springs, CO: Maize Press, 1984.

——, ed. *Chicano Cinema: Research, Reviews, and Resources*. Binghamton, NY: Bilingual Review/Press, 1985.

———. *Zapata Rose in 1992 & Other Tales*. San Luis Obispo, CA: Maize Press, 1992.
———. *Zapata Lives!* Colorado Springs, CO: Maize Press, 1994.
———, ed. *Hispanics and United States Film: An Overview and Handbook*. Tempe, AZ: Bilingual Press/Editorial Bilingüe, 1994.
———, ed. *Miguel Méndez in Aztlán: Two Decades of Literary Production*. Tempe, AZ: Bilingual Review/Press, 1995.
———. *Contemporary Chicana and Chicano Art: Artists, Works, Culture, and Education*. Vol. 2. Tempe, AZ: Bilingual Press/Editorial Bilingüe, 2002.
———, ed. *Chicano Art for Our Millennium: Collected Works from the Arizona State University Community*. Tempe, AZ: Bilingual Press, 2004.
———. *Good Bandits, Warrior Women, and Revolutionaries in Hispanic Culture*. Tempe, AZ: Bilingual Press, 2010.
Keller, Gary D., and Francis M. Nevins, eds. *The Cisco Kid: American Hero, Hispanic Roots*. Tempe, AZ: Bilingual Review Press, 2008.
Keller, Gary D., and Amy Phillips, eds. *Triumph of Our Communities: Four Decades of Mexican American Art*. Tempe, AZ: Bilingual Press, 2005.
Keller, Gary D., Vernon E. Lattin, and Rolando Hinojosa, eds. *Tomás Rivera, 1935–1984: The Man and His Work*. Tempe, AZ: Bilingual Review Press, 1988.

5

Luis Leal

Chicano Literary History

LUIS LEAL IS A friend, scholar, and progressive thinker. The term "model" may be overused in some cases, but not here, not when one talks or writes about Luis. One of his students, the now deceased and sorely missed Richard Reeve, wrote the first doctoral thesis on Carlos Fuentes in the United States and did so under Luis's guidance and direction, as did John Garganigo, who defended his thesis on the Uruguayan writer Javier de Viana. These are but two of the more than forty theses Luis directed at the University of Illinois. Years later, during a two-year stint as a visiting professor at Stanford, aside from teaching a full load, he also directed two doctoral theses. Luis's publication of a brief but on-target essay, which appeared in Revista Chicano-Riqueña, *directed by Dr. Nicolás Kanellos at the University of Houston, legitimized Chicano literature. Here was a universally known scholar writing about a literature that was struggling to break into the academy. No one to date has invested as much time and talent in revealing the merit of Chicano literature as a field of study at the university level. To date, again, no one has devoted more time to and produced more PhD's on this literature, which, at times, has been undervalued, and at other times, rejected—challenges that have always been overcome by the prestige of this old friend.*
—Rolando Hinojosa-Smith

Luis Leal (1907–2010), or don Luis as he was affectionately known, was born in Linares, Nuevo León, Mexico, on September 17, 1907. When he was nineteen years old he left his home country to pursue his university studies at Northwestern University, in Evanston, Illinois. Leal served in the U.S. Army during World War II and returned to pursue graduate work at the University of Chicago. He worked at the University of Mississippi and Emory University before accepting a tenured position at the University of Illinois, Urbana-Champaign, where he taught until his retirement. In 1976, he moved to California and worked at the University of California, Santa Barbara, dedicating most of his research to Chicano literature and soon becoming the unofficial dean of this field of study. Leal's contribution to Chicano letters, specifically to its literary history, is immeasurable and inspiring. His book Aztlán y México: Perfiles literarios e históricos *is a landmark text in the study of Chicano literature. In 1998, when Leal was ninety-one years old, he founded, with Victor Fuentes,* Ventana Abierta: Revista Latina de Literatura, Arte y Cultura, *a journal that publishes academic and creative works in Spanish by Latinos/as in the United States.*

Luis Leal's seminal article on the periodization of Chicano literature ("Mexican American Literature: A Historical Perspective") begins with the "Hispanic Period (to 1821)" and "The Mexican Period (1821–1848)," during which Spanish was the primary language for most Mexican Americans. Works written in both languages are part of the literary landscape in the "Transition Period (1848–1910)," the "Interaction Period (1910–1942)," and the "Chicano Period (1942 to the Present)," with English surpassing Spanish as the preferred language of choice for most Chicano and Chicana writers. With this in mind, the following interview deals specifically with the demise of Chicano literature in Spanish and the uncertain future that awaits it.

This interview was conducted at Leal's home in Goleta, California, in 2004.

* * *

Professor Leal, why is it important for Chicano writers to continue to write in Spanish?

It is very important that Chicano writers continue to write in Spanish for various reasons. The most important one, in my opinion, is that it is necessary that el pueblo Chicano maintain its culture.

Language is the most important way to do it. If language is lost, culture is lost. The way of reasoning, the way of seeing the world, the way of imagining, the way of conducting oneself, and even of dreaming, are different in the two cultures. The presence of the non-acculturated Chicano adds variety to North American culture. It is not possible to maintain a culture with a Mexican background without maintaining its language, and literature is one of the most efficient ways to do it. Another reason is the presence of a Spanish-speaking reading public that requires works to be published in Spanish. There are a great number of new immigrants who do not read English. A third reason would be to sustain cultural relations with Mexico and other Spanish-speaking countries. Few Chicano books written in English are translated into Spanish.

Is it important for the critics of this literature to write their literary criticism in Spanish?

To be consistent with my answer to the first question, I have to say that it is necessary that the Chicano critics write their criticism in Spanish. However, this is less important than the creative literature being written in Spanish. Generally, the critics write for other critics and rarely for the pueblo. I do not know of any critic that is not able to read in both languages. Chicano criticism, more and more, is being written by critics coming out of English departments and consequently is being written in English. What is more serious is that some of them do not know Mexican or Hispanic American literature. But if we were to make Chicano literature known in Spanish-speaking countries, like Mexico, then it would be better if the critic wrote in Spanish. Salvador Rodríguez del Pino's book on the Chicano novel written in Spanish *Cinco autores comprometidos* was very successful in Mexico due to the fact that there was no other book written in that language. I prefer to write my criticism in Spanish, but I am frequently asked to write it in English.

Do you think that Chicano literature written in Spanish will continue to exist?

During the 1960s it was common to write novels in Spanish, maybe because of the influence of Tomás Rivera and Rolando Hinojosa, or as an act of protest. But Rudolfo Anaya wrote in English and his work had greater diffusion than that of the other novelists, like Miguel Méndez or Aristeo Brito. I believe that the Chicano novel written in Spanish won't disappear as long as there exists a reading public that prefers to read in that language, a fact that depends on a constant wave of immigrants to increase the Chicano population in the United States. As long as that immigration is not completely stopped, Chicano novels will continue to be written in Spanish because a reading public will continue to exist. The latest tendency is to translate and publish Chicano literary works originally written in English into Spanish. For example, the novels of Sandra Cisneros, Rudolfo Anaya, Víctor Villaseñor, and others have already been translated into Spanish.

* * *

The following interview is one of the last ones conducted with don Luis Leal (April 5, 2009, in Leal's home in Goleta, California). At the time he was 101 years old and still active in his research and his writings. Although he was still lucid and alert to the questions, Leal had problems hearing them, and Francisco Lomelí—who was also present—generously assisted in making sure Leal understood them.

* * *

Professor Leal, What do you think distinguishes the literary critics of Chicano literature who study in Spanish graduate programs from those who study in English graduate programs at U.S. universities?

Well, you know, the majority of the critics of Chicano literature are found in English departments because they are interested in North American literature. Therefore, they see Chicano literature as a branch of North American literature. However, critics in the Spanish departments do not see it from the same perspective. If anything, some, including myself, say that Chicano literature might be part of Mexican literature. However, there is great opposition to this point of view. They say that Chicano literature in an autonomous literature that has nothing to do with Mexican literature. The division is very clear. Those who speak English are interested in the Chicano writers who write in English. The critics that are in Spanish departments are interested more than anything in those who write in Spanish. A great number of them write in English because they study in English departments. On the other hand, in Spanish departments no interest is given to Chicano literature. Why? Because they say that it is written in English. Some authors, like Miguel Méndez, might be read because he writes in Spanish, but the majority of Chicano authors write in English. Also, Chicano literature is not considered part of Hispanic literature but of North American literature.

Then, there are some philosophical differences between the groups?

Yes, I believe so. I've been criticized because I always try to connect Chicano literature with Mexican literature. Critics say that Chicano literature is an independent literature. There is no doubt that it is independent, but many connections exist between the two literatures. Chicano literature's roots are in Mexican literature. But it should also be said that many Chicanos do not know Mexican literature.

Francisco, how would you answer both questions?

I believe that there are some fundamental differences. In effect, those of us who studied in Spanish departments tried to link Chicano literature with Latin American and Mexican literature in one way or another. This leads to our interest in literary history, with don Luis Leal leading the way and helping us to understand it. Our colleagues in English departments, especially in the 1970s, were more interested in studying European and North American theories. Those of us in Spanish departments were also interested in theory, but not in the same theories that our colleagues in English departments preferred. Also, we were interested in literature in relation to its social, economic, and political contexts. Many times those in English departments were interested with lo norteamericano. They were especially interested in books written in English because they did not read Spanish. We did. We worked both fields. Therefore, I believe that the fundamental differences lie in the different theories that were used and the sociohistorical contexts that were practiced. We were interested above all in the social context and in the idea of a cultural revindication.

Professor Leal, one speaks of Chicano literature as a working-class literature, a blue-collar literature. Do you believe that there are parallels between writers and critics, as far as this is concerned? In other words, does a working-class critic exist in Chicano literature?

Not that I know of. Besides, that opinion to me seems to limit much of Chicano literature because Chicano literature is not written exclusively for a specific social class. Yes, a lot of Chicano literature has been written for the working class, but they are not reading it. It is others that read about the working class. Now, if Chicano literature is written for the working class, then they should react to it, but there is no reaction. In other words, the critics that talk about Chicano literature do not identify themselves as belonging to a certain class. We don't know what they are. Some of them could be working-class. For example, Miguel Méndez used to be a laborer, a bricklayer, but that doesn't mean that he considers himself working-class. Therefore, I don't feel that it is accurate to say that.

Are there class differences among Chicano critics and Mexican and Latin American critics?

Well, the social divisions do not exist only between those groups; they exist within all groups. If you go to a Modern Language Association (MLA) conference on North American literature, one could find an African American speaking of a literature that is not African American. Therefore, if there is an interest in an author who is not African American, and the critic is African American, then the work is no longer social criticism but literary criticism that is interested solely in the text without regard to the racial or cultural makeup of the author.

Professor Leal, tell us about your critical formation. (Note: Professor Leal did not seem to hear the question clearly due to his hearing problems and based on his response, he understood it to deal with the existence or presence of Chicano literature when he studied literature in Chicago.

Lomelí, however, after Leal's response, provided an answer based on his profound personal amistad—as a loyal colleague and friend—with Professor Leal.)

It has always been in Spanish departments. When I started to study Hispanic American literature, Chicano literature did not exist. Well, better said, it did exist, but it was not studied. There were Chicano poets who wrote in newspapers published by Chicanos, but the word "Chicano" was not used at that time. Nobody considered that such literature existed, much less that it was studied at universities. It wasn't until 1969, at the MLA conference, that a critical work on Chicano literature was presented. But before that there wasn't any Chicano criticism, or better said, it did exist but it was not known. It wasn't read. On the other hand, from that time until today, criticism has taken great strides in dealing with the study of Chicano literature. Since then it has passed through several literary approaches, from the social to the aesthetic. Another thing, Chicano literature could not be taught because there were no texts, there were no textbooks until the novels of Miguel Méndez, Rolando Hinojosa, and others began to be published. When this happened, Chicano literature classes began to be taught. If there is no text, there is no criticism. As a result, the professor had to improvise the criticism of that literature. Many times those observations turned into a book. So, as you can see, the presence of Chicano literature depends on universities offering Chicano literature courses and professors who are interested in that literature and in the publishing of their research.

(Note: It is at this point that Lomelí gestures with his hand that he wants to add something to Leal's response. He talks while looking at Leal, assuring his approval.)

I am going to add a little more of what you, don Luis, could have said but forgot to say. You had a more classical literary training because in the past an academic career tended to be more classically oriented. When I studied in Chile, I noticed that one had to study Latin and literary theory. In the United States, at least in my field of study, at that time one did not have to study literary theory, only the texts themselves. So the fundamental difference is that in the classical approach one needs to study, first, the classics, the philosophers, and then also the critics from all over the world. In the United States those who study in English departments study North American and European critics, especially the English and the French; while in Latin America, according to what I experienced, first they read Latin American critics and then European, and not only French but also Austrian, Russian, Spanish, among others.

Professor Leal, since you were trained in Spanish departments, is it important for you to write your work in Spanish?

Well, I believe that in my case it is. Why? Because to me it is easier to write in Spanish than in English. I believe that it is not common for the literary critic to write in Spanish. Now, if I do write criticism in English it is because I am asked to do it in English. But I prefer to write it in Spanish. Today it would be common for a writer to write well in both English and Spanish, but to choose Spanish instead of English to write his work in? I doubt that that would happen. Why? Because the reader is going to read in English and the critic will have in mind his reading public. If the reading public is able to read in both languages, it will still ultimately prefer to read a text in English and not in Spanish. Now, in a bilingual book in which both languages are used, the reader is able to choose the language that he or she wants to read. Other than that, if there is no translation of a text, English is the language of choice.

I want to add that my first study on Chicano literature was published in Spanish; it is included as the last chapter of *México: Civilizaciones y culturas*, published in 1971, which by the way, when the second edition of the book was published, a critic from Texas said that adding that chapter had ruined the book. But that study was first published in English; "Mexican American Literature: A Historical Perspective" was in English. I wrote it in English. I don't know why. Now if you ask me why I chose English and not Spanish I cannot give you a satisfactory answer because, well, whatever it was, maybe I felt like writing it in English. Many times one cannot explain the motivations that makes one choose A or B.

For undergraduate students who are fluent in both Spanish and English, what do you think is the principal factor that leads them to choose a graduate Spanish program or a graduate English program?

Well, that can't be answered because each case is personal and cannot be generalized. Each person has his or her motives by which he/she chooses one department over the other. We do not know what the motives are. Maybe the father is an americano and tells his son or daughter, look, go study in the English department, not the Spanish one, or the mother might be mexicana and tells him or her to study in the Spanish department, not the English department. One doesn't know. It's a matter of personal motives, which makes it difficult to understand sometimes.

Francisco?

I would answer this a little bit differently. I would say that, in effect, one cannot know with certainty why an undergraduate student chooses a graduate Spanish program or a graduate English program, but I believe that there are certain inclinations that might justify the choice. Those who study in English departments acquire a good training in English and they feel comfortable with the language. Also the choice could be the result of an assimilation process or a challenge to prove that one can succeed in an English department. Those who attend Spanish departments might have more cultural closeness with the subject matter, the texts, and the Spanish-speaking countries that they study. Many times they also want to polish and improve their Spanish, whatever that means.

Professor Leal, what is the future of Chicano literary criticism? Where is it heading?

Well, I am not a pessimist, but it seems that Chicano criticism is blending more and more with the literature of Latino studies. This tendency of not studying Chicano literature exclusively but of including it in a comprehensive literary program that includes all the Latinos in the United States is harmful for Chicano literature. It's harmful because if studied individually one can compare it with other Latino literatures and highlight its richness. Chicano literature can compete very well with any other minority literature. One should not feel that by mixing critical studies and Latino literatures, Chicano literature will disappear one day. It's impossible. The sheer number of Chicanos in the United States will prohibit that from happening. Primary consideration should be given to Chicano literature over any other minority literatures because of the great number of Mexicans living in the United States.

Professor Leal, to conclude this interview, what themes will Chicano literature deal with in the future?

The topics that future Chicano writers will address will undoubtedly reflect the existing social problems of their time. However, more general topics will be added to the ones voiced by the present Chicano community. Some topics dealing with science fiction, fantasy, and detective narratives are now published. Their reading public will not be solely academic but will also consist of a Chicano, urban, middle-class reading public that is rapidly growing, as well as a Mexican reading public from the northern part of the Mexican Republic, especially from the border areas. The most overwhelming concerns of Chicano literature will no longer be that of identity and a craving for justice. Other future concerns will be those dealing with economic improvement, higher education, and entertainment, especially television, a media outlet that already monopolizes a large number of Chicanos from all social and economic levels.

Selected Works

Leal, Luis. *México: Civilizaciones y culturas*. Boston: Houghton Mifflin Co., 1955.

——. *Breve historia del cuento mexicano*. México: Editorial Studium, 1956.

——. *Bibliografía del cuento mexicano*. México: Editorial Studium, 1958.

——. *Mariano Azuela: Vida y obra*. México: Editorial Studium, 1961.

——. *Historia del cuento hispanoamericano*. México: Editorial Studium, 1966.

——. *El cuento hispanoamericano*. Buenos Aires: Centro Editor de América Latina, 1967.

——. *Mariano Azuela*. New York: Twayne Publishers, 1971.

——. *Breve historia de la literatura hispanoamericana*. New York: Alfred A. Knopf, 1971.

——. *Corridos y canciones de Aztlán*. Santa Barbara, CA: Xalmán, 1980.

——. *Juan Rulfo*. Boston: Twayne Publishers, 1983.

——. *Aztlán y México: Perfiles literarios e históricos*. Binghamton, NY: Bilingual Review/Press, 1985.

——. *Don Luis Leal: Una vida y dos culturas: Conversaciones con Víctor Fuentes*. Tempe, AZ: Bilingual Press, 1998.

——. *Decade of Chicano Literature, 1970–1979: Critical Essays and Bibliography*. Santa Barbara, CA: Editorial La Causa, 1982.

6

Francisco A. Lomelí

Ambassador of Chicano Letters

My admiration for Francisco Lomelí began when I first read a critical analysis of my Cuentos i poemas *in his* Dictionary of Literary Biography *(1989). It was shocking to see that the incipient work of an apprentice had been included in his work. He was giving merit to a collection of short stories that I had considered unworthy of literary commentary. Instead, he had validated the work through its mere inclusion, thus making it part of the Chicano voice.*

This kind of attitude and keen perception is what sets Lomelí apart from other critics. His ability to find meaning in writings that perhaps others would consider devoid of literary merit is what makes him unique. He reads historical texts and makes connections with the literature of other countries—Mexico, Spain, Latin America. He finds literary kinships that shed a broader light on Chicano writings. His tireless research, which spans more than three decades, has contributed immensely to the perception that the Chicano literary canon is a universal literature. Through his superb scholarship, exceptional Chicano writing is given the recognition it deserves: world-class status.

—Aristeo Brito

Francisco A. Lomelí (1947–) was born in Mexico to parents who originated from the proud state of Jalisco. After working in various places in Mexico, Lomelí's parents settled in Southern California, in San Diego, where he would receive his early academic education. At the University of New Mexico Lomelí became involved in the growth and development of Chicano literature by helping create courses and publishing his literary research on that subject. Lomelí has spent most of his academic career at the University of California, Santa Barbara, teaching in both the Department of Spanish and Portuguese and Chicana/o Studies Department. His contribution to the field of Chicano letters, particularly in the development of Chicano literary history, is monumental. Of major significance is his commitment to presenting Chicano letters to international communities in Europe and Latin America, making him an admirable ambassador of Chicano literature.

The interview with Francisco was conducted in Goleta, California, in 2009 and in a number of e-mail correspondences from 2005 to 2013.

* * *

Francisco, where were you born? Describe your childhood and the place where you grew up.

I was born in Sombrerete, Zacatecas, Mexico, on April 13, 1947, although my family was living on a ranch at the outskirts of the city. My parents, originally from los Altos de Jalisco, had moved from Aguascalientes to earn their living. My father had served as a police officer in Aguascalientes for seven years, but the government, limited in their economic resources, demanded that its police force not only use the uniform to maintain social order but also to find ways to receive bribes from businesses like hotels, restaurants, stores, brothels, bars, and other places. Clearly, those actions compromised police officers and encouraged them to behave inappropriately, and my father wanted no part of that. Therefore, he opted to leave the police force and work at a ranch so he could use his farming skills in the caring of crops and livestock, in horse training, in the slaughterhouse, and so on. One of my father's rich uncles offered him a job as a foreman of his ranch, and my father saw that as an opportunity to return to his jaliscience roots, even though the ranch was located in Zacatecas. That uncle was of a strong character and always got into trouble because of his ruthless treatment of others. As was to be expected, a man took revenge on my uncle by gunning him down.

Consequently, my father's work ended immediately and our family had to return to Aguascalientes, forcing my father to become a bracero and work on the railroad in Chicago. Then he decided to try his luck as a ranch worker in San Diego, California, and took the family to Tijuana, between 1952 and 1954, until our official immigration documents arrived. The many changes in our life forced me to identify with the immediate place where I lived, realizing that I wasn't really of one particular place. In the summer of 1954 we arrived in Vista, a town located in the northern part of San Diego County. We settled permanently there. We were a versatile family who worked in a great variety of jobs: irrigation, carpentry, horse care, farm work, avocado and macadamia nut harvesting, gardening. The entire family began to work for Mr. Wells Miller, a very kind, considerate, and generous man. He treated me as a son and I bent over backward to impress him with my work at the ranch and in sales at his subtropical tree nursery. I developed several sales skills there and the man always rewarded me for my efforts, which strengthened my work ethic and allowed me to shake off my childhood shyness. This was important for me because at the tender age of fifteen I was able to obtain a certain confidence in what I did and how I presented myself publicly. The pace of work undoubtedly formed my work ethic, even as it reminded me of my social status in this country. The ranch was a social laboratory, my place of development, the place where the patrón rewarded me for my work. Above all, it was a place where I rubbed elbows with my father and mother as fellow workers and where they counted on my English language skills to communicate instructions, plan commercial strategies in the nursery, organize work projects, and negotiate salary issues, among other things. That's how I saw myself my first twenty-one years while I struggled to master the English language and learn as much as possible in my academic fields of study. Balancing the material interests of my family and my intellectual aspirations was not easy. But my family environment, characterized by love, solidarity, and humor, helped tremendously to make me feel part of something that was greater than myself. Every day I felt a sense of accomplishment. My Mexican family circle was impenetrable, and it did not let social insinuations, discrimination, or cultural insults break us. On the contrary, these challenges made our family stronger.

When does your academic and critical formation begin?

Upon entering school I faced the North American world with all its complexities and implied laws. I forced myself to compete, socialize, and learn the ins and outs of my school environment. I learned the rules of the game and participated in discussions, sports, long-distance running, student government, and club organizations, like the Key Club. In school I was one of the few Mexicans that moved between multiple social circles with pride. I felt like a spokesman or a representative of la mexicanidad. Repeatedly, even at the university level, I would experience the "innocent" or "ignorant" ninguneo directed at me when I was asked if I was Mexican every time that I excelled in some type of activity. Without hesitation, I would always answer them with a plain and straightforward "yes." I realized that I had to fight my own battles and prove my worth in anything that I wanted to accomplish. To embrace the term "Chicano" in the middle of the 1960s was critical for me because I already had a clear ideology and a readiness to fight for my people at the university level. The sense of justice that I shared with my parents and brothers was easily transferable to a larger social environment. Therefore, when I arrived as a third-year student at San Diego State in 1968, I discovered that something was fundamentally wrong with the place. I found out that I was one of the only sixty-two Latino students at a university with a student population of eighteen thousand. These statistics impacted me tremendously. I reflected upon the situation and later I began to question it. This led me to advocate for a greater Latino enrollment at institutions of higher education, and in 1970 I made an effort to assist in the recruitment of freshman Latino students. If, at the beginning, my main academic goal was to become a high school Spanish teacher, that soon changed when in 1969 I studied for a year at the University of Concepción in Chile, at the time considered the Berkeley of South America. There, I immersed myself in the study of literary theory, Latin American literature, university politics, global politics—specifically Latin American politics—and, of course, what it meant to be a Latino in the broader sense of the word. Also, I experienced something very intriguing: if in the United States my mexicanidad was consistently challenged, in Chile it was celebrated. Sometimes people who I barely knew would invite me to their homes to talk or exchange ideas and impressions. If in the United States my mexicanidad was a burden and a cross to bear, in Chile it was acknowledged and applauded. I gained more confidence and vigor in my convictions. That motivated me to use literature as a way to know and understand the Chicano world. When I returned to San Diego State I became involved in the Movimiento Estudiantil Chicano de Aztlán (MECHA) to get rid of the hegemonic North American cultural complacency that had created invisible borders of exclusion. With literature, I felt motivated to prove that we had a past, a present, as well as a future. I participated in efforts to document the emerging presence of Chicano literature through newspapers, artistic-literary festivals, and academic conferences. In San Diego, I participated intimately with outstanding people of the movement, like Alurista, Gustavo Segade, Carlos Vélez-Ibáñez, Juan Felipe Herrera, Francisca Rascón, Ernesto Chávez, and others. Such a background motivated me and provided me with the tools to promote a vision of the world where the Chicano could think critically. All this prepared me to pursue a doctorate in 1974, boldly heading to the University of New Mexico without knowing the place and surrounding myself with outstanding professors and a new generation of colleagues. It was an important decision, for it stimulated my intellectual development and at the same time placed me in a region of the country where our people had deep roots dating back to the Hispanic presence in the sixteenth century and our indigenous cultural past. At last, I felt at home and I was able to confirm that we were not only products of a most recent immigration but also of nomadic pueblos centuries old that had traveled and covered all the cardinal points. From this experience emerged my strong interest in literary history. I became involved in institutionalizing advanced graduate courses on Chicano literature, demanding that the Department of Modern and Classical Languages at the University of New Mexico offer a graduate course on that theme. The course was created and approved in the spring of 1976 thanks in part to Sabine R. Ulibarrí, chair of the department, who was surprised by the perseverance of the graduate students. I felt that I had reached a high point, because it could not be said that such a course was exotic or rare but an integral part of the program of study. With the approval of the course we had succeeded in opening and modernizing our department.

When does your interest in Chicano literature begin?

I remember that in 1970 several of us from San Diego State were interested in writers from Mexico: Octavio Paz, Mariano Azuela, Carlos Fuentes, and Agustín Yáñez. I had majored in Hispanic American literature and my second major was in Chicano studies, making me one of the first generations, in spring 1971, to enter that field of study. I took several courses in literature, education, pre-Columbian philosophy, and creative writing, but what motivated me, as far as Chicano literature was concerned, was to find Chicano literary texts that linked the present and the past. Since I had just returned from Chile, I found out that other colleagues, in 1971, had already organized the first annotated bibliography of Chicano literature, *Bibliografía de Aztlán*. I examined the literature section of the manuscript before sending it to the editorial board, and I remember how terrified they were when they realized that the manuscript included Mexican works and not Chicano ones. The difference between the two had not occurred to them. That same year we made an overwhelming discovery; we came across José Antonio Villarreal's *Pocho*, published in 1959. I felt vindicated. As a result, I began to return to the past and dig up Chicano literary works written before 1965. I was interested in finding these Chicano and Chicana voices and appreciating the social concerns that existed at the time. Unfortunately, we initially found that the literary work of our people was minimal, almost nonexistent. But I could not accept that. I knew that the works existed somewhere and could be found. In doing so, I felt like the unbending miner who knows that he will find gold somewhere but has yet to find where. I sensed its existence.

One of my first publications, a collaborative work with my graduate colleague Donaldo Urioste from the University of New Mexico, collected critical reviews on Chicano literary works for a special issue of *Latin American Studies* published in 1975. In 1976 Urioste and I decided to expand the project by including our own critical reviews of these and other works with the purpose of ambitiously collecting ALL the books we could find written by Chicanos and Chicanas up to that time, including some unedited manuscripts lent to us by authors like Rudolfo Anaya and Bernice Zamora. The result was the publication of our book *Chicano Perspectives in Literature: A Critical and Annotated Bibliography* published in 1976, which was the first extensive critical and annotated bibliography of Chicano literature. As a result of this publication, many students from all academic levels, other colleagues, and even foreign scholars wrote to thank us for our work. Without realizing it, we had given cuerpo y cara, in other words, literary substance to Chicano literature. It was a gutsy act because at this time critics were not interested in "criticizing" Chicano literature. In other words, they weren't interested in pointing out its defects as well as its merits. Of course, as expected we found a little bit of everything. We strived to classify and compile all the literature we could find, from the most recently published to the most remote. We managed to put together a more substantial body of literary works and categories than anybody had before. We also added a new category that we classified as "literatura chicanesca," to point out a type of production that defined the perspective of the non-Chicano writer. The work was an immediate success for it created a profile of our literature. Some criticized our category of "literatura chicanesca" as unnecessary, but we felt motivated to stop or at least describe the process of "Chicaxploitation," that is, the exploitation of themes of Chicano characters by those who had not lived the Chicano experience, whatever that may be. In that book we also proposed a definition of our literature that to this day we consider the most convincing or correct. But we discovered that it was impossible to satisfy all the critics.

In spite of the criticism, the work yielded great results, which led me to pursue other major projects. For example, in 1990 Nicolás Kanellos asked me to join the Recovering the U.S. Hispanic Literary Heritage Project housed at the University of Houston. This collaboration was a dream come true for me. We discovered that the quantity of writings and works by people like us far exceeded that of other groups, except for the works of the Anglo Americans who documented their conquest of the American Southwest in the eighteenth and nineteenth centuries. Nevertheless, today we count, thanks to various important collections like Nicolás Kanellos's *Herencia* and *The Norton Anthology of Latino Literature*, edited by Ilan Stavans.

Also, among several significant literary discoveries, we found two short novels written by Eusebio Chacón in 1892 in New Mexico, and later the polemical work, *The Squatter and the Don*, written by Amparo Ruiz de Burton in 1885, in California. Thus, Chicano literature has flourished through these findings from the past, which prove that we have a rich and varied literary legacy. In addition, I began working with mainstream editorial presses, such as Greenwich Press and Gale Research, in an effort to spread our literature to more diverse literary circles. At the same time, I tried to promote our literary production at the international level by participating in various conferences, such as those held in Germersheim, Germany, in 1984, Paris in 1986, Madrid in 1990, Bordeaux in 1994, Málaga in 2002, León, Spain, in 2010, and other places. As you can see, we have left the barrios and the closed circles of our national regions to promote Chicano literature in distant lands.

One speaks of Chicano literature as a working-class literature, a blue-collar literature. Do you believe that there are parallels between writers and critics, as far as this is concerned? In other words, does a working-class critic exist in Chicano literature?

The question could be a bit biased because, in effect, it creates divisions. I believe that in the 1970s there was an inspiration or a sociopolitical impetus that came from the working class. The majority of us came from the working class and that was our point of departure. But when we got involved in literary criticism, in reality we stopped being part of the working class because that discipline required a certain type of sophistication and cosmopolitan orientation. In the 1960s we advocated for the working class, especially because of the influences of the many -ismos that existed. We also influenced literature, criticism, and the Chicano movement. There existed a revindicated political scene that addressed the political issues and social problems of the Chicanos, and the critic could not be separated from that compromiso. But with time, we realized that it led to a dead-end street. I believe that Marxism was not as effective as it could have been because one saw its limitations. The idea was that everybody should identify with the working class, including the writers, the critics, and the readers. However, not everybody could maintain being working-class because once one begins to work at a university one stops belonging to the working class, right? Slowly, the concept of the working class turned into something nostalgic because there is a rupture within the community. We started dealing with more sophisticated literary issues that become global rather than regional.

Tell us about your critical influences in the department of Spanish where you were trained.

I was influenced not only by departments of Spanish and Portuguese in the United States but also by my participation in an academic study abroad program in Chile. Critically speaking, in Chile a more advanced critical discourse was practiced between my colleagues and professors, at least at the undergraduate level. Because of this experience I was able to study literary critics, especially Chileans, Argentines, and others, who promoted cutting-edge ideas, among them, Enrique Anderson Imbert and Raúl Jara. These critics were not well known in the United States because Latin American literature was not vigorously studied until the 1960s. The 1960s was the decade when the explosion—the "Boom"—in the study of Latin American literature took place. But in Latin America there was no such thing as an explosion because that literary tradition had already existed there for some time. In Chile we studied, in depth, the works of South American critics, and aspects of literary concepts, that in 1969 were rarely dealt with in the United States. I believe that because of my experience in Chile I was able to polish my writing and refine my knowledge of Latin American literature from a Latin American point of view. This knowledge helped me grow academically when I returned to my literary program at San Diego State and later on at the University of New Mexico.

Are there class differences among Chicano critics and Mexican and Latin American critics?

I believe that at certain international conferences the socioeconomic differences between the participants manifest because many times it is felt that most Latin Americans and Europeans come from the upper class, while many of the Chicanos and Chicanas come from a more humble, and unassuming, lower social class. This difference makes the Chicanos and Chicanas feel a little strange in an academic environment. I believe that this uneasiness manifested itself mostly in the 1970s and 1980s. But by the 1990s the academic playing field had evened out. Now, who questions whether or not the person belongs to the working class? Probably someone who is new to academics or who possesses some type of social class complex might make this an issue. In Mexico we might see differences in class more often. For example, wealthy Mexicans would see a Chicano academic with the last name Pérez and identify it with a common name from a common nobody, as opposed to their last name of a European origin. These wealthy people feel a certain social contempt for us because they see the Chicano as a bola de huarachudos (a bunch of nobodies). Let me add that the concept of the rasquache, introduced by Tomás Ybarra-Frausto, was embraced by many of us. It influenced the Chicano cultural identity in the 1970s. That was a working-class concept. Because we valued the rasquache in our literature and in our Spanglish—our unique way of expressing our reality—nos tachaban as belonging to a lower class. Lo rasquache was part of breaking away from the norm, of reversing values, of going beyond the conventional and the orthodox. But the fact that we have made social progress and that we no longer fit the stereotypes of the Chicano huarachudo and rasquache did not matter to them. The Chicano critics, on the other hand, have demonstrated that they were able to cross those socioeconomic borders in a very efficient and real way.

Where do you think Chicano literature fits within the Latin American and North American literary experience?

Whether Chicano literature fits within the North American, Mexican, or Latin American literary tradition, or if it is an independent and autonomous production, has been an object of discussion and debate. It's a little difficult to determine due to the reception it has received in different academic departments. In reality, its critical and theoretical makeup leads it to be considered as an independent literature, especially because nobody claims it as his or her own. It is ignored and expected to simply disappear or cease to exist. But instead of fulfilling this catastrophic wish, our literature is now used to this criticism and to the retrograde traditionalists who believed that Chicanos did not have anything valuable to say. I believe that that reasoning is no longer valid, for our writers possess great creativity in handling two worlds, two cultures, at least two languages, and an endless number of personal perspectives similar to an intrahistoria. It is true that we form part of the North American world, but our acceptance into that world has not been easy. Sometimes they put up with us and include us as an act of tokenism, but rarely do we form a "natural" part of their critical environment. With a few exceptions, Chicano and Chicana works are still not included in the mainstream literary canon. Mainstream critics tend to say that they do include us by offering a course on the topic, but it is worth noting that Chicano and Chicana authors are never included among the rest of the canonized North American authors such as John Steinbeck, Ernest Hemingway, e. e. cummings, and others. In other words, we still find a certain degree of "ghettoization." This may change as there is a lot of interest in Chicano literature now, but it will take time for it to be fully accepted.

What do you think of U.S.-Mexico border literature?

Border literature is one of the most revealing phenomena of today. Before 1980 this genre was not even mentioned or conceived of. Since then there has been an unprecedented resurgence in this literature. I remember having attended a conference in Tijuana in 1981 where critics and writers from both sides of the border got together for the first time to discuss, debate, and propose new views on the subject matter. Since then, the critical approaches have been nourished considerably by border literature and have opened new fields in cultural and theoretical discourses. This has allowed us to examine more carefully political, economic, artistic, and cultural aspects of literature. In the process, we realized that the world was becoming smaller, thanks to new means of communication and global rapport. Border literature allows us to better understand such phenomena. Instead of thinking in terms of dichotomies or perennial dualities, we should think in terms of fusion and amalgamation as part of our postmodern realities. The border has become a type of aleph, such as the one described by Jorge Luis Borges. This expression is encouraging because it provides glimpses of a promising future that has yet to arrive. This future could itself turn into one of the most prominent themes of U.S. and Mexican literatures.

What is the future of Chicano literature written in Spanish?

Chicano literature written in Spanish has its dilemmas. It continues to be a very useful vehicle of expression for our community, but unfortunately, the reading public does not easily consume it. When it is read, it is appreciated very much and pega where it is supposed to pegar. More and more there is a public that seeks our literature, or at least consumes what our writers offer. Nevertheless, the common reader typically disdains translations, complicating the purchase, dissemination, and acquisition of such works. But, I propose that one must keep on writing in the language that the author desires to write in, without sacrificing the quality or the cultural perspective that it contains. Let's look at Miguel Méndez, for instance. He has been consistent in writing all of his work in Spanish, and it is true that for that reason he has a limited reading public. But more and more he has achieved an international importance, and that is what counts. The important thing is to write, desahogarse, manifestarse, challenge the world, and explore the functionality of life to explore one's realities. Therefore, I believe that Chicano literature written in Spanish has a future, especially if it is written with a profoundness that touches the human soul.

What is the future of Chicano literature, in general?

This is difficult to say, but I don't see it disappearing. On the contrary, I believe that Chicano literature offers a lot of nerve and a keen eye toward touching on delicate topics and thus unmasking realities that tend to be ignored. There is still much to say concerning topics dealing with future borders, cultural interactions, internal family problems, the feminine psyche, the world of gangs, the meta-myths, the legends, the internationalization of economic problems, diseases, humor, racial syncretism, and the eternal themes of identity and culturalización. Our literature sometimes has been successful in dealing with some of these themes, but there is still a lot to be done. The fact that it has grown and been accepted at the national and international levels indicates that it's on the right path. It will continue to grow because there will always be a need for authentic voices to express our realities. Chicano literature has positioned itself to search for truths that allow us to focus on a dynamic world of creations for the well-being of our community. I am not worried about where our literature is heading, but I hope that it continues to provide new ideas and concepts for better understanding our dualities. If this is done, we can count on having a vibrant and innovative literature for years to come.

Any last thoughts concerning your role or function as a critic of Chicano literature? What do you think has been the major impact of your work in relation to Chicano letters? Also, do you see yourself as an ambassador of Chicano letters?

I believe that part of my motivation for opening ground for Chicano literature began in 1968 when as a student I became consciously involved at San Diego State University in cultivating a unique Chicano literary expression and at the same time identifying those new writers that had begun to make a name for themselves. I remember perfectly well when Alurista came to my Spanish for Native Speakers class at SDSU in the fall of 1968 and gave us a presentation on "the bilingual expression," Aztlán, the Chicano movement, and other related topics. His presence created excitement among all of us because he represented the ambience of great political-cultural activism that was emerging among our people. That class served as a springboard for exploring new means of communication and for valuing that skill in expressing oneself in both languages. It was a great revelation that we could live a double cultural sensibility without compromising one or the other. I realized that, in effect, I myself fell into this group of students that felt very comfortable expressing themselves in two languages. That completely changed my world-view, including the role that I saw language had in our psychic-personal formation. It also changed my attitude toward the so-called forced assimilation and how North American values served as a means to foster contrary cultural attitudes toward our community interests. I felt the need to recuperate my Spanish language with its unique Mexican subtleties and help create a sociocultural awareness for others to follow. I felt that my university education needed a pragmatic purpose that would benefit not only myself but also my community. Around this time, Rodolfo "Corky" Gonzales, with his poem *Yo soy Joaquín*, was the only author that I knew through a book. His work talked directly about our pueblo, its history, its relation with Mexico, its relation with the Anglo Saxon world, and the dynamics surrounding the great disadvantages that we lived as a people in this country. I felt inspired to search for fundamental changes to such conditions through literature. In an effort to construct a literary history of Chicano literature, I dedicated myself to the translation of short newspaper pieces and to searching for other authors from our literary past. At the beginning that search was like stepping out of a train in the middle of the desert, but soon I found them: authors with a wealth of unique voices, life experiences, and points of view. I soon found out that a number of people shared with me the same interests, and I saw that in effect I was not alone in this effort. There were others in search of something similar to what I was looking for.

From this interest stemmed my commitment to being a literary archeologist of Chicano literature. I have shared my findings with various colleagues from France, Spain, Germany, Russia, Costa Rica, Africa, Italy, and other places. For this reason it was very satisfying for me to travel to Moscow and Siberia with María Herrera-Sobek and María Teresa Márquez and present a series of talks and interviews for the purpose of making our literature accessible to any reader and breaking international barriers and borders in the process. The purpose was to cultivate and encourage new critical voices to emerge. I am pleased to say that through these efforts we can now find excellent academics who have contributed valuable approaches to the study of Chicano literature on almost every continent.

As far as being an ambassador of Chicano letters, let me say that that label carries considerable implications. To begin with, it represents a great deal of responsibility and praise because I know of several other colleagues that in their own way also promote our literature at the national and international levels. I don't feel that I hold an exclusive passport as ambassador, but I do feel that I have succeeded, en escala menor, in promoting our Chicano and Chicana writers and in continuing to expand the valuable work of other critics like Luis Leal, Américo Paredes, Aurelio Espinosa, María Herrera-Sobek, Nicolás Kanellos, Tey Diana Rebolledo, Genaro Padilla, Cordelia Candelaria,

Anselmo Arellano, Gabriel Meléndez, and many others. It is a great honor to have worked with them in this field of study because each one of them has contributed something very unique and significant in presenting Chicano literature to the world.

Selected Works

Lomelí, Francisco A. *La novelística de Carlos Droguett: Poética de la obsesión y el martirio.* Madrid, Spain: Playor, 1983.

Lomelí, Francisco A., and Rudolfo A. Anaya, eds. *Aztlán: Essays on the Chicano Homeland.* Albuquerque, NM: Academia/El Norte Publications, 1989.

Lomelí, Francisco A., and Juan A. Martínez, eds. *Chicano Literature: A Reference Guide.* Westport, CT: Greenwood Press, 1985.

Lomelí, Francisco A., and Gabriel Melendez, eds. *The Writings of Eusebio Chacón.* Albuquerque: University of New Mexico Press, 2012.

Lomelí, Francisco A., and Carl R. Shirley, eds. *Chicano Writers. First Series. Dictionary of Literary Biography.* Vol. 82. Detroit: Gale Group, 1989.

——, eds. *Chicano Writers. Second Series. Dictionary of Literary Biography.* Vol. 122. Detroit: Gale Group, 1992.

——, eds. *Chicano Writers. Third Series. Dictionary of Literary Biography.* Vol. 209. Detroit: Gale Group, 1999.

Lomelí, Francisco A., and Donald W. Urioste, eds. *Chicano Perspectives in Literature: A Critical and Annotated Bibliography.* Albuquerque, NM: Pajarito Publications, 1976.

——, eds. *De Colores: Journal of Chicano Expression and Thought: Chicano Literature and Criticism.* Vol. 3, no. 4. Albuquerque, NM: Pajarito Publications, 1977.

——. "Hard-Core Barrio Revisited: Violence, Sex, Drugs, and Videotape through a Chicano Glass Darkly." Introduction to *Barrio on the Edge / Caras viejas y vino nuevo*, by Alejandro Morales, 2–21. English translation by Francisco A. Lomelí. Tempe, AZ: Bilingual Press/Editorial Bilingüe, 1998.

Lomelí, Francisco A., Nicolás Kanellos, and Claudio Esteva-Fabregat, eds. *Handbook of Hispanic Cultures in the United States: Literature and Art.* Houston: Arte Público Press; Madrid, Spain: Instituto de Cooperación Iberoamericana, 1994.

Lomelí, Francisco A., Víctor A. Sorell, and Genaro M. Padilla, eds. *Nuevomexicano Cultural Legacy: Forms, Agencies, and Discourse.* Albuquerque: University of New Mexico Press, 2002.

Lomelí, Francisco A., et al. *A Decade of Chicano Literature (1970–1979): Critical Essays and Bibliography.* Santa Barbara: Editorial La Causa, 1982.

7

Felipe de Ortego y Gasca

The Chicano Reinassance Man

ARCHITECT OF fine prose and literary critic par excellence, Felipe de Ortego y Gasca stands at the center of Mexican American literature as an author of monographs, poetry, fiction, plays, essays, and hundreds of critical articles. Considered the founder of Chicano literary history, Ortego y Gasca coined the phrase "Chicano Renaissance" to describe the flowering of Mexican American literature in his celebrated essay "The Chicano Renaissance," published in the Journal of Social Casework, *in May 1971. As a scholar and respected writer, Ortego y Gasca became a mentor to hundreds of writers and academicians learning to climb the uncharted peaks of Mexican American literature and discover the terra incognita of Chicano thought. With his eloquence, Ortego y Gasca could mesmerize an audience. And yet, Felipe was distinctly a gentleman scholar in the British slant of the word. No other writer of such magnitude and scope of vision could have catapulted Chicano literature from the margins of American letters.*
—Rafael C. Castillo

Felipe de Ortego y Gasca (1926–) is considered one of the pioneers of Chicano literary history. His parents originated from Guanajuato, Mexico, and arrived in the United States soon after the end of the Mexican Revolution in 1921. The family worked as migrant farm workers throughout the United States, eventually settling in the Midwest, were Felipe was born.

Ortego y Gasca began his academic career majoring in Spanish, and even though he would later change it to English, his love for Hispanic letters never diminished. His PhD dissertation, "Backgrounds of Mexican American Literature," is considered the first work to deal with Chicano literary history. In that study he introduced the term "Chicano Renaissance," a concept that inspired a generation of future Chicano writers, primarily those writing in the 1960s and early 1970s. Ortego y Gasca also edited We Are Chicanos, *one of the first anthologies on Chicano literature published by a major American press—Simon & Schuster. He has worked for more than fifty years at various universities including Arizona State University, the University of New Mexico, New Mexico State University, the University of Houston, San Jose State University, the University of Texas at El Paso, and Sul Ross State University, where he is Professor Emeritus of English. Currently he is scholar-in-residence at Western New Mexico University in Silver City, New Mexico.*

The interview with Felipe was conducted in his home in Kingsville, Texas, in 2006 and continued in a number of e-mail correspondences from 2006 to 2012.

* * *

Felipe, where were you born? Describe your childhood and the place where you grew up.

My father was born in 1900. He used to tell us that when he was a young man he participated in the Mexican Revolution. He was not a soldier—in 1910 he was only ten years old—but he was in charge of taking water to the guerrilleros. What's interesting of his anecdotes is that with the passage of time his memories of the Mexican Revolution were aggrandized. When he told us the same story of the revolution years later, he used to say that he was Pancho Villa's main advisor: "Pancho Villa did not move a finger without first consulting Luis Ortego." My father liked to tell many stories. He came to Texas in 1921 from Guanajuato, Mexico. A branch of my mother's family settled in San Antonio in 1731. So from her side we have deep roots in Texas. When my father crossed the border he stayed three years, until 1924, scouring the United States. That year he went back to Mexico for my mother. About my mother's marriage to my father, she told us que se la había robado, meaning he eloped with her. In

July or August of 1926 they left for Minnesota as migrant workers, harvesting beets. Upon their return to Texas they passed through Blue Island, Illinois, a suburb of Chicago where my uncle José, my mother's brother, lived. My birth certificate lists me as "Felipe," but when I began to attend the segregated schools in San Antonio, Texas, my name was changed to Philip. That was the Americanization process for mejicanos. In fact that's the name that appears on my driver's license. But in the 1960s, in 1966 to be exact, when I met Octavio I. Romano, I reclaimed the name "Felipe" once again. I give Romano credit for converting me into a Chicano and for teaching me to value the importance of that reclamation. I have a brother and two sisters. Rebecca is three years younger than me. Marta is three years younger than Rebecca and my brother, José, is three years younger than Marta. The death of my parents in 1936 was unexpected; it affected me so much that I did not attend their funeral. I was so angry with them for having abandoned us. "Didn't they know that I needed them? How could they have gone?" I asked myself. It wasn't until I turned twenty-six that I finally gave closure to this trauma of my life. It was then that I realized that they were not the cause of my behavior. After my parent's death, my sisters and brother and I went to live with our uncle José in Chicago.

How was your family life? What impact did your parents and your environment have on you?

My parents' death affected me so much that in school I was incorrigible. At the same time, when I began school in 1932 I was held back a year; I had to repeat the first grade for being a Spanish speaker. When I reached the fourth grade, I was held back another year because I still had not made sufficient progress in English. In 1940 my uncles from Chicago were not able to support us and sent us to live with different families in Pittsburgh, Pennsylvania. I ended up with Ernesto Méndez, a relative from my father's side of the family. He lived with Mrs. Lucy, a black lady. I lived with them in the black neighborhood of East Pittsburgh, from 1940 to 1943, when I then decided to enlist in the U.S. Marines. Mrs. Lucy taught me to play the guitar, the blues. She saw the great interest I had for music, an interest that after World War II was going to play a major role in my life. I served in the Marines for three years, from 1943 to 1946. I served in the Pacific and in China at war's end and was discharged as a platoon sergeant. Later I would learn that of the 16 million American men and women in uniform during World War II, one million of them were Hispanics, mostly Mexican Americans, who won more Medals of Honor than any other group.

When does your academic preparation begin?

In 1946, when I was discharged from the Marines. I returned to Pittsburgh and worked in the steel mills from 1946 to 1948. One day after my 3 to 11 p.m. job shift, upon crossing Monongahela River on my way home—on the South Side of Pittsburgh—I stopped in the middle of the bridge to meditate over the moon's reflection on the water. Something happened to me in that moment because it was there that I decided to do something with my life. In the following days I went to the offices of the Veterans Administration in Pittsburgh and informed them that I wanted to go to college but had finished only a year of high school. They told me that the University of Pittsburgh was provisionally accepting any veteran from the war, regardless of any academic record. In August 1948 I entered the university as a freshman and that first semester was very difficult. I finished with two As and three Fs. I received the two As in Spanish. The three Fs were in chemistry, history, and English. The school notified me that since I was a provisional student one of the Fs would have to be changed to a D for me to continue with my studies. I could not convince my chemistry and history professors to change their grades. I had better luck with my English professor because we had both served in the Marine Corps. He was a first lieutenant and I a platoon sergeant. When we spoke we connected well, we even exchanged stories about our military life. The professor said to me, "You know, Mr. Ortego, I can't promise you anything, I am going to review your work and if it's possible to change the grade from an F to a D, I will let you know." In a few days he called and told me that he could change the grade, so the following semester, spring 1949, I took the second semester of English with the same professor and I received a D. I often ask myself whether the professor's kindness encouraged me to study for the doctorate in English. At Pitt I was a comparative studies major in English, Spanish, French, Italian, and Russian. I earned a lot of credits in French and Spanish, but more in English.

What literature in Spanish did you read at that time?

I read Spanish writers, like Benito Pérez Galdós and works such as *El libro de buen amor* and *Lazarillo de Tormes.* I also read Hispanic American books such as *La Araucana.* At that time I didn't think there were Mexican American authors. I felt so ill prepared in my readings that I spent a lot of time in the library. I always carried books with me. When I was a boy, I read in Spanish. My parents insisted that I read in Spanish. My mother taught me from some blue books that peddlers brought with them to sell to the general public. At war's end, I read Miguel de Unamuno's *Del sentimiento trágico de la vida.* That book saved my life. What happened is that five of us marines went from our base in Tsingtao to a nearby swath of pines to get a Christmas tree. After cutting it we put it in the truck, and when we were about to return to our base a group of Chinese Communists appeared out of nowhere and surrounded us. Their uniforms did not have insignias, therefore we could not tell who was in charge. Even though we didn't carry any weapons we were not afraid of them. We had survived the War of the Pacific and if the situation turned ugly we knew we could handle it. At last, one of the communist soldiers, who seemed to be the leader, approached the truck, saw Unamuno's book, and asked in Spanish, "¿Y este libro de quién es?" "And this book, who does it belong to?" I answered him in Spanish that it was mine. "Oh, good," he answered. He placed it back on the seat and proceeded to leave with his troops. Unamuno saved my life because who knows what could have happened if the leader had not spoken Spanish.

Did you finish your BA at the University of Pittsburgh?

I did not, even though I did have enough credits to earn the degree. I wanted to learn so much! So to provide for myself I earned extra money playing music. I studied the guitar with two very good guitarists. They taught me a lot. I joined the musicians' union and traveled with musicians through Ohio, Illinois, Indiana, Washington, DC, Maryland, New York, and New Jersey. But then in 1952, I went into teaching. Even though I did not have the BA degree, I did obtain the certificate to teach Spanish, French, and English. I had completed the necessary courses for certification in Pennsylvania. I taught French at Munhall High School near Pittsburgh until 1953. Since I had participated in ROTC at Pitt and had been appointed a second lieutenant in the Air Force reserve, I promptly joined an Air Force Reserve unit in 1952. In 1953 my reserve unit was mobilized. The commander of the reserve group asked me if I was interested in pilot training school. I did not answer him right away, and he suggested that I think about it. I did and I filled out the application never thinking that they would accept me, but they did. However, the Air Force did not accept applications for flight training from people who were twenty-seven years of age. I was twenty-six and a half at the time and had to get a special waiver from the Secretary of the Air Force to apply. I had to report to Goodfellow Air Force base in San Angelo, Texas, before my birthday, which is August 23. On August 21 I took the train from Pittsburgh to San Angelo. I arrived at the base on August 22 at 10 p.m. Had I arrived at midnight I believe that they would not have accepted me because I would have turned twenty-seven at that hour. After flight school I spent the next nine years in the Air Force. I left the Air Force in 1962 as a reserve major. After the Air Force I taught French at Jefferson High School, known as "la Jeff," in El Paso, Texas. In the spring of 1964, Newman Reed, who was the chair of the Department of English at New Mexico State, recruited me as an instructor of English at New Mexico State University. In 1966, I completed the MA degree in English at Texas Western College (renamed the University of Texas at El Paso in 1967). That was the year Texas Western College basketball team won the National Collegiate Athletic Association (NCAA) championship. Newman Reed advised me that if I wanted to continue as an academic I had to study for a doctorate. In 1967 I was accepted into the doctoral program in English at the University of New Mexico (UNM) and started taking courses for the doctorate in English.

Did you earn your doctorate from the Department of English?

Yes. It's interesting because when I started the MA at Texas Western it was in Spanish with a minor in English. Later, I changed my major to English with Spanish as a minor. I had good professors. Some of the most famous specialists in the study of Shakespeare and Chaucer taught at Texas Western. I wrote my thesis on *Hamlet*, and when I went to UNM I was going to get the doctorate with a dissertation on Chaucer. But in July 1969, when I had finished taking all of my graduate courses and had written three chapters of my dissertation, the director of the new program in Chicano studies at UNM asked me to prepare a class on Mexican American literature. I accepted because I was the only Mexican American in the department. That September I taught the first course on Mexican American literature at UNM, which turned out to be the first course taught on Mexican American literature in the country.

Who helped you to organize the course?

The librarian at UNM and two recently hired young professors, who became members of my doctoral committee, helped me. With the New Mexicans I met in New Mexico, I desperately began to search for Chicano reading material for the class; there wasn't much to find at the time. In 1966 I had met Octavio Romano, the founder of *El Grito*, the first journal dedicated to Mexican American studies, so I had an idea of where to look for advice. One hundred and twenty five students enrolled in that first class. Among the works I used were ones by John Rechy, Floyd Salas, Ray Barrios, and Alurista. I did what was possible with the paucity of materials available.

Was this course in Chicano literature responsible for your decision to change the topic of your dissertation?

Yes, after this experience I spoke with the Chair of the English Department and told him that I wanted to change the topic of my dissertation. He gave me the OK. "It's highly unusual to allow it," he told me, but he gave me permission to change it. However, he warned me that I might have a problem organizing a committee that would be familiar with the theme. But three young professors from the department agreed to be part of my committee. It took me a year to finish the dissertation. I titled it, "Backgrounds of Mexican American Literature." It was the first study on Mexican American literary history, though at the time I didn't know that. From this study the term "Chicano Renaissance" emerged. I remember that Juan Bruce Novoa asked me what "renaissance" I was talking about? He was right, I wasn't sure either, but I think that once in a while one has to be daring. When I reread the dissertation, or parts of it, I ask myself, "Did I say that?" But because of it, I discovered writers such as Vicente Bernal, a New Mexican poet who wrote *Las primicias*, and Andrew García, the Texan who went to Montana in 1880, and Miguel Antonio Otero, the Governor of New Mexico who wrote about Billy the Kid. I found bits of literature here and there, like an ignis fatuus.

Did Spanish and Latin American literature influence you in the preparation of "Backgrounds of Mexican American Literature"?

Yes, I conceptualized the dissertation in two parts—Part I: Roots, the Indigenous and the Spanish; Part II: Traditions. First, I discussed indigenous literature and then the literature from Spain, suggesting that when the Spanish brought their literature to Mexico, they helped shape the Mexican culture because of the creation of the mestizos. I had to study more of what I had learned of Spanish Peninsular and indigenous literature.

Was it the knowledge of this work that led you to edit the anthology We Are Chicanos: An Anthology of Mexican American Literature?

In 1968 I was part of the National Council of Teachers of English task force on Racism and Bias in the Teaching of English. In 1971, the national conference took place in Las Vegas, Nevada. Black, Native American, Asian, and Chicano caucuses were present. In a conference room a group of us gathered the presidents and vice presidents of the major publishing houses of the country and we "Mau Maued them." In other words, we cornered them so they could listen to our complaints. One of the representatives of Simon & Schuster asked me if I would be interested in organizing an anthology on Chicano literature. I accepted and finished it in two years, in 1973. Other anthologies had been published on the subject, but this was the first to include a critical literary perspective and not just an accumulation of texts.

How did you face the challenge of not including Chicano writers that express themselves in Spanish, since the anthology was directed to an English speaking public?

It was a difficult decision not to include them. The anthology was in English and I decided not to include literature in Spanish. If I were asked to organize it again, this time I would publish it in a bilingual edition.

What do you think of the Chicano writers who in their works search for Mexico as a type of cultural refuge? Do you think that something is missing in their identity because they feel distanced from Mexico?

I say yes, that since 1848 Mexican Americans have felt abandoned by the United States. It's a fact that Mexico was forced to surrender more than half of its sovereign territory for $15 million. Maybe, in that sense, they look to Mexico not so much as a refuge but as a way of demanding, "Look, you abandoned us, and look how we have developed." Because of that, the symbolism of the Chicano movement—which includes icons of ancient Mexico and its indigenous roots—emerged with so much passion.

What do you think of Chicano literature written in Spanish? Do you believe that it has a future?

Oh, yes. Definitely. But probably we don't find it so much now because there are so few places that publish it, and if it is published the distribution is not very good. But I think there is plenty of Mexican American literature that is written in Spanish. Possibly, we are giving credence to the propaganda that says that this literature is not in tune with reality and so it is said that "nobody reads it." But in our present, yes, it is being read and taught.

What do you think is the most important development of Chicano literature from the 1960s to the present?

The strongest change has been in the genre of the novel and in prose. We now have more prolific and focused writers than we had in the 1960s and 1970s. Now, as opposed to past years, when there was an intent to discredit the stereotypical images that were imposed upon us, we can write works that focus on the multiple experiences of our reality. One change from the writers of 1960s and 1970s is that they are now writing their biographies. Something interesting is that when reading them we are going to revise or revaluate history in their terms, because in their remembering the authors sometimes tell us something different and distinct from what actually happened. For example, when I read José Angel Gutiérrez's, *The Making of a Chicano Militant: Lessons from Cristal*, a book that talks about his development as a Chicano, I said to myself, "I don't remember this part, this seems a little different than what really happened." This is not to deprecate the work. On the contrary, the Chicano writer is giving us more content than we otherwise were aware of.

What do mexicanos think of Chicano writers?

A few years ago I went to a conference on Chicano literature at the Universidad Nacional Autónoma de México (UNAM), and I believe that there is an effort on the part of some Mexicans to know us, to really know us. However, there are many others, like Carlos Fuentes and Octavio Paz, who knew us only superficially. But this in not Mexico's fault; it's our fault. We have to write more. We have to organize symposiums, go to Mexico, present ourselves, and say, "this is who we are; we are a great part of Mexico outside the country." Somos el México de afuera; el otro México. It's our responsibility to make these efforts possible.

I suppose that for Chicanos to be taken seriously in Mexico they have to perfect their Spanish, correct?

Yes, absolutely. You're right. We have to learn the language, but of equal importance is that they also understand English. This reciprocal communication would be beneficial for both sides. Importantly, however, Mexico must acknowledge that despite our historical context and circumstances, we have preserved Mexican culture and have done our best to maintain the language. We have created an American form of Spanish, sometimes called Spanglish, con orgullo.

On what project are you currently working?

At the moment I am finishing an essay that I will present in a reading for the Texas Historical Association; it's called "Demography and Destiny: Hispanic Texas in the 21st Century." I am also finishing an extensive essay about the origin and the development of Tejana/o literature, one that is different from Hispanic and Mexican American literature. Also, I am involved as editor-in-chief with the ABC-CLIO Greenwood *Encyclopedia of Latino Issues Today*. We hope that it's published in 2014. It's a two-volume encyclopedia that, based on the demographic projection of Latinos—that by 2040 a third of the United States' population will be Latino—I believe will help increase the understanding of the historical and intellectual presence of the Latinos in the United States.

Any last thoughts concerning your role or function as a critic of Chicano literature?

This is a difficult question because of its self-evaluating nature. It is always problematic to determine one's own influence in any discipline or area of study. I see that now I am quoted in many critical works on Chicano literature. It's true that without knowing it, I wrote the first literary history on Mexican American literature. And from that study emerged "The Chicano Renaissance," the essay that identifies me with the beginning of the Chicano literary renaissance. It was published in May 1971 in the *Journal of Social Casework* because no other journal cared to publish it at the time. It can be determined that the impact it had on the development of Chicano literature has been positive. Although my voice was un llanto solitario en el llano, it carried enough urgency to darle gas and say with our Mexican American consciousness que somos mejicanos en los Estados Unidos and that we have a literature as valid and worthy as the literature of our origins—Mexico.

Selected Works

Ortego y Gasca, Felipe de. "Backgrounds of Mexican American Literature." PhD diss., University of New Mexico, 1971.

——. *Montezuma's Children*. El Paso, TX: Chicano Research Institute, 1971.
——. *Selective Mexican American Bibliography*. El Paso, TX: Border Regional Library Association/Chicano Research Institute, 1972.
——, ed. *We Are Chicanos: An Anthology of Mexican-American Literature*. New York: Washington Square Press (Simon & Schuster), 1973.
——, ed. *Contemporary Perspectives of the Old Spanish Missions of San Antonio.* San Antonio, TX: Institute for Intercultural Studies and Research, 1979.
——. *Milestones in Chicano Literature: A Guide and Reading List*. San Antonio: Texas Commission for the Humanities, 1982.
——. *The Cross and the Pen: Spanish Colonial and Mexican Periods of Texas Letters.* Washington, DC: The Hispanic Foundation, 1983.
——. *Chicano Literature: Development and Criticism* (the Sabal Palms Lectures). Austin, TX: Caravel Press, 2004.
Ortego y Gasca, Felipe de, and David Conde, eds. *The Chicano Literary World: 1974*. Albuquerque, NM: National Education Task Force de la Raza, 1975.
Ortego y Gasca, Felipe de, and Arnoldo De León, eds. *The Tejano Yearbook, 1519–1978: A Selective Chronicle of the Hispanic Presence in Texas*. San Antonio, TX: Caravel Press, 1978.

8

Tey Diana Rebolledo

Mujer Singing in the Snow

Tey Diana Rebolledo is a pioneer Chicana literary critic, educator, mentor, and activist. She has had the pulse of Chicana feminism since the early 1970s, because she not only "talks the talk" but "walks the walk." As a divorced mother in her thirties, she returned to university studies (where we met) to pursue her doctorate. Her critical models (feminist studies, discourse analysis, and semiotics) suited the "in your face" writing of contemporary twentieth-century Mexicana and Chicana writers and poets. By the late 1970s she had begun to focus on texts that, as a New Mexican–born Chicana, spoke to her. The catalyst for her feminist rage? A 1960s psychological experiment that occurred during a college course, where she had been the sole Chicana. Diana believes that her/our opinion counts, and she has been and is a powerful advocate for our voice. She also maintains a positive view of life, enjoying humor, appreciating the ironies, and believing in change. One of her numerous, insightful, and original pioneering publications has the pithy title "Chicana Poetry: The Quiet Revolution." If you have read my work, you may see why we have been hermanas since graduate school. She is my role model, and she is awesome: "Though she be but little, she is fierce . . ." (This Shakespeare-like quote will make her laugh, but if you know her, well!)
—Margarita Cota-Cárdenas

Tey Diana Rebolledo (1937–), a native of New Mexico, received her PhD degree in Spanish from the University of Arizona. She has taught at the

University of North Carolina at Chapel Hill, the University of Nevada, Reno, and since 1988 at the University of New Mexico. Rebolledo is the author of The Chronicles of Panchita Villa and Other Guerrilleras: Essays on Chicana/Latina Literature and Criticism *and* Women Singing in the Snow. *She has also coedited several books including* Women's Tales from the New Mexico WPA: La Diabla a pie, *and* Infinite Divisions: An Anthology of Chicana Literature. *Rebolledo has been the recipient of a Rockefeller Fellowship and a Danforth Fellowship. She has also been named a Distinguished Professor, a UNM Regent's Professor, and a New Mexico Eminent Scholar. Rebolledo is a tireless scholar who has enriched the field of cultural studies, focusing her research on Chicana/o literature and contemporary Southwest Hispana/o literature and culture.*

The interview with Tey was conducted through a number of e-mail correspondences from 2008 to 2012.

* * *

Tey, where were you born? Describe your childhood and the place where you grew up.

I was born in 1937 in a small pueblo of New Mexico called Las Vegas. When I was a young girl, the pueblo was very rural. On the weekends the cowboys and ranchers came to the pueblo and my mother said that they left their horses close to the house and that the horses ate the grass that she had planted. She complained a lot about that. I don't know if that's true because my mother was a great storyteller and always exaggerated things. The pueblo was divided between Anglos and Hispanics. The Hispanics mainly lived in the old pueblo that was constructed around a plaza and surrounded with adobe houses. The Gallinas River separated the old pueblo from the new one. In the new pueblo, the houses were constructed during the railroad era. Some were huge Victorian houses, others very modest ones. My father was a professor of Spanish in Las Vegas Normal School, the school for teachers. Now it is called Highlands University. We lived in the new pueblo and my family was one of the few that crossed the river that separated the Anglos and the Hispanics.

I grew up during World War II, and I had a great fear of planes. When I heard the sound of planes I was completely sure that they were Japanese and that they had come to bomb us. That was sure to happen, I thought, because we lived close to Los Alamos, the secret place where the United States government was experimenting with nuclear bombs. To prepare us for any possible enemy invasions we had "blackouts" and closed the curtains at night so that the Germans and the Japanese would not find us. My mother would laugh and comment that Las Vegas was such a small pueblo that the "blackouts" were inconsequential, that no matter what they did, they would never find us.

How was your family life? What impact did your parents and your environment have in your early life?

I am a daughter of immigrants. My mother was born in Mexico and my father in a small pueblito located in the mountain ranges of Peru. My mother married at a young age a very important lawyer in Mexico and had two children, my brother Guillermo and my sister Angeles. She divorced her husband and several years later she met my father when he went to Mexico on vacation. At the time my father was a professor who had received his doctorate from a university in Spain. They married and had two children: me, a mischievous and spoiled girl, and my sister Gloria. Even though my mother did not complete more than a few years of secondary education in the convent that she attended, she was a very intelligent woman. She was a great storyteller, una mentirosa that loved to read. She was also very gorgeous. She had her genio, as we say. My father was a very studious man, also very handsome and tolerant. Both of them influenced me very much because as a girl I liked to listen to their stories and to my mother's lies. When I was a girl I read a lot. I always had my nose stuck in a book, something that I still do today. My mother missed Mexico very much; therefore, for her it was a continuous coming and going to visit her extended family there. I was the first daughter of my father and since my sister Gloria was born six years after I was, for many years I was the consentida of my father and I could literally do whatever I wanted. When I was ten years old or so, my father was offered a faculty position and the chair of the Spanish Department at Connecticut College for Women, in New London, Connecticut. Since my mother was from Mexico City, she wanted to move from Las Vegas to a larger pueblo; therefore my sisters Gloria, Angeles, and I moved with my parents to New London. There were no Hispanics there! In the beginning this was a big shock, but after that I got used to it.

When does your academic preparation begin?

As you can see, education was very important for my parents and for me too. When I was fourteen years old my father died of a malignant brain tumor, leaving my mother a widow with two young daughters. My mother suffered a lot, but she moved on and went to work as a librarian. Those were very difficult years for us. When I was in my third year of high school, my mother decided to relocate to California, to Chula Vista, where one of my uncles had a small factory. Once again, we experienced a very big change in our life. The following year she decided to return to Mexico. I didn't want to go there and lose my senior year at school, so a Jewish family—who were great friends of my father—invited me to live with them in New London so that I could finish my studies. I have always had great love for this family because they helped me a lot with my studies and my career. Even though the parents have died, I still keep in touch with their daughter, who is my age. We see each other not as friends but as sisters. Like me, she followed an academic career and is an art history professor in New York.

Connecticut College awarded me a scholarship, and I was able to study there for four years. Then I decided to return to New Mexico to study for my MA in Latin American studies at the University of New Mexico. I studied sociology, history, history of art, and a little bit of literature—I had a class with the great professor Sabine Ulibarrí. There I also met my first husband, a historian, and we had a daughter, Tey Marianna Nunn, who is the director of visual arts at the National Hispanic Cultural Center in Albuquerque.

When did you discover your interest in literature, in general, including U.S., Mexican, Spanish, and Latin American literature? What authors influenced your academic career?

For several years I stayed at home, taking care of my daughter. During the time of the Chicano movement, I was against the war in Vietnam and participated in public protests. I also took part in the grape and lettuce boycotts and performed dramas at the supermarkets in support of the farmworker's struggles. One day César Chávez came to Portland, Oregon, where we were living at the time, and my chiquita and I had the honor of meeting him and participating in a march. That moment has remained a very important one for us.

In 1974 I divorced and enrolled at the University of Arizona in Tucson to study for my doctorate. At that time, I decided to study Latin American literature because I had previously received my bachelors in Spanish. The years in Tucson were magnificent. I studied with Professor Eliana S. Rivero in one of the first classes that dealt with Latin American women writers. In the class was another Chicana who studied with me, Margarita Cota-Cárdenas. One day Margarita invited me to a poetry reading where some students were going to read their creative work. There I listened to Margarita's poetry—she read poems from her book *Noches despertando inconciencias.* Her poems were the first feminist poetry that I had ever heard. Her reading impressed me tremendously because the poems spoke to me; they were talking about many of the experiences that I had lived. I understood them. Also, Juan Rodríguez was at the University of Arizona working as a professor in the Spanish department. Later that year, the Chicano professor Arturo Madrid came to the university to give a conference on Oscar Zeta Acosta's *Autobiography of a Brown Buffalo.* It was at the University of Arizona—and through the people mentioned above—that I realized that Chicano literature existed. I finished my studies with a doctorate in Spanish, writing my dissertation on the Mexican poet, Rosario Castellanos. I also studied pre-Columbian literature, which has always interested me, with Professor Miguel León Portilla.

In the various faculty positions that I held at the University of North Carolina at Chapel Hill and later at the University of Nevada, Reno, I continued my interest in Chicano literature. I collected works of poetry and narrative wherever I could find them and incorporated them into my classes. I also began to attend conferences that dealt with Chicano studies. Professor Rivero and I applied for a National Endowment for the Humanities (NEH) grant to prepare a book of Chicana criticism, and when the grant was awarded to us, I began to travel to various universities and libraries in search of Chicana writers. I spent, more or less, two years on this project. While the research was in progress, Eliana and I decided that besides organizing a book of criticism—it was badly needed for there was not much written about Chicana women at the time—it was equally important to include an anthology on the literature that we were gathering. Therefore, our anthology, *Infinite Divisions: An Anthology of Chicana Literature*, was the result of this project and was published by the University of Arizona Press in 1995. It is one of the first anthologies published on Chicana writers, and it is still used in literature classes today. Later, in 1990, I published a book on literary criticism titled *Women Singing in the Snow: A Cultural Analysis of Chicana Literature*, also by the University of Arizona Press. Since then I have continued my interests in Chicano literature, publishing articles on women of New Mexico and another book, *The Chronicles of Panchita Villa*, published by the University of Texas Press in 2005.

In 1984 I came to the University of New Mexico as a professor in the Department of Spanish and as the director of women studies. Here in New Mexico I have met more Chicano and Chicana authors, and I have had the good fortune of having as colleagues and conspiradores people like Sabine Ulibarrí, Rudolfo Anaya, Erlinda Gonzales-Berry, and Enrique Lamadrid. Erlinda, Enrique, and I were able to start a MA degree program in Southwest studies and also a doctorate in this field in our department. Also, in my research, writers and academics such as Pat Mora, Sandra Cisneros, Norma Cantú, and María Herrera-Sobek have supported me very much. They are excellent friends. One important thing to bear in mind is the fact that the world of Chicana writers and critics is a very small world. We follow our literature with interest and almost all of us know each other. I have seen Chicana creative and academic writing mature and grow in importance during these years.

What do Chicana and Latina writers have in common? Differences?

I think that the literature of the Chicanas and Latinas in the United States have many characteristics in common as well as major differences. It's a fact that Chicana writers have a long historical tradition in the United States; in other words, some are second, third, and fourth generation residents of this country. Also, these writers have lived in a rural environment and come from the working class. They, as well as their parents and grandparents, have suffered a great deal of social, economic, and educational discrimination. Consequently, they are constantly in search of their place and their identity inside this diverse country. Their literature is political and reflects a social reality. They have been poor and hard working, and they want to leave behind not only their personal story or that of their family but also the story of their community. In their writings they incorporate myths and pre-Columbian images, criticize the Catholic education that has limited their personal development, and fight the machista attitudes that exist in our society. Through their writing they search and find the strong voice of themselves and of women. They write mainly in English, with cultural concepts and selected words or phrases presented in Spanish. The ones that write their literature in Spanish, like Cota-Cárdenas, have a lot of difficulty finding a place to publish their work.

Many of the Latina writers in the United States come from an educated upper class. Many are immigrants of first-generation families, and if they are from Central America or the Caribbean, they come from urban centers and their experience in the United States is one of the city, generally New York or another East Coast city. They write on themes dealing with cultural shock, discrimination, or the return to their countries of origin. I am thinking of writers such as Julia Alvarez, Cristina García, and Isabel Allende. The sense of community and the history of that community in the United States are not as noticeable in their work. Many times they write their work in Spanish, and then it is translated into English.

And Latin American writers?

I would say that the differences between Chicana writers and Latin American writers are more or less the same. The Latin American writers come from an educated upper class. They have a longer publication tradition. They are more careful in expressing their thoughts, while I believe that the Chicana writer, in general, no tiene pelos en la lengua. In other words, Chicana literature contains daring taboo topics and is expressed in a strong, harsh language that responds to the rejection and the limitations that this culture put upon them.

Does Chicano culture have any influence on Mexican culture?

I don't know if Chicano culture influences Mexican culture very much, even though general U.S. popular culture does. I believe that Mexicans do not read a lot of Chicano and Chicana literature. But what is clear is that Chicanos and Chicanas are influenced by Mexican culture, and we incorporate a lot of Mexican popular culture into our literature: pre-Columbian myths, cultural figures like la Malinche, la Virgen de Guadalupe, and la llorona, music, sayings, food, cinema, art. Mexican culture influences our culture and our literature. One cannot read Sandra Cisneros, Pat Mora, or Denise Chávez without seeing Mexican popular culture being combined with American popular culture.

What do you think of Chicano literature written in Spanish? Do you believe that it has a future?

Since I work in a Spanish department, of course I support Chicano literature written in Spanish. But, unfortunately the works that are published are very limited in number due to the lack of demand of the reading public. Also, it is a fact that for many Chicano and Chicana writers English is their first language and they feel more comfortable writing in that language. I understand that, for we have to master the language that controls our environment. But what always surprises me and what I deeply appreciate is the number of writers that do speak and write in Spanish. Writers like Margarita Cota-Cárdenas and Erlinda Gonzales-Berry have written their short stories and novels in Spanish but have had problems finding a press that would publish their work. I believe that in the United States we lack a Spanish reading public. Maybe the ideal solution would be for presses to publish our literature bilingually.

On what project are you currently working?

I am working on a manuscript on Chicana autobiography and another on the connection between creativity and the Chicana artists and writers. But I still have a long way to go.

Any last thoughts concerning your role or function as a critic of Chicano literature?

Well, I hope that my work has helped disseminate Chicana literature to a wide reading public. I believe that when you read Chicana literature, your worldview changes—that is, you never see Chicanas in the same way. You understand their struggles and their triumphs. It is a very powerful literature. I love it when my students tell me they have given the books they read in class to their sisters, brothers, mothers, boyfriends, and girlfriends because they see something of themselves in these books and want to share them. That's absolutely the best part.

Selected Works

Rebolledo, Tey D. "The Wind and the Tree: A Structural Analysis of the Poetry of Rosario Castellanos." PhD diss., University of Arizona, 1979.

——. "Walking the Thin Line: Humor in Chicana Literature," in *Beyond Stereotypes: The Critical Analysis of Chicana Literature*, edited by María Herrera-Sobek, 91–107. Binghamton, NY: Bilingual Press, 1985.

——. "The Politics of Poetics: Or What Am I, A Critic, Doing in This Text Anyhow?" In *Chicana Creativity and Criticism: Charting New Frontiers in American Literature*, edited by María Herrera-Sobek and Helena María Viramontes, 129–38. Houston, TX: Arte Público Press and Mexico/Chicano Program University of California, Irvine, 1987.

——. *Women Singing in the Snow: A Cultural Analysis of Chicana Literature.* Tucson, AZ: University of Arizona Press, 1995.

——. Introduction to *Romance of a Little Village Girl*, by Cleofas M. Jaramillo, xv–xxvii. Albuquerque: University of New Mexico Press, 2000.

——. "Las Hijas de la Malinche: Mexicana/India Captivity Narratives in the Southwest, Subverting Voices," in *Nuevomexicano Cultural Legacy: Forms, Agencies, and Discourse*, edited by Francisco A. Lomelí, Víctor Sorrel, and Genaro Padilla, 129–50. Albuquerque: University of New Mexico Press, 2002.

——. *The Chronicles of Panchita Villa and Other Guerrilleras: Essays on Chicana/Latina Literature and Criticism.* Austin: University of Texas Press, 2005.

Rebolledo, Tey D., and Teresa Márquez, eds. *Women's Tales from the New Mexico WPA: La diabla a pie.* Houston, TX: Arte Público Press, 2000.

Rebolledo, Tey D., and Eliana S. Rivero, eds. *Infinitive Divisions: An Anthology of Chicana Literature.* Tucson: University of Arizona Press, 1993.

Rebolledo, Tey D., Erlinda Gonzales-Berry, and Teresa Márquez, eds. *Las mujeres hablan: An Anthology of Nuevo Mexican Writers.* Albuquerque, NM: El Norte Publications, 1988.

Rebolledo, Tey D., Erlinda Gonzales-Berry, and Millie Santillanes, eds. *Nuestras mujeres: Hispanas of New Mexico: Their Images and Their Lives, 1582–1992.* Albuquerque, NM: El Norte Publications/Academia, 1992.

9

Juan Rodríguez

The Communicator (*sin pelos en la lengua*)

"THERE'S NO GREATER PAIN," the Nicaraguan poet Rubén Darío wrote, "than not to know where we come from or where we are going." The role of all great educators, as Paulo Freire taught, is showing the way such a journey takes, of pointing others toward legitimate self-definition. Furthering that pedagogical consciousness is what has guided "El Profe Rodríguez" in his teachings on his own intellectual journey. But that responsibility to help define, or redefine, the Chicano experience now passes to another generation, the one José Angel Gutiérrez has named "Panethnic Latinos." Juan Rodríguez, and others like him, have already shown the way by personal example, beginning in the cotton fields and reaching up to some of the most prestigious universities in the country. An intimate friend whom I have known for over thirty years, Rodríguez has produced a singular curriculum vitae worthy of careful study by all serious scholars who wish to continue providing due relevance to such a vital area of study. But seeing is believing or, as St. Thomas or someone with a similar-sounding name has said, sound advice for good listeners. It's still the same.
—Saúl Sánchez

Juan Rodríguez (1942–) is a tejano from South Texas. His parents, originally from Linares, Nuevo León, Mexico, were migrant farm workers, and for years, Rodríguez worked with them in farm fields in various parts of the United States. After teaching at several universities, he returned to his native state of Texas, where he has worked at Texas Lutheran University for more than thirty years as a professor of English and Spanish and as the head of the Mexican American studies program. Rodríguez is a highly respected Chicano literary critic who has written on Chicano literature for more than forty years. His seminal articles on Chicano literary history and the Chicano short story have contributed immensely to this subject matter. In addition, his contribution to the recuperation of nineteenth-century Chicano texts is fundamental in the reconstruction of Chicano literary history. Rodríguez's legendary Carta abierta *served as an essential means of informing readers of new Chicano/a writers and the current state of affairs of Chicano literature and culture.*

The interview with Juan was conducted at his home in Seguín, Texas, in 2003 and continued in a number of e-mail correspondences from 2003 to 2013.

* * *

Juan, where were you born? Describe your childhood and the place where you grew up.

My parents and grandparents are from Linares, Nuevo León, Mexico. During the Mexican Revolution—in which my grandfather participated—his family crossed the Rio Grande/Río Bravo into Texas. I was born in Edinburg, Texas, in the Valle de Lágrimas. The raza there call it "Linburgo." Specifically, I was born on a ranch, el Rancho de Santa Cruz, but my birth was registered in Edinburg several days after the fact. After several years of near starvation in El Valle, we entered the working cycle of migrant workers. We traveled north every year during the cotton season, and in the mid-1950s we ended up in a small farming community near Lubbock, Texas, a city that Mexicans refer to as "Lóbica." I grew up there and attended Texas Tech University. After that, I attended the University of Iowa to pursue doctoral studies. Later on, I worked at numerous jobs because I continued to live the life of a migrant. I became an academic migrant worker. I worked two years at the University of Arizona, in Tucson, two years at the University of California, San Diego, two years at the University of California, Berkeley, one year at the University of Washington, in Seattle, two years at the University of

Texas at Austin, and for many years at Texas Lutheran University, in Seguin. Furthermore, during the summer and in several semesters I worked at other institutions. For example, I taught summer school at the Universidad Autónoma de San Luis Potosí, Mexico. I have also taught at the University of Wisconsin–Milwaukee, St. Edward's University, and for ten years as an adjunct at the University of Texas at San Antonio.

Why did you decide to study at the University of Iowa? Did you work as a migrant worker in that area and wanted to live there as a student?

No, fíjate que at the University of Iowa they have the Writers' Workshop and the International Writing Program. One of my professors at Texas Tech suggested that I apply to Iowa. Iowa interested me because it was far away; I had never been to Iowa. When we worked as migrant workers we only traveled as far north as Arkansas to pick cotton and pecans. I went to Iowa because my professor recommended the school and because I was interested in writing and in the International Writing Program located there.

Did you participate with the group of writers?

Not officially. But when I arrived at the university I audited those classes, sometimes as a pirata. What I did do was socialize with many of the writers who participated in the writing workshop, particularly the Latin American authors, many of whom in later years found some fame: Oscar Hahn, Enrique Jaramillo, Carlos Cortines, Grinor Riojo, and others. But the most important thing, as far as my own personal development was concerned, was that I began to participate in the protest activities against the Vietnam War. I became involved with the Chicano movement through my activities against the war. I was a university student leader of the Chicano movement, which coincided with the Native American and African American civil rights movements. These progressive movements came from students who were experiencing retrograde conditions in many academic departments at the university, including the Spanish department. These departments manipulated the students and treated them like children. In Spanish our department's control of the students was to such an extent that an old, female professor mandated that those of us who were doctoral students should not speak with those studying for their masters, that the married students should not speak with the unmarried ones, and so forth. Since I was involved in organizing campus activities against the Vietnam War, it was natural for me to also organize the graduate students in the department. After a number of confrontations with our administrators, we were able to organize a graduate student union. Of course, in the process of organizing it, I learned that educational institutions and education itself embody political and ideological platforms. This radically changed my life. I went to Iowa with a master's degree but with the feeling that I really had not learned much in school. Let me explain it another way. In the classroom, I encourage my students to know how to read a text, to be literate in a text. I tell them that most educated people know how to read a text at one level or another. They know what a text SAYS, but far too many don't know what a text MEANS. They know how to read the word, but they don't know how to read the world. I arrived in Iowa knowing how to read a text; in other words, I knew how to memorize titles of books, names of authors, plots, and so on. But really, I was a very ignorant person as far as ideology was concerned. For me, all the critics were the same—they were critics. All the writers were the same—all were writers. I could not distinguish between a Marxist critic and a formalist or a reactionary one. In Iowa, se me prendieron las luces, as they say. Suddenly, literature was an integral part of political life, in other words, of human life. The two could not be separated from one another. I joined the Chicano movement because at that time—we're talking of the mid- to late 1960s—I was becoming aware of César Chávez and the Chicano concerns in California and other parts of the country. Soon, I began to organize the few Chicanos that attended the University of Iowa to request a course in Chicano literature in our Spanish department. The request for the course was denied because the faculty argued that no such thing existed. But, after we threatened to organize a strike and demonstrations, they allowed us to offer it. I was the person assigned to teach the course, but unfortunately, I left Iowa for Arizona and was not able to do it. What's interesting is that one of the professors who was againt the formation of such course was the first professor to teach Chicano literature at Iowa! When I arrived at the University of Arizona, I knew that my duty and responsibility were to explore, develop, and institutionalize Chicano literature at the university level. In the beginning, in the early 1970s, when those first classes on Chicano literature were offered in California, New Mexico, and Texas, we didn't have a large body of Chicano literature texts. What we brought to the classroom was what we knew of Mexican and Latin American literature. I remember that in those early Chicano literature classes most of the syllabi involved the study of Juan Rulfo, Carlos Fuentes, Nelly Campobello, and, of course, Octavio Paz's *El laberinto de la soledad*, specifically the chapter on pachucos. But, regardless of that fact, these courses were still regarded as Chicano literature courses.

I assume that that ideological and political context did not exist at Texas Tech.

You are right, it did not exist at Texas Tech at the time, nor does it now, I suspect. But my ideological level of understanding was not the problem when I was enrolled there. The problem was that I did not have any money. There were none of the financial aid or other financial opportunities for Mexican Americans that exist today. At Texas Tech there were few Chicanos in the early 1960s, maybe ten or twelve of us. Curiously—and this happens in many universities, even today—we Chicanos, when we saw each other in the hallways, ran from each other because we had entered the university denying that we were Mexican. When we saw another Mexican, it was like seeing our image in a mirror or in a photograph. We ran because we had negated ourselves for so long and didn't want to be Mexicans. What we did do, Francisco Carrillo and myself—he was one of the other Mexicans at Texas Tech—was start a club, "Los Tertulianos." The name of the club reflected my ideology. In other words, I was not political at all. The club, in fact, was a social/cultural club. But our idea of culture was very superficial in this organization. It was all tacos and enchiladas in a nonpolitical context. We were contributing to stereotyping Mexicans rather than clarifying the importance of culture in the struggle for social justice. In contrast, in Iowa we started "The Chicano and Native American Union." The name itself reflected my transformed political consciousness. At Texas Tech there was very little political activity. Nephtalí de León, the most political young person at that time in Lubbock, distributed a Spanish-language newspaper to the local community. It was called *La voz de los llanos.* Nephtalí condemned the racist system of segregation and exclusion and promoted poetry and culture from a political point of view. Many people do not know that Nephtalí made great contributions to the Lubbock Chicano community, mostly by helping many Mexicans find their cultural and political voice. If anyone was truly doing something serious in the 1960s in Lubbock, it was Nephtalí de León, not me or the other handful of Mexican American students at Tech who considered ourselves "Spanish" rather than Mexican.

Which were the first works of Chicano literature that caught your attention?

It was Luis Valdez and his writing. California Chicano movement newspapers reached us in Iowa. It was there that I first read Chicano literature. At one time we invited Daniel Valdez (Luis's brother) to Iowa through our newly founded Chicano and Native American Union. He made Chicano poetry and music real for us. After that initial experience I started to connect with a group of Chicanos from Chicago, especially those from the Pilsner District.

When did you start Carta abierta?

I was in San Diego from 1974 to 1976, and as part of my effort to teach a graduate seminar in Chicano literature, I desperately began to search for anyone who might have anything to contribute to an academic course in dire need of material worthy of study in an institution of higher learning. It did not take me long to realize that I was writing more or less the same thing to all of my correspondents. This happened before we had access to computers! Again, se me prendió el foco. I thought, "why not come up with a general letter to all my friends, and that way I don't have to work so much?" That idea gave birth to *Carta abierta. Carta abierta* lasted fifteen years, maybe eighteen, I don't really remember. In any case, *Carta abierta* quickly became the only medium of diffusion of Chicano literature across the country, a medium that provided literary information from donde fuera for people who did not have access to it or were unaware of it. I wanted to promote Chicano literature and confirm and affirm that it was a developing body of literature that merited serious attention from critics and writers. Also important was for Chicano literature to create an impact in political and ideological terms. This last goal was something that interested me the most for I was very concerned that writers who identified themselves as "Chicanos" truly reflected the Chicano/Mexican American experience, be it rural or urban. The intent to keep Chicano literature Chicano, if you will, was the most controversial aspect of *Carta abierta*.

Why did Carta abierta *end?*

Carta abierta ended for two reasons. One, I started Relámpago Books and Relámpago Press. I did not have enough energy to do anything else. The other reason, the more serious one, was that I was very honest when people asked me to talk about a particular book. On the one hand, I was in the business of selling books, but on the other, as an academic I had to analyze the texts. I could not do both things. I left *Carta abierta* because at the time I felt that the distribution of Chicano literature was more important. People knew about Chicano literature but didn't know where to buy it, because most Chicano literature was being published by small presses and the texts were hard to find. For example, copies of Aristeo Brito's published work were stored in the closet of his house! If one wanted to buy a copy of *El diablo en Texas* you had to get in touch with Aristeo so that he could send it to you from his closet space!

Then, how to do it? How does one distribute Chicano literature? I started Relámpago Books when I left Berkeley for Seattle in 1979. When I made presentations on a particular Chicano text, *Bless Me, Ultima*, let's say, I knew that people would ask me where they could buy a copy. I would tell them, "Well, I don't know, the publisher or author sent a copy for me to review. That's how I got my copy." To address this problem of getting the texts into readers' hands, I began to carry with me extra copies of the texts I was going to present in my lectures. For example, if I was going to talk about Tomás Rivera's *y no se lo tragó la tierra* or Hinojosa's *Estampas del Valle*, then I would get in touch with Herminio Ríos at Quinto Sol Publishing in Berkeley and ask him to send me fifty copies of the books. I would pay him and take them to Milwaukee or Kansas City or wherever I was invited to lecture. After the presentations, people would ask me where they could buy the book. "I have them here," I would answer them. But the funny thing is that during the Q and A part of my presentation, I would get so involved in the discussions that my books would swiftly disappear! My ex-wife told me that if I was really serious about distributing Chicano books, I needed to start an independent distribution company. I did know everybody in the Chicano literary world, so I founded Relámpago Books in 1979/1980 and turned it into the first national distributor of Chicano literature. In addition, Relámpago Books turned into an international distributor, sending a great number of books to Germany, Spain, France, and the Soviet Union. In time, business grew so much that I couldn't keep up with it. I had two full-time jobs, the one at the university and the one as a distributor. It was too much; I just couldn't keep up with the pace. I worked every night, every weekend. I would do everything. I would package the books, write all the labels, fill out the necessary information, travel. But because of my ignorance, I got in trouble with the IRS over taxes. I was making money from the sales but did not have a separate account for taxes. I got involved in tax problems that took six or seven long years to settle. That, and the fact that I went through a divorce, ended Relámpago Books. Two or three years after my divorce, I started another distributor called AMBROWN that lasted around five years. But by then I felt exhausted and lacked the energy to continue the distribution business. Besides, Arte Público Press and Bilingual Press began to take over as the two main distributors of Chicano texts.

Does El toque *have the same function as* Carta abierta?

Yes. When I read Chicano literature and its critics, I find that there are very few honest voices in Chicano criticism. Most, if not all, critics of Chicano literature practice our craft as employees of a college or university. We are all limited by the rules of the academy, which impose a language and an approach that determine what is valid and legitimate to the academy. All of this is quite counterproductive to the understanding of authentic Chicano voices. So when I started *El toque*, I very much wanted to continue the honesty I had practiced in

Carta abierta. With *El corto, El toque's* electronic versión, I wanted to publish Chicanos whose work I liked. I wanted to present their work, discuss it, criticize it, sin pelos en la lengua.

What changes have you seen in Chicano literary development from the 1960s to the present?

Perhaps the most important change is that the so-called Latinos have marginalized it. Today, after years of struggling to legitimize our literature in the academy and at a national cultural level, I feel that Latinos are reaping the fruits of our struggle. Another change is that with Tomás Rivera we buried the rural aspect of Chicano literature. Now, from the 1990s onward, Chicano literature is highly urbanized. As a result of that, Chicano literature is influenced by questions of feminism and homosexism. The homosexuals and the feminists have monopolized the attention of the reading public and of the critic. Not so much the critic, but rather the Chicano literary and academic market. In the past, one could talk about readers, now we talk of a market, a market that is controlled by capitalists from New York and Los Angeles. The mainstream publishing houses that control the literary market in this country have identified particular authors and promoted them so much that the majority of the readers in that market read only those writers. In sum, the changes that I see are the following: Chicano literature is more urban, more feminist and gay; it has been displaced by Latino literature; and it has become a space controlled by the capitalist and academic systems that leave very little room for the production of an authentic criticism of it, in other words, a criticism that should define our literature as one that is alive and dynamic rather than dead, like Shakespeare.

For example, as far as criticism is concerned, you can find academic books and doctoral dissertations that have little impact in promoting Chicano literature among the common readers—the readers from the pueblo. These works have little impact because the language they use is very specialized and the references that are made are self-references in the same critical line that the university has used for centuries. In other words, academics have to prove the legitimacy of our literature by citing critics who would have been unable to understand our literature. I believe that most Chicano critics of the 1960s and 1970s—once they earned tenure at the university and thereby found the comforts of the bourgeoisie—abandoned Chicano literature to write about more "legitimate" things. That in itself has brought a change in the production of literature. Now everybody wants to be a poet. We have more poets than readers. We have more creative writers of Chicano literature than critics. We have more writers than readers because everybody apparently believes that they can be writers. On the one hand, this can be quite positive; but on the other, unfortunately, the people that start to believe that and act on that belief are persons that are so alienated from the core of the culture and of the pueblo that what they are producing is alienation itself. How great it would be if the voice of the pueblo—the one of a panadero, for example—would find its own means of communication and of expression. Instead, what we have are people, many like the ones from the "Poetry Slam" and "Chicano Rap," that really don't have an expression beyond their own alienation.

Your answer leads one to ask if Chicano literature remains a working-class, blue-collar literature or if it has lost its connection with that community?

What has happened is that a lot of Chicano literature has been personalized, giving us several autobiographies and memoirs. For example, works by John Phillips Santos, *Places Left Unfinished at the Time of Creation*, *The Farthest Home Is in an Empire of Fire,* and Richard Rodríguez are more about underscoring the individual than the community; they talk more about the "I" than the "we." That inward step is part of an American middle-class individualism. Another thing is that Chicano literature explores topics that have not been well thought out. Now Chicano literature deals more with self-expression than communal-expression. Also, Chicano literature has been taken over by Latino or Hispanic forces who, as grateful immigrants, came to the United States as a fallen middle class. These were mainly urban individuals who were far removed—in their own countries of origin—from the rural, from the working class. It seems that we have returned to the past when Mexican and Latin American literatures were incorporated into those early Chicano literature courses. Now, the Latin Americans have entered this Chicano field and have monopolized it. They have imitated the Chicanos to a certain degree. This hispanization of Chicano literature—some call it tropicalization—has taken away a lot of attention from the Chicanos. That hurts me because whatever ground was gained in the past these immigrants have taken away from us. It's a type of colonization imposed upon ourselves, by our brothers and colleagues. Hispanic literature in the United States is really a Latin Americanized literature written in English and in Spanish. Chicanos carved out a literary space at the national level that was lost to the Latino writers, who have claimed it as their own. Their success is due in large part to the fact that a EuroAmerican audience, where money and fame are found, rewards a "minority" literature that silences or sugarcoats the harsh historical and contemporary realities of the Chicano experience.

Are there differences between Chicanos and other Hispanics from the United States?

There are very profound differences, but unfortunately there is an attempt by the common market to invalidate them. The market cannot stand distinctions.

What other themes stand out in Chicano literature?

In the 1990s, homosexuality and feminism began to dominate the Chicano literary scene. On the one hand, such a move was very positive, because, truth be told, the Chicano movement was both sexist and homophobic. But, on the other hand, it has had an intimidating effect on the Chicano literary world insofar as it functioned as an anti-male force. As a result, it became taboo to criticize it. This makes it very difficult for someone to say that such a razing attitude represents a crass feminism, a crass homosexualism. Literary criticism, unfortunately, has followed the same pattern. We have academic works, like Sonia Hull's on feminism, that are very insensitive. For example, it's very easy for her to say, "This man said 'hembra,' then it's sexist!" I think that sexism is misunderstood at a deep ideological level. It has been very easy to denigrate and attack male critics from the 1970s and 1980s. Many of these critics feel very intimidated and are silenced. I present Sonia Hull as an example here because she attacks several persons, including myself, as being sexist. But she has not read carefully several of the critics she mentions, or she has misunderstood what they write—which is something very common in a critic. This is due, as far as language is concerned, to the fact that the critic doesn't have the adequate language skills in caló, pachuquismo, code switching, or in the cultural practice of cábula. Let me give you an example: the mere fact that someone uses the word "güisa" to refer to a female does not mean that he or she is sexist, but rather that "güisa" is part of the common popular Chicano speech and is used because in that speech the word "bata" does not exist, "bato" being the word used for males.

But just so you don't think all Chicana writers do this, let me talk a bit about another Chicana writer. In contrast, Diana López—from Corpus Christi and who now lives in San Antonio—in her first novel, *Sofía's Saints*, explores something that I call the habits of the heart. She explores culture at a deeper level. Diana explores the meaning of love, success, and friendship, among other themes, through characters that are authentic and that belong to a particular community. Her characters, by struggling and surviving in life, are expressing a cultural definition of what it means to live in a specific historical moment. Diana writes in a more subtle way. Her writing is more complex, more profound, without being pretentious.

What does the future hold for Chicano literature written in Spanish?

Unless more intimate and profound ties with Mexico are established—at the northern Mexican border and México, DF—there will not be much future for Chicano literature in Spanish. This is truly unfortunate because I consider that some of the best Chicano literature we have is written in Spanish. It is the literature that has been able to express the vital experiences of the Chicano. Unfortunately, it's a dying art among Chicanos, and it will perish unless those ties with Mexico are established. Chicanos have to start reading Mexican authors and vice versa. Axel Ramírez was the director of the El Centro de Estudios Chicanos at the Universidad Nacional Autónoma de México (UNAM) for eight or ten years. However, not too much was known of that Centro or of its activities on this side of the border. He knew many of the Chicano writers and critics and had the opportunity to make that intimate and profound connection between Mexico and the United States, but he never took advantage of it. Why? I don't know. An opportunity was lost there. Years before, during the 1970s, the Mexican government established an excellent educational program called "Becas para Aztlán" that produced important results for the Chicano movement. We need Mexico to establish more programs like that. But we also need Chicano studies programs in the United States—at the University of California, Santa Barbara, the University of California, San Diego, the University of Texas—to invite Mexican scholars who are interested in Chicano studies, particularly Chicano literature.

As far as the literary influence of Chicano authors, do you think that there is a tendency for them to lean toward North American literary influences?

Yes, almost exclusively. Few are the Chicano writers and critics who know Latin American literature or criticism. A great number completely ignore the Latin American critical, philosophical, or ideological literary currents. In fact, they don't know much about Latin American writers, not even the great ones such as Carlos Fuentes, Gabriel García Márquez, and Juan Rulfo. Until we have that exchange and the centers that I have mentioned, the separation will continue to exist.

Do you think that Chicano literature has touched the sensibility of the Mexican? Do you believe that Mexico understands the Chicano?

No. What Mexico knows about the Chicano are stereotypes. There's a lot of ignorance on their part, just as there is a lot of ignorance in this country about Mexicans. We reciprocate in that sense. But most Mexicans and Chicanos do not know each other very well. I believe that the best-known Chicano writer in Mexico is Miguel Méndez. Although el monstruo of Mexican criticism, the late Carlos Monsiváis, did much to connect Chicanos and Mexicans beginning in the mid-1960s, not many Chicanos know Mexican writers, and vice versa.

What is the future of Chicano literature?

It will have more impact in the common market, and I think that there will be a reaction against it. There will be a reaction against this present feminist and homosexual literary current. I think that at a certain point, young writers will arrive at a literature that will return to its Chicano roots. There will be more awareness of the direction this literature will take. For the time being, I think that the market is offering many economic and material benefits to its favored writers. This posits a difficult situation because this favoritism turns itself into the patterns and models for young writers to follow. But at a certain point in time, there will be a reaction to this. A type of "Tuércele el cuello al cisne" will take place. I hope that this return will come true so that there will be more open discussion about Chicano literature. A strong connection with Mexico—particularly its border writers—and the use of the Spanish language in our literature will truly be the key elements that will save us from the alienation that the common market has brought.

Any last thoughts concerning your role or function as a critic of Chicano literature? Also, what do you think has been the major impact of your work in relation to Chicano letters?

It's really for others to rule on the role or function, if any, I have played as a critic of Chicano literature. That stated, however, I do believe that I was among the first to approach Chicano literature from an academic, as well as a rasquache, perspective. During the late 1960s and early 1970s, I saw the need to introduce Chicano literature as a legitimate field of study in academic circles and—at the same time—to promote and applaud it among our own raza communities. Therefore, I wrote in both academic and rasquache tongues, and I continue to do so to this day. In the former effort, I sought to define and give order to a body of writing in the process of discovery and intense creation. In the latter effort, I wanted to speak in the language of los rasquaches not only to communicate in a popular language but also, in so doing, to attack the pedantic and pretentious language of exclusion practiced in the academy. Sadly, this language situation has gotten worse in our day of appealing and appeasing the "tweeds," as Genaro Padilla calls them, who control the tenure and other reward tracks at the university. This sense of genuflecting before the academic gods grows out of an inferiority complex that can lead to burn out or even a premature death from a heart attack—rest in peace Tomás Rivera. Or so I believe.

Another role that I may have played in the early years of the Chiclit (Chicano literature) Renaissance, as my good friend Ortego would have it, was as a literary historian. Having taught one of the earliest Chiclit courses at the university level in this country, I quickly discovered that true Chicano literary texts were extremely sparse and ill-defined. The one or two Chiclit courses taught here and there around the country during those early years were really Latin American—particularly Mexican—literature courses with a Chicano text or two thrown in to complete a respectable bibliography. This was necessarily so because, at the time, we knew of only two or three Chicano titles, not enough texts, certainly, to make a standard university course, truth be told. So I—with the enormous help of some brilliant and dedicated students at UCSD—began an early, serious effort to find, study, and publicize "lost" Chicano texts: the short stories of Jorge Ulica, for example, which I compiled and published in *Crónicas diabólicas* in 1982. In the process, I began to define what was, and was not, Chicano literature. All of this happened, of course, long before Hispanics and Latinos dispossessed us of our gains and called them their own.

In closing, I would like to say that both *Carta abierta* and Relámpago Books brought me into contact with many, if not all, of the Chicano studies academics and artists of the time, an experience I shall treasure to the end of my days.

Selected Works

Rodríguez, Juan. "Temas y motivos de la literature chicana." In *Flor y Canto II: A Chicano Literature Anthology*, edited by Arnold Vento. Albuquerque, NM: Pajarito Publications, 1978.

——. "Notes on the Evolution of Chicano Prose Fiction." In *Modern Chicano Writers: A Collection of Critical Essays*, edited by Joseph Sommers and Tomás Ybarra-Frausto, 67–85. Englewood Cliffs, NJ: Prentice Hall, 1979.

——. "El desarrollo del cuento chicano: del folklore al tenebroso mundo del yo." In *The Identification and Analysis of Chicano Literature*, edited by Francisco Jiménez, 58–67. Ypsilanti, Mich.: Bilingual Review Press, 1979.

———. "La búsqueda de identidad y sus motivos en la literature chicana." In *Antología histórica y literaria*, edited by Tino Villanueva, 200–208. Mexico City: Fondo de Cultura Económica, 1980.

———. *Las crónicas diabólicas de Jorge Ulica*. San Diego: Maize Publications, 1982.

———. "The Chicano Short Story." In *A Decade of Chicano Literature (1970–1979): Critical Essays and Bibliography*, edited by Luis Leal, et al., 41–45. Santa Barbara, CA: Editorial La Causa, 1982.

———. "The Problematic in Tomás Rivera's . . . *and the Earth Did Not Part*." In *Contemporary Chicano Fiction: A Critical Survey*, edited by Vernon E. Lattin, 131–40. Binghamton, NY: Bilingual Press/Editorial Bilingüe, 1986.

10

Rosaura Sánchez

La pensadora chicana

AS I READ ROSAURA SÁNCHEZ'S INTERVIEW I once again reflect on the fact that in Chicano/a studies many of our critics are also writers, and that it is because of intellectuals like Sánchez that we now have permission, and in fact have established this precedent, to bifurcate our abilities. That Sánchez reconciles the past with the present in her academic work and research is no surprise given her work on the Recovery Project, and yet that is another element that is unique to the Chicano/a critic: uniting historical with contemporary events to turn out a literature that is intersectional but that also particularly addresses the needs and wants of a working-class readership. Sánchez and critics of her époque truly set a precedent in underlining the need for disciplines like working class studies, women studies, and transnational studies because they, as transnational thinkers, understood the importance of utilizing the rest of the world as a mirror for understanding the identity quest that internally colonized populations need as a base to solidify their identities as American identities.

—Gabriella Gutiérrez y Muhs

Rosaura Sánchez (1941–) is a professor of Latin American literature and Chicana literature at the University of California, San Diego. Her work on critical theory, cultural studies, third world literatures, and gender studies has been significant and highly praised by her peers, inside and outside of Chicano studies. Her book, Chicano Discourse: Socio-Historic Perspectives, *has made valuable contributions to the field of*

Chicano linguistics. Of equal importance is her work on Chicano literary history, writing, with Beatrice Pita, several important critical studies of María Amparo Ruiz de Burton's nineteenth-century novels Who Would Have Thought It? *and* The Squatter and the Don. *Sánchez is an accomplished scholar of literary theory who is constantly searching Chicanos' sense of place and space in this abstract and challenging field of study. In addition to her scholarly work, Sánchez is a talented writer of fiction.*

The interview with Rosaura was conducted at the University of California, San Diego, in 2008 and continued in a number of e-mail correspondences from 2008 to 2012.

* * *

Rosaura, where were you born? Describe your childhood and the place where you grew up.

I was born in Texas, in San Angelo, a town that now is a small city of 100,000 people located around 130 miles from the Mexican border in the middle of a plateau called Edwards Plateau. It is surrounded by ranches that raise sheep and farms that produce cotton and grains that feed cattle and chickens. The River Concho, surrounded by pecan trees, is divided upon entering the city and feeds two dams and a lake. What I most remember of my childhood are the periods of drought and the dust in the barrio, especially in the streets, for in those days they were not paved. When I was a young girl there also wasn't sewage in the barrio and it wasn't until later—I was about nine or ten years old—that we had a bathroom inside the house.

My father was a laborer. He worked many years for the state highway department. He liked to read and since we lacked books at home he read the newspaper and the Bible. I believe that my father, a Mason, read the Bible in its entirety several times. Readings from the Bible were the first literature that I read. Without any doubt, being working-class formed me as a person. I remember, for example, that when it snowed and the roads were frozen, my father's foreman would telephone him at midnight to see if he wanted to spray the bridges outside of San Angel—that's what we called the town—with sand and salt. It was a way of earning a few extra pesos, dollars that always were needed at home.

When my mother was a young girl, she worked with her family as a cotton picker. That tradition continued with her children. I remember when I was around six years old, my mother, my two brothers, and I spent a month with my grandparents and my aunts and uncles picking cotton in Tahoka, Texas. It was an unforgettable experience that us children saw more as an adventure than work, even though we picked cotton five days a week. Later, as a teenager, we picked cotton only on Saturdays and holidays, like Thanksgiving Day in November. I remember one time when I went with my aunt Enriqueta and her kids to pick cotton, the gringo owner did not want to pay us, saying that we had started working when the cotton was still wet because of the morning dew. From that experience I learned to feel anger due to the exploitation and the lack of resources that we suffered in the barrio. Years later, I would share all of these memories with Sherley Anne Williams, an African American writer and professor at the University of California, San Diego (UCSD), who died several years ago. She was the only professor at the university who, like myself, had lived the experience of picking cotton.

One cannot talk about one's personal life without talking about the family and the persons that one has known. One is, after all, the product of one's experiences and of the people with whom we share our lives. My parents were born in Mexico, both from the state of Coahuila. My father came to San Angelo when he was twenty years old, but my mother came when she was a small child, three years old. As a result, she grew up in Texas. The children, all four of us, were born in San Angelo. We are second-generation Chicanos. I have an older brother, Alejandro, and a younger one, Rubén. When the three of us were teenagers my sister, Nelda, was born. Now we all live in California, with the exception of my younger brother who lives in Maryland. My father died in 1974. My mother, who came to live in California with my sister and her daughter when she was eighty-seven, lived in Texas most of her life. Because of that I traveled to Texas often, despite having lived in California for so many years. My mother died two years ago at the age of ninety-two.

When does your academic preparation begin?

As far as education is concerned, in those days schools in the barrio in San Angelo were not very good. My brothers and I learned to read, write, and count before going to school, thanks to my father. We were fortunate that he taught us, because the academic preparation that I had in elementary school was dreadful. The teachers did not expect a lot from us, nor was it expected that we would ever study beyond the sixth grade. For them, we were destined to be laborers, housewives, or maids. They were only interested that we minimally knew how to read and write. Also, there were no libraries in school or in the barrio. There were no educational games in the classroom. Nothing. In those days—especially in the barrio—we also didn't consider that it was important for women to study. I was lucky that my mother wanted me to have what her parents had denied her. After six years of elementary education, the few of us who continued on to high school attended an integrated school with whites, but it wasn't until the end of the decade of the 1950s that blacks in San Angelo were integrated into our high school. Frankly, those were difficult years. One felt unappreciated by Anglo-Saxon teachers. One had to constantly prove something. Prove that one was not worthless; that one had brains and was intelligent; that one could earn an "A." Texas has always been a racist state. It's not surprising that in 1959, when I graduated from high school, there were only twenty of us Chicanos and Chicanas on the graduation list. From my high school senior class, only three of us—all of them women—attended San Angelo College, which later became Angelo State University. After San Angelo College only I moved on and attended the University of Texas at Austin to finish my degree. Fortunately, I had an older brother who was very studious and whatever he did, I wanted to emulate. So when he went to Austin, I set out to do the same when I finished with my academic program at San Angelo College two years later.

When did you discover your interest in literature, in general, including U.S., Mexican, Spanish, and Latin American literature and linguistics?

In the main library at the University of Texas at Austin (UT) I came across Charles Dwyer, a former professor at San Angelo College (SAC) who had moved to Austin to study to become a librarian. At San Angelo College, I had worked as a work-study student for him and another professor, Charles Moser, in the English department, then my favorite subject, and had known almost all the professors. At SAC there were good professors; the bad thing was that there were few Chicanos and Chicanas who attended the college. At that time there were no Latino professors at San Angelo College or in the San Angelo public schools. In Austin it was Dwyer who spoke to me about the possibility of working in the Latin American Collection. I needed to work and thanks to his recommendation I spent several years as an assistant in the Latin American Collection. It turned out to be a great learning experience for me, for I worked with people who were passionate about working with books. It was an honor to know professor-librarian Nettie Lee Benson and to work with her, even if my work consisted of fulfilling minor tasks in the great projects that she had, among them the building of what today is considered the best Latin American library in the country that now bears her name. It was there that my desire to know about the Latin American continent began. I was majoring in Spanish and English literature at the university, even though I must confess that at the beginning Spanish did not really attract me, until one semester I took a class with Professor Ricardo Gullón. He was a man fascinated by language, literature, and ideas. What started as a "double major" became a Spanish major. In Austin, the Department of Spanish and Portuguese leaned toward the study of Spanish Peninsular literature and because of that, my favorite authors at the time were Miguel de Unamuno and Benito Pérez Galdós.

When did you become interested in social justice themes and Chicano social issues?

Unlike other students at the University of Texas, for me, coming from a poor family, it was impossible to travel abroad. Therefore, I decided to join the Peace Corps. Other Chicano students that worked in the library at UT also decided to join the Corps. One was assigned to the Philippines, one to Brazil, and I to Ecuador. My interest in the indigenous world—my father always told us that we were part indigenous—led me to request a post in an Andean country y se me hizo. I spent two years in the mountain ranges of Ecuador working with the Indians and with the children of the pueblo de Guamote and the indigenous community of Mercedes Cadena. That experience profoundly changed my life.

At that time I was very conscious of the racism, exploitation, and oppression that affected the Mexican Tejanos and blacks in the

United States and the indigenous people in Ecuador. During my early years at the University of Texas I participated in marches against racism and segregation; one must remember that at the beginning of the civil rights movement, Texas was a state under Jim Crow laws. At that time, blacks could not live in the university dormitories where whites resided. I lived in a Methodist dormitory, where Latinas were accepted, but everyday I went by a cooperative of black women where my friend, Jolene Scott, also from San Angelo, lived, and I was able to witness segregation firsthand.

I thought I knew how the world that I was destined to live in worked, but I had not read Marx or undertaken any critical studies about capitalism or imperialism or even reflected on what all that had to do with one's everyday life. I lacked the theories that would help me explain what I saw. I analyzed social factors in terms of race. On my return from Ecuador, my oldest brother, Alex—who had been in Vietnam and had returned to Austin after he hurt his knee pulling a wounded soldier from the battlefield—and I joined the movement against the war and participated in marches and demonstrations. I remember very well running through Guadalupe Street with other students when the police threw tear gas bombs to disperse the demonstrators. At that time the Chicano movement had also been initiated in California and in Texas. The professor that encouraged us to participate in these political activities was Sergio Elizondo, professor of Latin American literature. We also began to protest the lack of Chicano and Chicana students at the university. The 1960s was full of student political activity, not only in Austin but also all over the world. We even marched to the state capitol to support the farm workers, who wanted to join a union. It was there that I first heard Reies López Tijerina speak.

In Ecuador I felt that literature era un lujo and not useful for helping the indigenous people of Mercedes Cadena—the indigenous community next to Guamote, where I worked. I felt that I should have studied something more practical, like engineering or medicine. I was angry with myself for not being able to do more for these people. What I did do was participate in a program of literacy for the Quechua-speaking Indians. For that reason, I decided that upon returning to the States I would study something more practical within my field of study: Spanish linguistics. The irony was that at that time Noam

Chomsky's transformational grammar was very popular and that's what I learned. As a field of study, it couldn't have been more abstract, but the irony was that I loved it. To keep my assistantship in the Spanish Department I had to keep studying literature and that's why I received my MA in Spanish/Latin American literature, writing a thesis on Argentine writers Ernesto Sábato and Leopoldo Marechal. But soon a doctoral program in linguistics in Romance languages was created and the three of us who studied with one foot in linguistics and the other in Spanish were able to transfer to that program. The following year a professor who taught courses in linguistics left the department, and I, even though I was only a teaching assistant (TA), had the opportunity to offer advanced courses in Spanish linguistics. Later on, José Limón, a fellow graduate student, and Professor Américo Paredes went to see the chair of my department and requested that I teach a course on Chicano Spanish. That course led me to write my essay "Nuestra circunstancia lingüística," which was published in *El Grito*. Later, I decided to use that work as the basis for my dissertation, which dealt with a transformational analysis of Chicano Spanish.

Were you offered a faculty position after you graduated from the University of Texas?

Before I finished the dissertation I had the opportunity to join the University of California, San Diego (UCSD), as an assistant professor, thanks to the recruitment efforts of Arturo Madrid, a professor in the Department of Literature at UCSD. At that time no Chicano or Chicana faculty had been granted tenure at UCSD, so I believed that one day I also would have to leave. But I finished the manuscript that would later be my first book, *Chicano Discourse*, and was granted tenure. What's interesting is that after twenty years or so, I returned to what from the beginning was my passion, literature, and I left linguistics behind. Today, I teach courses on Latin American literature, Chicano/Latino literature, and literary theory. I teach my classes in both Spanish and English.

Viéndolo bien, San Diego is where I developed intellectually. Here I met Professors Carlos Blanco and Fredric Jameson and a series of graduate students who were more or less my age. I learned a lot from them. I began to read Marx, Lukács, Benjamin, Brecht, and Lenin. Those readings changed my life, my perspective. Today, to read Jameson, Eagleton, Caffentzis, De Angelis, Harvey, Negri, Hardt, and other critics is as important as reading the latest Chicano-Latino or Latin American literary works.

I am also interested in seeing what critical race theory has contributed to criticism. There is a woman, Kimberly Crenshaw, who speaks in terms of the intersection of a series of factors. She speaks of the intersection between gender, class, and race, and that is of great interest to me because one cannot see only class, one has to see class in relation to ethnicity and race as well as gender. One has to see things through that intersection, that interrelation that always exists in all one does. This concept of intersection has interested me and I have used it in my work, although I do think that not all factors are equally important and that one must think in terms of contradictions and dominant structures.

What do you think distinguishes the literary critics of Chicano literature who study in Spanish graduate programs from those who study in English graduate programs at U.S. universities?

There is a generational difference because the critics who are interviewed for this book, including myself, studied literature at a time when Chicano literature did not exist as a field of study. Most of us studied Spanish, Spanish Peninsular, and Latin American literature. At the University of Texas, in the 1960s, the majority of the professors in the Spanish Department worked in Spanish Peninsular literature. There were only two people doing Latin American literature at UT then. At UCSD, by the time I joined the faculty, there were a couple of people doing Latin American literature, but the others focused on Spanish Peninsular literature as well. Of course no one was doing Chicano literature. In fact not until Juan Rodríguez arrived at UCSD were Chicano literature courses offered. When he left, we hired Marta E. Sánchez, who was one of our students, to cover his courses. For a while, I did not teach Chicano literature because I did not want to make it seem like I could replace people in that field of study. Even though I wrote critical essays on Chicano and Chicana literature, I did not teach it. I taught Latin American literature and critical theory. But after Marta left, I began teaching those Chicano and Latino literature courses because I felt that the subject matter was very important and that it would be a long time before we would replace Marta. I began to teach Chicano literature in Spanish. Today I teach Chicano and Latino literature in English. I believe that the critics interviewed for this book are the ones who invented the field of Chicano literature, in spite of their lack of previous training in it.

I believe that people who work on Chicano literature today have a better preparation in Chicano studies than those of us who were trained in Latin American literature in departments of Spanish and Portuguese. On the other hand, we have a good foundation in Latin American and Spanish Peninsular literature, while more recent and younger critics and writers have training in U.S. literatures. As far as our literary criticism is concerned, it is based more on U.S. and European theories than on Mexican or Latin American criticism.

Besides this difference in training, are there other differences, for example, in how they see or read a Chicano text?

Well, I believe that the majority of the critics interviewed for this project belong to the working class; therefore from the start there was an interest in presenting the social problems of the Chicano working-class community. This concern is present everywhere. Within early Chicano criticism there is clearly a type of cultural, nationalist criticism oriented toward issues of identity, toward what it means to be Chicano; this includes issues of indigenous/mestizo identity and relations with Mexico. But it seems to me that it wasn't really a connection with Mexico but with Mexican myths––for example, the interest in Aztec myths initiated by Alurista––which for me did not and do not represent the reality of Mexico today; they represented something more remote and exotic. They did, however, provide Chicano criticism, and especially Chicanas, with new discourses. The Revolution was also something very important in the Chicano movement, although we tended to idealize it. I believe that we lacked a historical background; we had not studied history and we didn't know a lot about theory.

How did you get interested in the Recovering the U.S. Hispanic Literary Heritage Project?

In the 1980s I began to have an interest in the nineteenth century, particularly in the testimonios of the Californios who were interviewed years after losing the territory of Alta California to the North American invaders. From this study came my *Telling Identities,* a book that analyzes these testimonios, which are stored in the Bancroft Library at the University of California, Berkeley. It was this interest that led my colleague Beatrice Pita and I to work on the two books by María Amparo Ruiz de Burton. One of them was the novel *The Squatter and the Don* (1885). The novel had been photocopied by my colleague Juan Rodríguez, who began to do some critical work on it but later left the project and gave it to Lauro Flores. Lauro, an ex-student of ours, now a professor at the University of Washington, was interested in an autobiography project and realizing that this novel did not deal with this genre left it on a bookshelf in my office before returning to Seattle. At first, the book did not interest me, but then as I read it, I realized that this work was tied to my project on testimonios. That is how Beatrice and I began our research and found the letter correspondence between Mariano Guadalupe Vallejo and María Amparo.

Our research on the project lasted several years. With the creation of Recovering the U.S. Hispanic Literary Heritage Project, Nicolás Kanellos, director of Arte Público Press, published a new edition of *The Squatter and the Don* that included a long introduction written by Pita and myself. After that Beatrice and I proposed a new edition of *Who Would Have Thought It?,* a novel also written by Ruiz de Burton. Arte Público eventually published the novel, with our introduction and annotations. Years later we published, once again with Arte Público, *Conflicts of Interest: The Letters of María Amparo Ruiz de Burton*, providing context for Ruiz de Burton's life in Alta and Baja, California, and on the East Coast of the United States during the Civil War. By editing and analyzing those letters, we were able to understand the life of the writer and her transnational history.

Our work on Ruiz de Burton's nineteenth-century novels has taken us to a new project about "enclosures," about the dispossession of the land and the means of production and subsistence, a phenomenon tied to the capitalist development of yesterday and today. Lately, plenty has been written, at the theoretical and economic levels, about what critics call "new enclosures." We use these theoretical works for our study of the representation of "enclosures" in Chicano, Latin American, and Native American literatures. This project will take us on a trans-American and transethnic analysis that has also demanded a lot of research and possibly will take a couple of years more to finish.

One speaks of Chicano literature as a working-class literature, a blue-collar literature. Do you believe that there are parallels between writers and critics, as far as this is concerned? In other words, does a working-class critic exist in Chicano literature?

Well, I believe that in the beginning it was important to emphasize that the Chicano was working-class, but that emphasis later lost ground. Now, there is a distinction between those who emphasize the question of class and those who emphasize culture. Today some critics emphasize ethnicity or gender or sexuality more than they do class. For some of us class is still defining, even though all the other factors are also important. This week in class, we were discussing the theme of liminality, the notion of an in-between space, of being between or belonging to two spaces or cultures. Well, liminality could be true for a first-generation person who has a Mexican culture and who comes to the United States and sees another culture and feels in the middle, not knowing where he or she is located. But for those of us born in the barrio in this country, we don't have that "other" (Mexico) and we also are not "gringos" (Anglos). We do not feel "gringo." We don't, however, see lo nuestro as being in the middle of anything. We have constructed our own space and it is here and there. So there is a difference, as far as the approach to literature, that has separated us within the field, in spite of being—as I believe most of us are—part of the working class.

Do you think that Chicana critics, because of those negative concepts connected to the Chicano, for example, being identified as "pochos" by Mexicans, feel uncomfortable when they participate in conferences alongside Mexican critics, or in fact, Latin American critics?

Yes, that has been the case in the last two or three decades, in the encuentros between Chicano and Latin American writers and critics. I remember that in the 1980s there was a news report in some Mexican newspapers that in some conferences the Chicanos who attended were criticized as being pochos, of not knowing how to speak Spanish properly or knowing how to conduct themselves. That type of criticism is also made of the Chicano writer and critic, even today, as is evident in some Tijuana blogs.

I believe that for those of us who study Spanish, the criticism was not valid, but for those in other fields of study, where the language was/is English, it was difficult to communicate in Spanish. But I saw other types of differences, differences of class and not of language, in exchanges between Chicanos/as and Mexicans. For example, in the 1980s, several encuentros de mujeres were organized in Tijuana and sponsored by the Colegio de México and other institutions. In one conference, some Chicano graduate students from UCSD came up to me on campus and told me that things were not going well there; that they, los mexicanos, were attacking us. Soon I realized that el encuentro, the conference, had become a nationality issue. The professors from the Colegio de México who attended the conference showed a condescending attitude toward the Chicanas, acting as though we were academically deficient and unsophisticated and that they needed to teach us how to do things correctly. To me, that display of class arrogance me revienta. No more encuentros have taken place between them and us. Why? Because I see their arrogance, not of race, because we are all Mexican, but of class. They see us as inferior to them. They feel that we are not academically prepared, that they need to come and educate us and to pinpoint our deficiencies. I find that offensive.

Does it still continue to exist today, because you say that this happened in the 1980s?

Yes, it still continues.

Concerning Chicanos and issues of class, does this class distinction exist between the first and second generations of critics of Chicano literature?

No. I believe that the differences are not of class because for the most part we all come from working-class families. The differences can be traced to perspective and focus: What do critics emphasize in their analyses? What factors are central to their analysis of a text? Those are the differences that have existed among critics. There have been theoretical differences as well; for example, those Chicano critics that were influenced by Frederic Jameson had a different perspective and approach to literary criticism. Other critics and theorists came to affect our work as well. In the 1980s, for example, I began to study work in cultural studies and found the essays of Stuart Hall to be just what I was looking for. His work interested me very much because of the connections that he made between ideology and historical materialism. I remember telling Blanco that there was a *tipo* that was expressing what I wanted to say. I didn't know at the time that Hall was black, that he was from Jamaica. When I later knew this, it seemed to explain a great deal. Hall had a way of understanding things dealing with questions of class, history, race, culture, everything. Because of discoveries like these, I found that I had more in common with particular Chicano critics of another generation in spite of their having studied in an English department and I in a Spanish one.

Rosaura, tell us about your critical formation in the department of Spanish where you were trained.

Well, the critical training that I received as a literature student in Texas was a formalist training; that was what Gullón did. But afterward, when I came to UCSD, I re-educated myself. I began to study Marxist criticism and found many different Marxist approaches. More recently I have found many other critics who are working on the concept of enclosures. I fall in love with new critics all the time.

How about Spanish and Latin American critics—have you fallen in love with any of them?

No. I'm interested in reading them but I'm not as taken by them. Some critics, even though they are writing about something totally different, provide approaches that are useful for literary analysis in Chicano/a literature. Eagleton, for example, writes about the relationship between the Irish and the English, how Irish writers react to British colonialism and domination. Well, I find there something that speaks to me and that is telling me something. I like critics that see the text in terms of ideological discourses. I want to do social criticism that takes into account economics and politics. I want to read critics who speak to me about imperialism, class structure, social space, and even ecology. I search in their work for a connection that will help me with the things that I do, primarily criticism on Chicano, Latino, and Latin American literature.

How about any from la frontera, Tijuana—do any of the critics from this border area speak to you on issues dealing with the U.S.-Mexico border?

Critics exist, but they do not speak to our issues.

Do you believe that Mexican critics ignore the Chicano critics?

It's not that they ignore Chicano critics but that they underestimate them. They don't see them as important. And within their context, we are not important. What's important for them, for example, is immigration, something that is extremely important to us, too. Too often we write from one national perspective that ignores the other. Thus, when they speak about the frontera, it's in relation to the Mexican side, and when we talk about the border, it's from the perspective of this side. I believe that there are certain problems that we have in common with them, but there is little or no interaction. The fault lies with both sides. At the critical level, I am interested in what Monsiváis has to say, what Joaquín Blanco has to say. But I can't say that what they write influences my work.

What do you think of Chicano literature written in Spanish? Do you believe that it has a future?

It was my generation who began to teach Chicano literature, primarily in Spanish. Today that literature is written mainly in English and taught in English departments or in Chicano studies. I believe it will continue to be that way until we become the majority in this country. Beatrice Pita and I just finished an essay on the Latino population that appeared in the journal *Aztlán*. In that article we see the problems and the contradictions that distinguish this growing population that will become the majority in less than a century. Maybe by then, the bilingual population will write literature in both Spanish and English. But for now English predominates in the literary scene. There are many writers, both male and female, not only Chicanos and Chicanas but also Latinos and Latinas, who write and publish their works in English in renowned publishing houses. Unlike before, today there is an ample repertoire of texts that one can choose from for Chicano and Latino literature classes. In the 1960s and 1970s only the journals *El Grito*, *Revista Chicano-Riqueña*, *Bilingual Review*, and *Caracol* published in Spanish. Today, I believe that *Ventana Abierta* and *Puentes* might be the only ones that still publish works in Spanish.

Is it important for you to write your academic work in Spanish?

Well, I have written some essays in Spanish, but my books and most of my articles have been written in English. The work on testimonios of the nineteenth century, I did that in English. The work on María Amparo Ruiz de Burton by Beatrice Pita and me was done in English. We are working on another project dealing with the dispossession of land, and we are doing that in English as well. English has become the language of criticism for me, but once in a while I'll turn to Spanish. For example, some time ago I was asked to speak in Tijuana on "What is Chicano literature?" Well, I prepared that presentation in Spanish. Today, I teach my Latin American literature classes in Spanish, but my courses and seminars on Chicano/Latino literature are in English because all the texts I use for those classes are written in English.

For undergraduate students who are fluent in both Spanish and English, what do you think is the principal factor that leads them to choose a graduate Spanish program or a graduate English program?

When students graduate with a BA they begin to think in terms of future work and ask, where are the jobs? If they want to teach Latin American literature, then clearly they need to apply to a Spanish department, but if they are interested in Chicano/Latino literature then they need to apply to an English department. Chicano literature positions are not found in Spanish departments today. They are found in English departments. Sometimes there are positions in Chicano studies departments, but there are very few Chicano studies graduate programs in the country. The majority of graduates that specialize in Chicano and Chicana literature teach in English or American studies departments. These departments look for someone who can teach ethnic studies and at the same time have a specialty in Latino/a literature. I want to prepare students for those types of positions. The majority of my students read texts written in English and write their dissertations in English. That is our reality today. It seems to me that the reality of things demands that one train students for English positions, knowing that obviously it is important to know Spanish, but there are no Spanish programs that are hiring Chicano literature professors, that I know of.

When does your creative writing begin?

Research and teaching occupy almost all of my time. For fifteen years, the graduate students from the doctoral program that I work with have been my special interest and I have had the pleasure to see several of them receive their doctorates. The classes, the lectures, the duties as a professor do not leave a lot of time to write my short stories, even though I am always "writing in the air," as one might say, making notes and cutting newspaper articles that would be the basis of a new short story. I believe that the narrative side of my work comes from my mother. She loved to narrate things of the past and the people that she knew. I began writing while I was a student at the University of Texas at Austin but never published anything until I came to UCSD and Juan Rodríguez suggested I send some of my stories to the University of California, Irvine, Chicano writing contest. They published some of my stories. Some years ago, the University of New Mexico published a bilingual edition of *Entró y se sentó*, a collection of my short stories written in Spanish and translated to English by Beatrice Pita. The collection includes some old short stories and some recent ones. Almost all the old ones deal with Texas themes, but the ones from the last twenty years deal with California. Almost all of them have to do with the working class, the class that I come from and that I know best. Some deal with feminist issues, others are historical, all of them, in their own way, are political. Some of my short stories have appeared in texts for the teaching of Spanish, and almost every year I receive e-mails from high school male and female students who want to know why I write such things and whether they have to do with my personal life. I respond that the short stories are what they are, short stories, works of fiction based on many things that are not necessarily autobiographical. The short story writer that I like the most is Julio Cortázar, and I believe that in my recent stories, his influence can be detected.

Do you prefer to write your creative work in English or Spanish?

I used to write in Spanish. I did not write in English until recently. Beatrice and I have collaborated in writing a short science-fiction novel published by Calaca Press. I find that the everyday conversational language in English does not come out so easily for me. In other words, my English is more academic. For example, to say any pendejada—anything one wants to say without apprehension—comes out spontaneously in Spanish for me. In English I have to think about what I want to say. Sometimes I articulate phrases that come out as if they were extracted from a book. They don't carry the fluency of a dialogue. Beatrice is fortunately fully bilingual in Spanish and English. Like they say, one has languages for different functions, different uses, and for me, English has not been the home language. I spoke Spanish at home and today I code-switch constantly. So, common things, the small things that one knows how to say, comment, criticize, y mandar alguien a la chingada, those types of things, I would have to think about how to get just the right nuance in English but not in Spanish. For that reason, I generally wrote in Spanish. In spite of having been born in the United States, Spanish is my native tongue, and maybe because of that the creative part comes out in Spanish. Lo otro, my academic work, I write primarily in English. I did however want to write something that was not criticism in English and now in a collaborative effort with Beatrice Pita, we have done it. I have also come to realize that collaborative critical and creative work, as a whole, produces superior outcomes.

On what academic/creative projects are you currently working?

Beatrice Pita and I have continued working on our research project on enclosures. I have also recently published an article on xenophobia in the *Latino Studies* journal. Beatrice and I have just finished writing an article on Caribbean-American texts that deal with the dictatorship of Trujillo, including a novel by Vargas Llosa and one by Vázquez Montalbán. We have submitted it to a journal and await their decision. We are also finishing up an article on "settler colonialism" that we plan to send off for consideration in a few days. We are currently translating Sergio Elizondo's *Muerte en una estrella*, a text that we consider one of our best Chicano novels.

Any last thoughts concerning your role or function as a critic of Chicano literature? Also, what do you think has been the major impact of your work in relation to Chicano letters?

The way I see it, my most important role in the field of Chicana/o and Latino/a literature has been as a teacher/mentor, as a professor at UCSD who has trained a number of stellar graduate students. As a critic I have tried to communicate my interest in Marxist theory, in historical and ideological analyses, and in cultural studies. My work considers issues of class, gender, sexuality, ethnicity, and race, as well as more macro-level issues like imperialism and how capitalism shapes everything. And finally I have never stopped being intrigued by language and discourse, the material stuff of which literature is made.

Selected Works

Sánchez, Rosaura. *Chicano Discourse: Socio-Historic Perspectives*. Rowley, MA: Newbury House Publishers, Inc., 1983.

———. "Chicana Prose Writers: The Case of Gina Valdés and Sylvia Lizárraga." In *Beyond Stereotypes: The Critical Analysis of Chicana Literature*, edited by María Herrera-Sobek, 61–70. Binghamton, NY: Bilingual Press/Editorial Bilingüe, 1985.

———. "Ideological Discourses in Arturo Islas's The Rain God." In *Criticism in the Borderlines: Studies in Chicano Literature, Culture, and Ideology*, edited by Héctor Calderón and José David Saldívar, 114–26. Durham, NC: Duke University Press, 1991.

———. *Telling Identities: The Californio Testimonios*. Minneapolis: University of Minnesota Press, 1995.

———. "Calculated Musings: Richard Rodríguez' Metaphysics of Difference." In *The Ethnic Canon*, edited by David Palumbo-Liu, 153–73. Minneapolis: University of Minnesota Press, 1995.

———. *He Walked In and Sat Down and Other Stories*. Albuquerque: University of New Mexico Press, 2000.

Sánchez, Rosaura, and Beatrice Pita. Introduction to *The Squatter and the Don*, by María Amparo Ruiz de Burton, 5–51. Houston, TX: Arte Público Press, 1992.

——. Introduction to *Who Would Have Thought It?*" by María Amparo Ruiz de Burton, vii–lxv. Houston, TX: Arte Público Press, 1995.

——. Introduction to *Conflicts of Interest: The Letters of María Amparo Ruiz de Burton*, ix–xxiii. Houston, TX: Arte Público Press. 2001.

——. *Lunar Braceros 2125–2148*. San Diego: Calaca Press, 2009.

Sánchez, Rosaura, Beatrice Pita, and Bárbara Reyes, eds. *Critica: A Journal of Critical Essays; Nineteenth Century Californio Testimonials*. La Jolla, CA: UCSD Ethnic Studies/Third World Studies, 1994.

11

Charles M. Tatum

Chicano Popular Culture

THE WORK OF CHARLES M. TATUM and other critics is thankless. For a critic to be accurate in his analysis he needs prophetic powers to properly assess, praise, or criticize an experimental, enigmatic, or elusive artistic vanguard. With the rebirth of Chicano literature, a new opportunity opened. After an exuberance of amateurish poetry, the landscape changed dramatically with the bildungsroman of Tomás Rivera, with the complex meditation Peregrinos de Aztlán, by Miguel Méndez, and with the "pícara" Estampas del Valle, by Rolando Hinojosa. To fully appreciate their artistic vision, with its enduring themes and carefully crafted prose, the critic needs rare bilingual and bicultural sensitivities and a universal perspective to properly value these gems of Chicano literature. From the start Tatum has been at the forefront of the evaluation of our artistic endeavors. Undoubtedly, he has carved himself a place among other experts of Chicano letters with his comprehensive analysis of our literature.
—Saúl Cuevas
(Translated by Saúl Holguín De La Cruz)

Charles M. Tatum (1943–) has been recognized as a pioneer and important contributor to the field of literary studies and Chicano popular culture. His book, Chicano Literature, *was published in Mexico in translation. It has been influential in introducing Chicano letters in both the United States and the Spanish-speaking countries. In 1980 he cofounded and coedited* Studies in Latin American Popular Culture, *an important journal that focuses on Latin American and Latino/a popular culture. Tatum has taught at the University of Arizona since 1987. He has been head of the Spanish Department and later Dean of the College of Humanities, where he authored a 160-page report, Chartering a University of Arizona Course Towards Becoming an Hispanic Serving Institution: Recommendations, at the request of Peter Likins, former President of the University of Arizona. Tatum has also served as an Arizona Humanities Council member and as the president and on the board of the Recovering the U.S. Hispanic Literary Heritage Project since the early 1990s.*

The interview with Charles was conducted at the University of Arizona in 2010 and continued in a number of e-mail correspondences from 2010 to 2013.

* * *

Charles, where were you born? Describe your childhood and the place where you grew up.

I was born in El Paso, Texas, in 1943, but I never lived there, even though my family often visited my mother's and father's families. My mother's family traces its Spanish/Mexican ancestry to Juan de Anza, who charted an inside route from northern Sonora to the San Francisco Bay area, where he founded the Presidio in 1776. I spent my childhood and part of my adolescence in Parral, Chihuahua, where both my father and mother were employed by the American Smelting and Refining Company (ASARCO). Spanish and English were spoken in our home as well as among my friends, who were mainly Mexican, American, and Canadian. My mother's family in El Paso, like typical border-region people, spoke both English and Spanish as well as that special border language with all its retruécanos, or puns. In sum, I spent my childhood in an intensely bilingual and bicultural environment, a true blessing. As a child I became progressively aware of class, national origin, and ethnic differences. There existed great differences between those from this side of the border and the parralenses (people from Parral), and those who belonged to middle- and working-class Mexican families, as well as the great majority of the Mexican population. Those class prejudices were very strong within my own Mexican American family. Our family was middle class. As far as being bilingual and bicultural, my childhood left a tremendous and completely positive impact on my formation as a person. For me, Parral remains, as parralenses often say, "la capital del mundo," although I have not visited there for many years.

How did your academic preparation begin?

My elementary education took place in a very small one-room school in La Prieta in Parral, Chihuahua, one of many mining camps established for employees of ASARCO. My mother was my teacher for all of my elementary school education. She was an excellent teacher who was very demanding. She was very good at admonishing me at school during the day and at home at night. The good thing is that as a child I learned very quickly how to dedicate myself to my studies even though I also was a travieso. At fourteen years of age, I left for Colorado to attend a Catholic Benedictine school in Canyon City. I spent my four years of high school there receiving a solid pre-college education, especially in math, science, and Latin. I received my BA degree from the University of Notre Dame, first majoring in pre-law, hasta que se me prendió el foco in my second year at the university when I took a survey course on Spanish Peninsular literature as an elective. I then concentrated for my remaining time at Notre Dame on taking advanced undergraduate courses in Spanish and introductory literature courses in Italian. I was fortunate in having very good mentors among the Spanish and Italian faculty. I graduated in 1965 and was awarded a Fulbright Fellowship to pursue courses for a year (1965–1966) in Madrid. Although I had grown up in Mexico, living in another Spanish-speaking country was very rewarding and contributed greatly to my intellectual development and cultural breadth. My second daughter was born in Madrid, so the experiences associated with this and raising a young family opened up for us a unique set of cultural and other experiences, such as trying to negotiate the Spanish medical system and trying to obtain a birth certificate at the ayuntamiento for our new daughter. My lexicon also expanded as I found that sometimes my Mexican Spanish was not readily understood; more than one shopkeeper corrected my usage sometimes with a tone of utter disdain. As a Fulbright Fellow, I spent my time in Madrid attending courses at La Universidad Complutense and reading the works of post–Spanish Civil War novelists, many of whom were in exile. I attempted to interview a few, but I was not always successful, mainly because of the dominant attitude of fear and suspicion that made such interviews difficult. The year in Spain (1965–1966) was a period when the Franco dictatorship was strong and particularly intolerant of dissent from any quarter, including that of students and intellectuals. The repression was manifested in the perpetual strikes and demonstrations at the university. It was common to witness the university student protests and the violent reaction from the municipal police—the much feared and hated grises who dressed in grey uniforms. I distinctly remember coming out of the subway La Moncloa—a transfer location from the trolley that ran to the university—to face a group of demonstrators fleeing the grises, who were moving through the crowd on horses wielding long, heavy clubs. The year in Madrid left an indelible mark on me in terms of my intellectual and political awakening.

When my young family and I returned to the United States in May 1966, the country was going through an intensive period of political and social upheaval associated with the beginning of the civil rights era, the beginning of the Vietnam War protests, the women's movement, and especially the Chicano, African American, and American Indian movements. I had chosen to pursue my MA in Spanish and Latin American literature at Stanford, a fortuitous choice in terms of my continuing concientización; the San Francisco Bay Area was one of the country's centers of social unrest and progressive political organizing. I soon became a member of the fledgling Peace and Freedom Party of California, a new far Left political organization that was trying to get its candidates on municipal and state ballots. The Stanford campus—where David Harris, the student body president, regularly challenged students at public rallies on campus to get actively involved in political organizing—provided a rich and rewarding environment for my further politicization. Although I did not participate in any of the César Chávez/Dolores Huerta United Farm Workers events in and around Delano during my two years in California, I was active in some of the early boycott activities in Palo Alto and Menlo Park. In my first year of MA studies at Stanford I became very disillusioned with my graduate program that at the time put a lot more emphasis on Spanish Peninsular literature than on Latin American literature. With the exception of a brilliant and student-friendly new professor from Harvard who made the study of Cervantes and the Golden Age dramatists both exciting and challenging, most of my professors seemed tradition bound in their approach to literary studies. So upon finishing the MA degree in 1968, I left for Albuquerque, where I began my doctoral studies at the University of New Mexico (UNM). My keen interest in Latin American literature was enthusiastically welcomed in a department that had several Latin Americanists on its faculty. This was to become one of the most important decisions in my academic trajectory. By contrast to the faculty at Stanford, my professors at UNM challenged us with the latest theories of criticism as they invited their graduate students to look at literary texts in very different ways. And although graduate courses in Chicano/a literature were not yet offered at UNM, my studies did afford me an opening in that direction that would set a course for my entire career.

How did you get introduced to Chicano literature?

In the 1969 spring semester, I was teaching a class for native Spanish speakers, as Heritage Learners were then known. The class consisted of students from throughout New Mexico. I remember distinctly when a group of these students approached me after class one day to request permission to miss several days of attendance. I asked them where they were going and what they would be doing during their absence. They excitedly told me that they would be attending the first Crusade for Justice youth conference organized by Rodolfo "Corky" González in Denver, Colorado, on March 27, 1969. I, of course, knew about "Corky" and his political activity in Denver, so I took a risk as a lowly graduate student with no real authority to grant them such permission, but I asked them to do written and oral reports on the conference when they returned. I remember how enthusiastic they were when they returned, particularly when I responded favorably to their request to organize a course on Chicano literature. At that time there was hardly any course material for such an endeavor. *El Espejo* and *El Grito* had been published, but no anthology of Chicano literature or other materials written in Spanish were readily available for classroom use. I asked the students to prepare the curriculum for the course themselves by, as a start, gathering proverbs, riddles, dichos, short stories, corridos, and other song forms from individuals in their families and their wider communities. I knew that northern New Mexico as well as southern New Mexico were areas that were rich in literary oral history passed on from generation to generation; I was confident that they would succeed. The students returned from their summer break inspired by what they had collected and ready to take the next step. Together we worked out a preliminary syllabus that I then took to the head of the Spanish Department to request that an experimental Chicano content literature and culture course be created. Happily, his response was positive and enthusiastic. This, then, was my introduction to Chicano literature, thanks in large measure to the commitment and vision of my students. I taught the course the next semester, supplementing the materials gathered by the Chicano students with photocopies of some literature in Spanish gleaned from the Zimmerman Library shelves. I had already committed myself to writing my PhD dissertation on José Donoso, a Chilean novelist, but the creation of that Chicano course completely changed my academic focus. The dissertation provided material for several articles and presentations, but my post-PhD research very soon turned decidedly toward the burgeoning field of Chicano literature, which along with Chicano popular culture has dominated my research and much of my teaching for over forty years. I, along with dozens of other graduate students and faculty members across the Southwest and California, received no formal training in Chicano literature. Most of us were trained to pursue our careers as professors of Spanish Peninsular or Latin American literature and a few as professors of American literature. I was fortunate to get to know Felipe de Ortego y Gasca, who was just finishing a dissertation in the English Department at UNM on the importance of Mexican American literature within the American literary tradition. Felipe, then, was a real pioneer in providing a strong intellectual foundation for this emerging field of Chicano literature. His PhD dissertation was titled "Backgrounds of Mexican American Literature." I quickly obtained a copy of it from dissertations made available by the University of Michigan, who published dissertation abstracts and whole dissertations on demand. His dissertation gave me a much-needed background in the history and development of

Chicano literature. It also served to dispel the notion that this literature burst forth in the 1960s, as a kind of isolated phenomenon.

I received my PhD in 1971 and my first academic work was in Minnesota, at a rural branch campus of the University of Minnesota located in Morris. I was very fortunate in making early connections with Nick Kanellos and Luis Dávila at a couple regional conferences. They had recently founded *Revista Chicano Riqueña*. I remember one memorable conference held at Indiana University Bloomington, where I met Rudy Anaya, Tomás Rivera, Rolando Hinojosa, and several Chicano critics such as Juan Bruce Novoa, Ray Paredes, and Frank del Pino. I felt welcomed into this small community of scholars who had a common purpose to put Chicano literature on the American literary map.

Did you teach Chicano literature at the University of Minnesota, Morris?

No. I was given responsibility for courses in Latin American literature as well as basic first- and second-year Spanish grammar courses. I did, however, write and publish my first articles on Chicano literature while I was there.

And after you left Minnesota?

After I left Minnesota, I took a faculty position in Massachusetts at Holy Cross College, a Jesuit institution, from 1974 to 1976. I didn't teach Chicano literature there either; most of the Spanish-speaking students were Puerto Ricans who had a greater interest in their own emerging U.S. literature. I did, however, invite Juan Bruce Novoa, who was then an assistant professor at Yale, to give a couple of talks at Holy Cross. On one occasion, he was accompanied by Rolando Hinojosa, who was visiting Yale. After Holy Cross, I moved with my young family to New Mexico State University (NMSU), in Las Cruces, where I taught from 1976 to 1987. Other than Chicano literature courses that I had offered Heritage Learners at the University of New Mexico when I was a graduate student, I had not had the opportunity to teach Chicano literary content courses until my arrival at NMSU, where my colleagues Sergio Elizondo and Guadalupe Valdés urged me to do so as soon as possible. These colleagues also served as my mentors and taught me a great deal about the culture, language, and literature of the U.S.-Mexico border region. I still owe both of them a debt of gratitude. Sergio, already a published writer, taught me how to navigate the sometimes treacherous waters of Chicano literary studies, especially how to deal with those who had little tolerance for an individual with an Anglo name doing such work. He introduced me to many people such as Américo Paredes, Aristeo Brito, Carlos Vélez-Ibáñez, and Miguel Méndez. He supported and encouraged me to write and publish my first book, *Chicano Literature*, in 1982. I did so with the aid of a yearlong National Endowment for the Humanities Fellowship. It was at NMSU that I regularly taught Introduction to Chicano Studies as well as Chicano literature and culture courses to undergraduate and MA students.

Did you teach Chicano literature when you accepted a position at the University of Arizona?

Of course! I came to the University of Arizona in 1987 as head of the Department of Spanish and Portuguese, and I immediately began teaching undergraduate and graduate courses in Chicano literature, but those courses were already being taught by other colleagues. In fact, Chicano literature and culture courses had been taught in undergraduate and graduate curriculum in the Department of Spanish and Portuguese at the University of Arizona since the late 1960s. Several PhD dissertations had been written on different aspects of Chicano literature in the early 1970s. Also, in the early 1970s, B. Guerrero, a farsighted and inspirational faculty member in the department, had established a strong Spanish for Native Speakers (Heritage Learners) program, one of the first, if not *the* first, in the country. Thus, I found at the University of Arizona a rich ambiente where Chicano literature and culture had been acknowledged and celebrated for almost two decades before I arrived.

Which Chicano authors did you read at the time that influenced your work?

I had already published, in my 1982 book, synopses of the work of many Chicano and Chicana writers including José Antonio Villarreal, Richard Vásquez, Orlando Romero, Fray Angélico Chávez, Nick Vaca, Luis Valdés, Estela Portillo Trambley, Tomás Rivera, Rudy Anaya, Rolando Hinojosa, Oscar "Zeta" Acosta, Lorna Dee Cervantes, Sandra Cisneros, Denise Chávez, Norma Cantú, Gary

Soto, Alberto Alvaro Ríos, Helena María Viramontes, and Alicia Gaspar de Alba. I was not hesitant to require that my students read at least some of these authors, who had published exclusively in English, but I also regularly included works in Spanish by Alicia Gaspar de Alba, Alejandro Morales, Sergio Elizondo, Ricardo Aguilar, Rolando Hinojosa, Miguel Méndez, and Aristeo Brito. I think that it is a disservice to students in Spanish departments if in their courses on Chicano literature we exclude the vast array of Chicano authors who have published only in English. I know that there are those who would disagree with the inclusion of such works in English, but the mix of works in English and Spanish simply reflects the current state of Chicano literature. I have balanced the inclusion of both by requiring that students conduct class discussions, write their papers, and take their exams exclusively in Spanish. The dilemma for those who teach Chicano literature in English departments, where most of the students—and most of the time, the professor—do not speak Spanish, is that they therefore are not comfortable reading Chicano authors who have published only in Spanish. There the dilemma is exacerbated when the course is structured to give students a panoramic view of the evolution of Chicano literature from 1848 on, and especially if one includes precursors such as Alvar Núñez Cabeza de Vaca, Fray Marcos de Niza, and early forms of Spanish poetry and song forms such as the romance, the decimal, and the canción. How does a course exclusively in English do justice to rich oral traditions of dichos, adivinanzas, corridos, and so on? Occasionally, I would also include some works in Spanish translation such as Villarreal's *Pocho* and, later, Cisneros's *Woman Hollering Creek*, but this is a less than ideal alternative.

How about your critical formation?

As stated above, much of my theoretical/critical approach to the analysis of Chicano literature came by way of "learning on the job" since I had received no formal training in examining these texts. I was, however, able to use my knowledge of structuralism and sociological, new historicist, and Marxist theory and criticism early on and, later, cultural studies, reader-response theory, and postcolonial theory proved to be useful. It is fair to say that critical theory has never been my strength. My recent publications are largely derivative, that is, syntheses of what others have theorized. I have thus not contributed theoretically to the field of Chicano literature or offered perceptive critical insights. I am mostly a literary historian and stand aside for my colleagues, including the new generation of young scholars, who are much more conversant with literary and cultural theory. Sometimes I think that twenty-five years as an academic administrator—ten as a department head and fifteen as a dean—have taken their toll in terms of my developing a deeper knowledge and comfort with theory and criticism.

What do you think distinguishes the literary critics of Chicano literature who study in Spanish graduate programs from those who study in English graduate programs at U.S. universities?

I do not believe there is a great difference in terms of the kind of theoretical/critical background and training that they are exposed to during the course of their graduate studies. However, there is a difference in that often those in English graduate programs are limited in their ability to read some of the early foundational texts as well as authors such as Hinojosa, Rivera, Morales, Elizondo, Aguilar, Méndez, Brito, and Gaspar de Alba in the original. Some studies of Chicano literature that are otherwise exemplary fail to include in-depth analyses of these and other authors. I believe that these authors are routinely omitted from courses and reading lists because the literary formation of many academics who teach these courses has been in English departments. Perhaps their lack of fluency in Spanish impedes them from closely examining Chicano authors who write in Spanish. The majority of scholars who study in Spanish graduate programs are Latin Americanists who can draw on the traditions and currents in, for example, Mexican literature in providing a more nuanced elucidation of at least some Chicano texts than those who do not have this academic background.

For undergraduate students who are fluent in both Spanish and English, what do you think is the principal factor that leads them to choose a graduate Spanish program or a graduate English program?

I don't know. Maybe they have the mistaken idea that English departments are superior in terms of their focus on theory; this is definitely not the case. But it is a pity because there is a need for young literary critics to be fully bilingual and to know how to read and write in English and Spanish as well as any other native speaker. Many of them have come from Mexico. Here at the University of Arizona a Mexican student recently finished writing his doctoral thesis on Chicano urban literature. There are also Mexican students who are finishing and others who are beginning their graduate programs. Recently a student from New Mexico came to me inquiring about the relations that existed between Mexico and the United States and between the Chicana and the mexicana. She asked me for a reading list on the subject. I suggested Ana Castillo's *The Mixquiahuala Letters*, Erlinda Gonzales-Berry's *Paletitas de guayaba*, and Sandra Cisneros's *Caramelo*, among other works.

One speaks of Chicano literature as a working-class literature, a blue-collar literature. Do you believe that there are parallels between writers and critics, as far as this is concerned? In other words, does a working-class critic exist in Chicano literature?

I don't believe so, but this is a very good question. I doubt it because that first generation of critics found its own literature that encouraged them to continue forward and earn a PhD and to participate actively in an academic life. I believe that today the new students that are entering the academy are different in nature; in other words they have a different perspective of the job market. More than anything they plan to obtain a PhD for job security. Of course, that was also *my* motivation; I had a family of three children when I finished my doctorate. But I believe that today students are motivated more by job security than by intellectual exploration and scholarly inquiry.

When does your interest in popular culture begin?

That interest began in 1971, when I was teaching at the University of Minnesota, Morris. My first year as a faculty member there, I was asked to explore establishing a summer study abroad program in Mexico, and in that same year we took our first group of students to Cuernavaca, Morelos, which is about a ninety-minute drive south of Mexico City. Being immersed once again in Mexican culture brought to the fore my growing up in Mexico within an ambience of popular culture including the movies of Tin Tan, Cantinflas, Pedro Infante, and Jorge Negrete, among other Mexican cultural icons. Also important during those early years in Mexico were boxing, lucha libre, baseball—from the various baseball leagues from Parral—radio programs, music: mambo, songs from Agustín Lara, and other famous singers from that era. As a child, I had read Mexican comics, among them *La familia Burrón*, but it had never occurred to me to study them and other forms of popular culture as part of my research agenda. I remember that one day in the second year of the program, one of our undergraduate students approached my colleague and friend, Harold E. Hinds Jr., a historian. The student respectfully but pointedly said, "You are missing the point, here on street corners in Cuernavaca there exists a thriving secondary market business in renting and selling an endless number of used Mexican comic books. Why don't you incorporate them into our program of study and into your teaching of the Spanish language and the history of Mexico?" That caught our interest in the subject. One thing quickly led to the next; Harold and I began talking about founding a scholarly journal that in the early 1980s became *Studies of Latin American Popular Culture*, which, now, forty years later, is published by the University of Texas Press. Harold also proposed that we write a book dealing with the Mexican comic book. That book project lasted fifteen years, from the day we started it to the actual publication of the book in 1992 under the title *Not Just for Children: The Mexican Comic Book in the Late 1960s and 1970s*. It would be a decade before I would return to popular culture with the publication in 2001 of my book *Chicano Popular Culture*. And ten years after this I would publish my book on lowriders titled *Lowriders in Chicano Culture: From Low to Slow to Show.*

How does one teach Mexican culture to the Chicano?

This question assumes that Chicano students are not already knowledgeable about Mexican culture. This is not the case at the University of Arizona, where many of my students are second- and third-generation Mexicans who continue to have very strong ties with their families in Mexico. The same is true of other students whose families go back several generations. Living only fifty miles from the U.S.-Mexico border gives the Chicano students at our university a unique advantage in terms of their familiarity with Mexican culture. Language and traditions remain vital within most Chicano families in Tucson. I have learned a great deal from these Chicano students, more than I have taught them about Mexican culture.

Is Mexico interested in the Chicano?

I believe that there are scholars and students in Mexico who are interested in the historical and sociopolitical circumstances of Chicanos, but I do not believe that the general population in Mexico is particularly interested in the unique experience of Chicanos in the United States. Occasionally in the past, Mexican government agencies such as the Secretaría de Educación Pública (The Ministry of Public Education) has had publishing and educational programs that focus on the Chicano experience, but such programs have been only sporadic. This agency translated and published in 1986 my 1982 book on Chicano literature. I am extremely grateful for their willingness to do so.

What is the future of Chicano literature written in Spanish?

The publication of Chicano literature written in Spanish is driven primarily by market forces. Generally speaking, those editorial houses that publish the works of, for example, Sandra Cisneros or Denise Chávez, as well as other Latino/a authors such as Junot Díaz, Oscar Hijuelos, Cristina García, and Julia Alvarez, do not seem interested in publishing in Spanish. In addition, tragically there are only a few writers who have sufficient mastery of the Spanish language to write their works in Spanish. On the other hand, writers such as Sandra Cisneros publish in English and soon afterward a translation is published by the same editorial enterprise. Editorial houses such as Vintage publish Chicano and other Latino writers whose works are then distributed in Mexico, Latin America, Spain, and here in the United States. The future of Chicano literature written in Spanish is bleak.

What are some of the changes that you have seen in Chicano literature from the past to the present?

One of the main ones is the use of the language. Most of the literature that is published today is written in English. I believe that the cultural and social commitment that existed until 1985, even 1990, has diminished. I believe that today's young writers are interested in themes that cut across cultures. They are more concerned about individual and generational issues and less about cultural and historical issues. Although there are exceptions, contemporary writers have largely abandoned an emphasis on social concerns.

Are you currently working on any new projects?

No, none. I retire this year from the University of Arizona.

Any last thoughts concerning your role or function as a critic of Chicano literature? Also, what do you think has been the major impact of your work in relation to Chicano letters?

My impact is minor. I say it with complete humility. I am not one of the pioneers of Chicano criticism, although I have contributed in helping to provide a historical overview of Chicano literature and popular culture and a delineation of some of their recent trends. My contributions have been modest.

Selected Works

Tatum, Charles M. *Chicano Literature*. Boston: Twayne Publishers, 1982.

———. *La literatura chicana*. Translated by Víctor Manuel Velarde. México: Secretaría de Educación Pública, 1986.

———, ed. *Mexican American Literature*. Orlando: Harcourt Brace Jovanovich, 1990.

———. *Chicano Popular Culture: Que hable el pueblo*. Tucson: University of Arizona Press, 2001.

———, ed. *The Literature and Popular Culture of the U.S.-Mexican Border*. Manhattan, KS: Studies in Twentieth Century Literature, 2001.

———. *Chicano and Chicana Literature: Otra voz del pueblo*. Tucson: University of Arizona Press, 2006.

———. *Lowriders in Chicano Culture: From Low to Slow to Show*. Santa Barbara, CA: Greenwood, 2011.

Tatum, Charles M., and Erlinda Gonzales-Berry, eds. *Recovering the U.S. Hispanic Literary Heritage*. Vol. 2. Houston, TX: Arte Público Press, 1996.

Tatum, Charles M., and Harold E. Hinds Jr. *Not Just for Children: The Mexican Comic Book in the Late 1960s and 1970s*. New York: Greenwood Press, 1992.

——. *No sólo para niños: La historieta mexicana en los años sesenta y setenta.* Translated by Francisco Ledesma. Aguascalientes, México: Instituto Cultural de Aguascalientes, 2007.

Tatum, Charles M., and Yvette E. Miller, eds. *Handbook of Latin American Popular Culture.* Westport, CT: Greenwood Press, 1985.

12

Tomás Ybarra-Frausto

Rasquachismo ¿y qué?

IN CONTEMPORARY CHICANO/A LITERATURE, Tomás Ybarra-Frausto will be remembered as a transcendent folklorist, an early graduate student in Chicano/a letters at the University of Washington, a pioneering professor at Stanford University, a charismatic lecturer, and an institutional builder via the Rockefeller Foundation.

The above image comes from witnessing his career up close and from afar: his competing for a teaching position at Stanford in the late 1970s; his classes featuring cutting-edge scholarship; his work with the Mexican Museum in San Francisco; his charming community presentations where he sang like a panadero in the barrio; his help in institutionalizing a doctorate in Chicano/Latino Literature at Stanford; his role in the eight-million-dollar grant that launched the Recovering the U.S. Hispanic Literary Heritage Project; his foreword to Velvet Barrios: Popular Culture and Chicana/o Sexualities *(2003), where he reflects on a post-Movimiento generation that interrogates "youth cultures, politicized spiritualities, constructions of machismo, and eroticized bodies"; his retirement; and his receiving the 2009 NACCS Scholar Award.*

At Arizona State University, I share my former professor's critical essays and books and narrate the Rockefeller grants that helped institutionalize Chicana/o literature and culture—a foundational and exceptional legacy.

—Manuel de Jesús Hernández-G.

Tomás Ybarra-Frausto (1939–) received his PhD in Spanish from the University of Washington. He has worked at the University of Washington, the University of California, San Diego, and Stanford University, where he was a tenured professor in the Department of Spanish and Portuguese. In 1989 Ybarra-Frausto accepted the position of Associate Director for Creativity and Culture at the Rockefeller Foundation in New York, an appointment he held for more than twenty years. In 1998 he was awarded the Joseph Henry Medal by the Smithsonian Institution's Board of Regents in recognition of his work for the institution, and in 2007 the Mexican government awarded him the "Order of the Aztec Eagle" for his lifetime achievement in building mutual understanding between Mexico and the United States through the arts and humanities. Ybarra-Frausto is coeditor of the seminal Literatura Chicana: Texto y contexto *and* Modern Chicano Writers *and has written extensively on Chicano theater and art, including his much acclaimed essay, "Rasquachismo: A Chicano Sensibility."*

The interview with Tomás was conducted through a series of telephone conversations and e-mail correspondences from 2011 to 2013.

* * *

Tomás, where were you born? Describe your childhood and the place where you grew up.

I was born in New Braunfels, Texas. My grandparents had lived there for several generations. My grandfather, Don Francisco Ybarra, owned a ranch where he grew cotton. Every year a family came to work for my grandfather and his sons. My mother, Libertad Frausto, came with her parents on one of those trips. The Fraustos came from northern Texas. At the ranch, my mother fell in love with my father, Nicolás Ybarra, and eventually married him. At that time, New Braunfels was a town completely made up of Germans. My grandfather belonged to the business class of that small population, so in order for him to do business with them he had to speak German. I grew up with my German friends who lived on ranches close to my abuelo's ranch. At home we spoke Spanish, and I learned German from them. When my grandfather lost all of his lands and personal possessions, my father brought him to San Antonio, where I lived most of my life. We lived on the west side of the city, which was the oldest Mexican barrio. I lived in a modest house with my grandfather, my grandmother, and my parents.

My grandfather's ranch was a typical northern Mexican ranch. When my ancestors settled there, the area was still Mexican territory. The ranch resembled the typical ranches in Mexico. I remember that it had long corredores. At the end of one of them there was a jamonera, a place filled with all kinds of abastacimientos: chorizo, hams, cheeses, everything. My grandfather had five sons. My father was his third born. At dinner, everybody sat together: my grandfather, my grandmother, their sons and their wives, the grandchildren, the entire family. When I was four or five years old I was given the responsibility of bringing the tortillas that were placed inside a basket that hung at the end of the hall close to the jamonera. This was a challenge because to do it I had to pass by menacing dogs that were constantly growling at me. But the errand made me feel very courageous. Basically, what I had to do was to lower the basket with a mecate and take the tortillas to the table without the dogs snatching them from me. When I delivered them, my grandfather would say, "Ay, you are a great hero, Tomasito, because you safely brought the tortillas."

At night after dinner, the men would sit in front of the house to talk and play cards. Since I was the first male born of all the grandchildren, I was el príncipe of the ranch; my grandfather always sat me by his side. I listened to the stories until I fell asleep smelling the tobacco that the men smoked. It was a machista culture that we lived in, and my grandfather was the one who mandaba. On several occasions he would tell me, "Look, when you grow up, I am going to teach you how to treat a woman, your wife." My grandfather always wore a white shirt and a watch fob; he was a rancher and dressed in the bourgeois style of those years. His sons' wives ironed all of his shirts and he would show them to me one by one, telling me to look closely at the shirt's collar and the cuffs and indicating that if they had a wrinkle not to wear it because "when you go out to the city you have to wear a well-ironed shirt." My grandfather was an autocratic type and since I was the firstborn male, he would always have me by his side.

It was an interesting life that I lived at the ranch and I remember it very well. Every 16th of September all the Mexicans that lived in the area came to a place where a dance took place. It was called "El salón quemado." It was given that name because a century before, a dance hall built in that same place had burned down. Every September 16, the dance hall was decorated with portraits of Miguel Hidalgo and other Mexican heroes and a platform was built where a person could go and deliver a speech; those who did always finished it with a "Viva México" or "México, beso tu suelo." I would ask my mother why those men bent down as if they were going to kiss the dance hall's floor. She would answer that it was only a symbolic gesture. Another tradition related to the dance hall was a religious one. At Christmas, the women would set up a small crib with a porcelain statue of the Baby Jesus in it. The crib was set up way in the back of the dance hall. As young men entered, they had to kneel and proceed on their knees all the way to the crib to "adorar al Niño" before they would be allowed to dance.

What part of Mexico are your descendents from?

From the north part of Mexico, I believe from the state of Coahuila, from a ranch named San Pedro de las Colonias. I have never been there.

Did the cultural life that you lived with your grandfather and parents influence you growing up?

Yes. In San Antonio there were many people who came from Mexico in the 1920s after the Mexican Revolution, joining those who had settled here from the seventeenth and eighteenth centuries. It was a very Mexican city with a strong Mexican ambience, and that influenced me growing up. For example, several weeks before entering my school—Ivanhoe Elementary—my father sat me down and told me, "Whatever your teacher tells you to do, you have to obey her because in school the teacher is like your mother and you have to do whatever she says." He also selected an atlas with a map of Latin America and told me, "Look, son, you are a Mexican and you speak Spanish. Look at this map. Let's see where Spanish is spoken." He then proceeded to trace with his finger the countries in Central and South America where Spanish was spoken. He said, "America is a continent not a country. You are an American, that's why you speak Spanish." I grew up with this understanding. That's why when my first grade teacher, Miss Moran, told us on our first day of class, "Okay, boys and girls, we're very happy that you are here but in this class we are only gonna speak English because you're in America," I raised my hand and told her, "Miss, miss, my father says that I am an American, that's why I speak Spanish." Bothered by this, she exclaimed "No! Go to the corner!" I was punished. In the 1940s speaking Spanish in school was not permitted.

Did you speak English at the time?

No, I spoke Spanish and some German. It was in school that I started to learn English. My parents told me to keep on speaking Spanish but to learn English, too, because a person who knew two languages "vale por dos." I then told my father, "I want to speak one hundred languages, so that I can be worth one hundred people." He said that the more languages I knew, the more I would become a man of the world. But in the school, we were not allowed to speak Spanish. In the classroom, we spoke English but when we went out on recess we spoke Spanish. Because of that, we had what the school called "language monitors." Every class chose a "language monitor" to report to the teacher which students spoke Spanish at recess. This was terrible because, as far as language was concerned, we served as spies against ourselves. The teachers would punish us. They would hit us with a ruler. "English only!" Think about it, English only! I would complain about this to my father. I would tell him, "You said that we were Americans and that we should speak Spanish." My parents went to school to speak to the teachers—all of them were gringas, and all of us were Mexicans. My father would tell them: "We want our son to speak English, but please we also don't want you to deny him to speak his Spanish language. It is a beautiful language, as beautiful as English. It is the language of our people and we want our son to be bilingual." Like I said before, at that time Spanish was not to be spoken in school, but slowly things began to change. I remember that the teachers taught us some bilingual rhymes. One of them said: "pollito is a chicken, gallina is a hen, el lápiz is a pencil, la pluma is a pen." Now, fíjate nomás how things have changed. Now my old school is named Cleto Rodríguez, a hero from World War II who was awarded the Medal of Honor. Now there are bilingual classes and all the information that is given in school is bilingual. Also, I would say that almost half of the elementary school teachers are Mexican Americans.

Describe San Antonio when you were growing up.

San Antonio in the 1940s had a significant mexicano community. Downtown was like any other Mexican downtown area. There were movie theaters that showed movies in Spanish; there were theaters, like the Teatro Zaragoza, where Mexican theater troupes performed their plays; there was a Mexican bookstore, many restaurants, and a marketplace where Mexican craftwork was sold. We grew up in a Mexican environment where at theater stage shows one listened to songs like "¡Viva México! ¡Viva América!" and where Mexican and U.S. flags were waved simultaneously. People felt that they belonged to two cultures. One felt belonging to what Américo Paredes referred to as "el México de afuera." In effect, this was truly a Mexico outside of Mexico where we added part of the Anglo culture. At home, we had a radio and always listened to Mexican radio stations. I grew up listening to radio programs that featured Inspector Lacroa, Detective Margot, and Dr. IQ on XEW and XEQ. As far as music is concerned, every Friday I listened to Agustín Lara's boleros on his radio program, "La hora azul." I also listened to Toña la Negra and all those artists who came from Mexico: "Desde la capital de México," announced the radio jockey. All the major artists from the Golden Age of Mexican cinema came. They performed in the Teatro Nacional or Zaragoza, the two oldest theaters in the downtown area. But every barrio had its own theater, like the Guadalupe or the Novedades. On Saturday mornings or noon, I went to either the Nacional or Zaragoza Theater. Also, I went to the O'Brien or the Majestic because they showed cowboy and *Tarzan* movies in English. The newspaper *La Prensa* of San Antonio played a major role in fostering a national and international culture in the city. Every Sunday, we received it, and the Sunday section of the newspaper contained literary works from various international poets and writers. Translations of literary works by writers like Charles Dickens were published. For example, my father used to read to us chapters of *Bleak House*. I thought that the author of that work was Mexican and that his name was Dickens! In that sense, we lived in a cosmopolitan culture, since we had within our reach European culture translated into Spanish via Mexico. We were Mexicans and Mexican culture was our culture, even though we had added a bilingual or bicultural layer to it. As far as social-class divisions, there were many rich people from the upper social class that came during the Mexican Revolution. These were Mexican businessmen who, with time, became Mexican Americans. They were the owners of stores and newspapers. Then, there was the middle class. My family belonged to the working class—poor but with steady jobs. Everyone had his or her own specific place in the social order.

But when you finished high school, did you want to leave your community and attend a university outside of Texas?

Fíjate que at that time I didn't think of options because I wanted to stay close to my family. When I was in high school, my family consisted of my parents, my sister, my younger brother, and me. We also had my uncles, aunts, and cousins who lived on the outskirts of San Antonio. I knew that universities like Harvard, Princeton, and Yale existed, but it never crossed my mind to apply to any of them. I was a good student with excellent grades, but I wanted to stay close to Texas and my family, and for that reason I only thought of attending the University of Texas. I arrived at the university at the time where there existed a Mexican American academic tradition. I worked with don Américo Paredes and I took classes with George Sánchez—the great academic from New Mexico—and Carlos Castañeda.

Did you study in the Spanish program?

I earned a BA in the humanities. After that, I declared a major in Spanish. When I was a senior, Tug Andersson, a great professor of French, came from Yale to teach at our university. He had an interest in promoting the teaching of multiple languages to children. I went to study in Italy, in Perugia, and when I returned, I began to work with Andersson teaching in the public schools as a master teacher, even though I had not yet graduated. He had a friend who organized a summer institute for teachers at the University of Washington and who wanted to learn different techniques for teaching languages to children. I was invited to be a master teacher at the institute. I accepted, and I loved the Pacific Northwest so much that I decided to stay in Seattle and finish my undergraduate degree and my doctorate at the University of Washington.

Who were the writers that influenced you?

At school I was immersed in the literature of Anglo America. Emily Dickinson and Walt Whitman influenced me very much. From the Spanish and Latin American world, I was interested in the essay, specifically José Martí's "Nuestra América," José Enrique Rodó's "Ariel," José Vasconcelos's "La Raza Cósmica," and Roberto Fernández Retamar's "Calibán." The literary text and its social context have always fascinated me. My dissertation dealt with Chicano poetry. I don't recall the title of the thesis, I believe it was "The Furrow and the Seed," but it was never published. The idea was that the seed was linked to the farm worker and that literature stemmed from the pueblo's working class. I viewed literature in a social context. One aim was to say that Chicano literature was rooted in the poetry and the everyday language of la gente. I emphasized my research on poets who wrote in newspapers, a source that was also important to my academic formation.

When does your interest in Chicano literature begin?

At the time, I was very involved in the Chicano movement, and I wrote an essay titled "Recuerdo, descubrimiento, y voluntad." The "Recuerdo" part dealt with remembering our cultural reality. The "descubrimiento" part dealt with discovering ourselves and with being proud of who we are. But even if some of us belonged to the upper class, los de arriba; the middle class, los de en medio; and the working class, los de abajo, all of us belonged to the same culture. The "descubrimiento" was that there existed a literature in each one of those social levels. The "voluntad" was the ability to face that reality and fight against racism. The themes presented in that essay could be seen in the writers of the time: Tomás Rivera, Rudolfo Anaya, Raúl Salinas, Abelardo Delgado, and Tino Villanueva, to name a few.

Joseph Sommers played a major role in my academic formation. He was my mentor, not only academically but also ideologically, for he dedicated his life to the most fragile of society: the poor, the marginal. He used to talk about his work in the South, with the African American community way before the start of the civil rights movement. Later, he became involved with the farm workers and the literature of the Mexican Revolution. I also worked with Luis Leal and José Luis Martínez, writers who shared Sommers's ideology. These three critics helped me in my development, for they highlighted the heart of the social, documentary, and protest functions of literature. To me, literature answers three basic questions: Who am I? Where do I come from? Where am I going? All literature is a response to these questions. Those are themes that we all deal with in one form or another. I was trained under this worldview. What I truly learned was that we, the literary critics, try to embrace and balance the tensions that exists between text and social context. All literature has these two elements. One challenge of the critic is to connect them.

How does Literatura Chicana: Texto y contexto / Chicano Literature: Text and Context *come about*?

The book was published in 1972. Joseph Sommers and Antonia Castañeda Shular were key in its formation. At the time, Antonia and I were Sommers's students. When I traveled to eastern Washington, I connected with the migrant workers and I discovered their rich culture. Their daily life experiences and their struggle to survive inspired me to form a theatrical group called El Teatro del Piojo. This was around 1964 or 1965. I gave it that name because when I was in elementary school, the school nurse would come into the classroom to inspect our hair for lice. If you had head lice they would douse you with a white powder. At recess, nobody would play with the kids covered with white powder. They were the piojosos, the unwanted ones, the outsiders. This rejection remained very much ingrained in my consciousness. As an adult, I wanted to turn this negative memory into a positive, and so the piojo became a symbol of social awareness. Since I had studied Spanish theater I presented entremeses, short plays, written by Lope de Vega to the farm workers. *Texto y contexto* was born out of these experiences. It was a book that consisted of three important elements: one, that Chicano literature had a historical background that preceded the Chicano movement of the 1960s; two, that Chicano literature was based on a dynamic culture; and three, that Chicano literature included Hispanic American writers. This last aspect met with some opposition because many critics questioned the inclusion of writers who were not Chicanos. But the purpose of their inclusion was to say that there existed a legacy, a shared cultural experience that belonged to all of us who spoke a similar language—Spanish—in "Nuestra América," as manifested by José Martí.

And Modern Chicano Writers?

That book was a continuation of those three elements found in *Texto y contexto*, but with the inclusion of more contemporary authors who presented fresh voices and literary nuances.

Describe your critical formation.

My critical formation began at the University of Washington, in the Spanish department, with Joseph Sommers and Jean Franco as my mentors. The work of Angel Rama and Fernando Alegría provided me with a critical knowledge of contemporary Latin American literature. I also learned a great deal from don Luis Leal. I would say that critical preparation and knowledge comes from what one studies in books and what one learns from mentors and colleagues.

When does the concept of "lo rasquache" and its cultural context originate?

Well, the genesis of "rasquachismo," or the idea of "lo rasquache," started when I read "Notes on 'Camp,'" the wonderful essay written by Susan Sontag. In that essay she talks about the homosexual community and its internal value systems and secret set of codes. Some of these value systems dealt with the way they dressed and behaved. When I read the article I immediately connected it with Chicanos, for we also had a particular set of systems that only we could understand. One of them dealt with the idea of survival. The base or core of lo rasquache has to do with the saying, "hay que hacer de tripas corazón." In other words, one must take advantage of what small or meager thing one has and make something useful out of it. It's a way of seeing the world, a particular type of existence. Since most Chicanos belong to the working class and are poor, this survival value system has to do with how we act and how we practice the "hacer de tripas corazón." To survive one uses what personal qualities one possesses, and humor is one of them. One uses what we call "las movidas," or strategies to move ahead in life. The Teatro Campesino's construction of the curtains used for the presentation of their "actos" out of material from sacks used to pack agricultural products exemplifies this concept. Members of the Teatro Campesino would sew these sacks together and use them as curtains. To me that was a clear example of how one uses what one has in hand to produce something useful or "hacer de tripas corazón." The rasquachismo concept falls between these lines. It's a result of knowing how to survive through the use of every day "movidas." I thought of this concept as a particular type of sensibility, not a style because a style is something that is frozen, but a sensibility of something that is always changing, like culture itself; a sensibility that is understood especially among the working class. And what is that sensibility? I remembered that as a kid growing up in Texas people said, "mira esa casita que se está cayendo, es una casita rasquache." Or if a person dressed in a shirt whose color did not match the color of their pants, people would say: "mira ese hombre anda vestido muy rasquache." I thought that lo rasquache was a sensibility that had to do with colors or with something that was not codified but was nevertheless understood by everyone. Rasquachismo was an aesthetic representation that belonged to the barrio. For example, if one begins to paint a wall pink and you run out of that color, but you have a can of a maroon color at hand, you would use that color to complete the job. People would comment on the odd combination as being very rasquache. It's an oppositional way of seeing things. I also believe that it has an aesthetic value system; it has a sensibility common to what we know of our culture. For example, I have visited modest homes where the walls are full of graduation, baby, grandchildren, and wedding pictures, all arranged like home altars. A barrio baroque style stands out from that display. One can fittingly say here what in English is referred to as "too much is not enough." In other words, all available spaces must be used. Similar to the baroque style of art, all spaces must be covered with ostentatious decorations. An extreme fear of emptiness or "horror vacui" is present here. We suffer from fear of lo vacio; that's why we cover all walls like altars. We decorate them with pictures, flowers, lights, and countless things. It's an aesthetic form born from envisioning a surplus where there is only the emptiness of poverty.

Tell us about your experience as a professor at Stanford University.

My years at Stanford University were life enhancing. When I arrived there, I was one of those young assistant professors who taught courses in Spanish grammar and literature. I arrived at a time when Chicano literature was starting to gain recognition. I also had the advantage of having Fernando Alegría and Jean Franco as colleagues there. When I arrived at Stanford, the Department of Spanish and Portuguese had a tradition that when new assistant professors were hired, the senior professor, in this case, don Fernando Alegría, would organize a welcome dinner for them. It's kind of an initiation into the academic fold for the new professors. All members of the faculty attend the dinner and one feels an academic family ambience at the gathering. In his welcome speech don Fernando Alegría talked of how literary disciplines changed with time. He commented on how, when he had arrived at Stanford, he and other colleagues introduced the study of Latin American literature. That was innovative because at that time Spanish Peninsular literature was mostly what was taught at Stanford. He said that with my hire things were changing once again, and that I was expanding the discipline because now I was introducing the study of Chicano literature in the department. He told me that I represented the future, while they represented the past, but that the future and the past worked together and that each one of us needed each other to maintain the three components of our literature: the Hispanic (Peninsular), the Latin American, and the Chicano. When he finished, I, being the newest member of the faculty, also had to give a brief speech. What I did was read a poem written by Alurista and emphasize that our Chicano literature was connected to the Anglo American literature—with its use of English—and to Mexican and Latin American literature—with its use of Spanish. I commented on the beauty of Alurista's bilingual poetry and of how it was constructing a new literary language with a new set of metaphors and endless bilingual possibilities. I also said that our literature belonged to that great body of Hispanic literature and that its presence served to enrich it, just as Latin American literature had done before. I was well received at Stanford, and all the new professors were given complete freedom to teach whatever they wanted within the departmental curriculum. I focused on the study of the Latin American and Chicano essay, as well as poetry and Chicano literature in general.

What do you think distinguishes the literary critics of Chicano literature who study in Spanish graduate programs from those who study in English graduate programs at U.S. universities?

I believe that there is a difference. For example, what I have seen and felt is that the literary critics in Spanish departments broaden the study of literature to a social context much more than those in English departments. Latin American literature and Chicano literature seem to emphasize historical and sociological contexts more than the literature studied in English departments.

One speaks of Chicano literature as a working-class literature, a blue-collar literature. Do you believe that there are parallels between writers and critics, as far as this is concerned? In other words, does a working-class critic exist in Chicano literature?

Well, I don't believe that there is necessarily a connection between the social class a writer belongs to and his or her view of the world. I would say that the majority of Chicano critics, including myself, belong to the working class, but not all of us have the same point of view or see literature in the same way. We recognize that there are writers who do not belong to the working class, as was the case of the nineteenth-century Californios—the rich Hispanic landowners from California. They wrote literature, mainly testimonies that dealt with their loss of land and power to the gringos. They feared the downfall of their Hispanic culture and their privileged world. These themes do not exist in working-class literature. What I'm saying is that even though critics might be from the working class, they don't necessarily write about it only. Some of them study the literature of the upper class. What both social classes do share in common is folklore, which exists in all classes because all share the same language and set of cultural traditions.

What do you think is the general attitude that the mexicanos have toward the Chicanos?

First, we have to understand that Mexican culture is highly centralized. People from the Federal District (e.g., Mexico City), the so-called chilangos, believe that they are the masters of the universe. Because of this attitude, people from other parts of the country feel a certain disdain for them. It is said that "donde empieza el cabrito termina la cultura"; in other words, it is believed that the farther one is removed from Mexico City, the more ignorant or uneducated one becomes. Thus, if you cross the Mexican border, north of the Río Bravo, then we Chicanos are considered even more ignorant and uneducated because we are farther away from the center. I remember a conversation that I had in Mexico with some very educated people about pochos. I told them that I was a pocho, but they didn't believe me. They said that I was a Mexican because I understood Mexican culture. I told them that all Mexicans have the potential to be Chicanos. I said that because so many people leave Mexico City to go north that they are bound to have a family member living in the border area or in the United States. Of course they are not going to identify themselves as pochos. I believe that the feeling of superiority that the Mexican has over the Chicano stems from a lack of understanding of one very, very important thing: that the Mexicans do not know what it means to survive in a hostile environment like the one that is experienced in the United States. They don't understand the struggle of the Chicano to maintain his language and culture. They only begin to understand it when a family member comes to this country, attends its schools, and starts to forget the Spanish language. I ask myself, why in Mexico do the indigenous people have to stop speaking their language and learn Spanish to be considered Mexican? We—the Chicanos—do not want to stop speaking Spanish and become gringos. We want to find a way to continue speaking Spanish and English just like in Mexico the indigenous people should continue to speak their indigenous language together with Spanish. Are the indigenous people the pochos of Mexico?

Is it important for you to write in Spanish? In English? Or does it matter what language is used?

I believe that in social and academic terms I have always been on the side of the underdog. I feel that within the academic world, Spanish departments and the language itself are underdogs. For example, for an assistant professor to be considered for tenure he or she needs to publish his or her work in English. That forces the critic to write more in English and less in Spanish. That's what happened to me, and as a result, most of my work is written in English, except when I participate in conferences in Mexico or when I submit a paper for publication in Spain or Latin America. It would be great if ethnic, Latino, or Chicano studies associations would organize conferences that include more panels in Spanish. The great majority of them are presented in English. Things need to change so that young scholars can have more opportunities to present their work in Spanish. But something important about migration today is that the new immigrants who come to the United States bring their language and write their work in a new and refreshing way. This is very important because they help to maintain the Spanish language. I would love the growing Chicano middle class to begin Saturday schools where boys and girls can learn their culture. Retired professors, who will also serve as teachers, would organize these schools. They would educate young people about their bilingual bicultural heritage.

Do you think that Chicano literature written in Spanish will survive?

New immigrants who come to this country from Mexico, the Caribbean, and Central and South America bring with them a new ideology of their experience as well as a refreshing use of the Spanish language. This is positive and rejuvenating because Spanish is spoken in most regions of the United States where Latinos reside. However, I feel that we need to do more to promote the language and practice it. For example, I have noticed that here in San Antonio—a city that is fully bilingual and bicultural—Spanish is losing ground because we don't speak it enough por flojera; it becomes easier for us to speak in English. There needs to be a social change in our attitude toward Spanish so that we can maintain and speak it to our sons and daughters at home and in the community. I believe that Spanish does have a future if we do all of this. Also, in Spanish departments we need to support literary journals written in Spanish like *Puentes* where students can publish their creative writing. In sum, we need to initiate a personal effort to make this happen so that Spanish does not disappear from our cultural identity.

For undergraduate students that are fluent in both Spanish and English, what do you think is the principal factor that leads them to choose a graduate Spanish program or a graduate English program?

I believe that those students who are bicultural have to understand that the language is part of a specific cultural heritage, like food or music. One must maintain this heritage, and even though this heritage is bicultural—Anglo, Hispanic—I would say that the more fragile of the two is the Hispanic culture. We must let the students know that one must have options. Language represents a worldview, and somebody who sees the world in two, three, four ways is better off than one who sees it from one point of view. To be a citizen of the world one must speak several languages.

What do you think of Chicano literature today? What are the most drastic changes that you have seen in Chicano literature in the last decades? How has it changed? Has it evolved or stayed the same?

The changes that I have seen in recent years deal with the experience of those groups that were ignored during the Chicano movement—in other words, the literature written by feminists, gays, lesbians, and other groups who in the past did not have a voice. Equally important is the presence of border literature, a literature that probably started in 1987 with Gloria Anzaldúa's book *Borderlands/La frontera: The New Mestiza*. Now there are new genres like science fiction and the detective and transnational novels. We also see groups of Chicanos in states where in the past they were not well represented, such as Georgia, Alabama, or Kentucky. In their work they express what it means to be Chicano in these regions. One must also mention themes that deal with drug dealers and emergent youth cultures as well as the formation of new Chicano contact zones within the Latino cultural world. In criticism, for example, one now sees comparative studies of Chicano literature and Puerto Rican literature.

Describe your experience working for the Rockefeller Foundation.

It was fantastic to work for an organization—the oldest philanthropic foundation in the United States—whose mission is "to promote the well-being of humanity around the world." I served as Associate Director of Arts and Humanities; the title later changed to Associate Director of Creativity and Culture. In the United States, my work was to facilitate or strengthen the humanities by funding university program projects that "made new knowledge." One of our largest was the Recovering the U.S. Literary Heritage Project that dealt with recovering Hispanic literature in all of its historical periods. Eight books have been produced by the project, all published by Arte Público Press in Houston, Texas. Other projects dealt with the publication of a recompilation of all the newspapers written in Spanish in the United States and a literary anthology called *Herencia*. In Mexico, I worked with the *Fidecomisca para la cultura México–Estados Unidos*, which promoted programs to decentralize the Mexican culture in that country. In other words, we supported the projects of scholars—in different areas of the arts and humanities—who worked outside of Mexico City. We also worked on many projects to strengthen the indigenous cultures in Mexico. A project that I liked very much was the forming of community museums throughout the country where the community could preserve the culture of that particular region. Another important project was the academic exchanges between public and private universities in Mexico and the United States to create bridges of knowledge and a mutual understanding between the two countries. In Latin America I enjoyed working on a project that developed a network of intellectuals who shared their country's particular cultural projects in different parts of Latin America. This network intended to later expand to include the United States and Europe.

Tell us about your latest projects.

All of my life I wanted to be a storyteller. For that reason, I am learning to become one, not through the written word but through the spoken one. I would like to narrate—in a language that everybody can understand—personal experiences that will make people understand the great struggle that we had to face to maintain our biculturalism. I want to narrate the social history of San Antonio, my hometown. For example, I want to write about what the locals did for entertainment, the places they went for recreation, the movie theaters they attended, their oral stories. I continue working with a lot of energy and ánimo on these types of projects.

Any last thoughts concerning your role or function as a critic of Chicano literature? Also, what do you think has been the major impact of your work in relation to Chicano letters?

Well, I belong to the group of compañeros who worked in the great project of cultural affirmation known as the Chicano movement. My role was to tell the story of the Chicano's literary production, in other words, to argue that Chicano literature had a historic base in the United States, one that began in 1848. In literature I promoted the folk base of the Chicano cultural experience. In the theater, I wrote essays on las tandas (variety shows) and las carpas (tent shows). In poetry, I wrote on the poets of the pueblo. I wrote essays on women, muralism, the visual arts, and regional cultural themes, focusing mostly on Texas and California. An essay of mine that is often quoted is the one I wrote on rasquachismo. Even though I don't identify myself as a working-class critic, I can see in reviewing my work that it is based on the everyday expression and speech of the common people. More than anything I feel very proud that my generation was the one that planted the seeds in those literary furrows that now are sprouting so magnificently.

Selected Works

Ybarra-Frausto, Tomás. "Poetry and History: Three Contemporary Chicano Poets." PhD diss., University of Washington, 1979.

——. "Alurista's Poetics: The Oral, the Bilingual, the Pre-Columbian." In *Modern Chicano Writers: A Collection of Critical Writings*, edited by Joseph Sommer and Tomás Ybarra- Frausto, 117–32. Englewood Cliffs, NJ: Prentice Hall, Inc., 1979.

——. "Rasquachismo: A Chicano Sensibility." In *Chicano Aesthetics: Rasquachismo*, 5–8. Phoenix, AZ: MARS, 1989.

Ybarra-Frausto, Tomás, and Alicia Gaspar de Alba, eds. *Velvet Barrios: Popular Culture & Chicana/o Sexualities*. New York: Palgrave Macmillan, 2002.

Ybarra Frausto, Tomás, and Shifra M. Goldman, eds. *Arte Chicano: A Comprehensive Annotated Bibliography of Chicano Art, 1965–1981*. Berkeley: Chicano Studies Library Publications Unit, University of California, 1986.

Ybarra-Frausto, Tomás, and Gerald E. Poyo, eds. *Recovering the U.S. Hispanic Literary Heritage*. Vol. 7. Houston, TX: Arte Público Press, 2009.

Ybarra Frausto, Tomás, and Joseph Sommers, eds. *Modern Chicano Writers: A Collection of Critical Writings*. Englewood, NJ: Prentice Hall, 1979.

Ybarra Frausto, Tomás, Joseph Sommers, and Antonia Castañeda Shular, eds. *Literatura Chicana: Texto y contexto / Chicano Literature: Text and Context*. Englewood Cliff, NJ: Prentice Hall, 1972.

Ybarra-Frausto, Tomás, et al. *Museum Frictions: Public Cultures/Global Transformations*. Durham, NC: Duke University Press, 2006.

References

Acosta, Oscar Zeta. *The Autobiography of a Brown Buffalo*. London: Charisma Books, 1974.

Aldama, Frederick Luis. *Critical Mappings of Arturo Islas's Fictions*. Tempe, AZ: Bilingual Press/Editorial Bilingüe, 2008.

Aranda Jr., José F. *When We Arrive: A New Literary History of Mexican America*. Tucson: University of Arizona Press, 2003.

Arias, Ron. *The Road to Tamazunchale*. Tempe, AZ: Bilingual Press/Editorial Bilingüe, 1997.

Bernal, Vicente. *Las primicias*, edited by Robert N. McLean. Dubuque, Iowa: Telegraph Herald, 1916.

Brito, Aristeo. *El diablo en Texas/The Devil in Texas*. Tempe, AZ: Bilingual Press/Editorial Bilingüe, 1990.

Brown, Claude. *Manchild in the Promised Land*. New York: Signet, 1965.

Bruce-Novoa, Juan. *Chicano Authors: Inquiry by Interview*. Austin: University of Texas Press, 1980.

——. *Retrospace: Collected Essays on Chicano Literature*. Houston, TX: Arte Público Press, 1990.

Cervantes, Lorna Dee. *Emplumada*. Pittsburgh: University of Pittsburgh Press, 1981.

Chacón, Eusebio. *El hijo de la tempestad; Tras la tormenta la calma: Dos novelitas originales*. Santa Fe, NM: El Boletín Popular, 1892.

Duke dos Santos, María, and Patricia de la Fuente, eds. *Sabine R. Ulibarrí: Critical Essays*. Albuquerque: University of New Mexico Press, 1995.

Garza-Falcón, Leticia M. *Gente Decente: A Borderlands Response to the Rhetoric of Dominance*. Austin: University of Texas Press, 1998.

Gonzales-Berry, Erlinda. "Chicano Literature in Spanish: Roots and Content," PhD diss., University of New Mexico, 1978.

——. "Vicente Bernal and Felipe M. Chacón: Bridging Two Cultures." In *Pasó por aquí: Critical Essays on the New Mexican Literary Tradition, 1542–1988*, edited by Erlinda Gonzales-Berry, 185–98. Albuquerque: University of New Mexico Press, 1989.

———. *Paletitas de guayaba*. Albuquerque, NM: El Norte Publications, 1991.

González-T., César A., ed. *Rudolfo A. Anaya: Focus on Criticism*. La Jolla, CA: Lalo Press, 1990.

Gurpegui, José Antonio, ed. *Alejandro Morales: Fiction Past, Present, Future Perfect*. Tempe, AZ: Bilingual Press/Editorial Bilingüe, 1996.

Gutiérrez y Muhs, Gabriella, ed. *Rebozos de palabras: An Helena María Viramontes Critical Reader*. Tucson: The University of Arizona Press, 2013.

Herrera-Sobek, María. *The Bracero Experience: Elitelore versus Folklore*. Los Angeles: UCLA Latin American Center Publications, University of California, Los Angeles, 1979.

———. Introduction to *Beyond Stereotypes: The Critical Analysis of Chicana Literature*, edited by María Herrera-Sobek, 9–28. Binghamton, NY: Bilingual Press, 1985.

———. "The Politics of Rape: Sexual Transgression in Chicana Fiction." In *Chicana Creativity and Criticism: Charting New Frontiers in American Literature*, edited by María Herrera-Sobek and Helena María Viramontes, 171–81. Houston, TX: Arte Público Press, Mexico/Chicano Program, University of California, Irvine, 1988.

———. "Solitaria." In "La mujer chicana y mexicana del siglo XXI: Ellas tienen la palabra," edited by Jesús Rosales. Special issue, *Puentes: Revista méxico-chicana de literatura, cultura y arte* 7 (Otoño 2009): 9.

———. "Fronteras." In "La mujer chicana y mexicana del siglo XXI: Ellas tienen la palabra," edited by Jesús Rosales. Special issue, *Puentes: Revista méxico-chicana de literatura, cultura y arte* 7 (Otoño 2009): 90.

Hinojosa-Smith, Rolando. *Estampas del Valle y otras obras*. Berkeley: Quinto Sol, 1973.

———. *Klail City y sus alrededores*. La Habana, Cuba: Casa de las Américas, 1976.

———. *El condado de Belken: Klail City*. Tempe, AZ: Bilingual Press/Editorial Bilingüe, 1994.

Kanellos, Nicolás. *A History of Hispanic Theatre in the United States: Origins to 1940*. Austin: University of Texas Press, 1990.

———. *Hispanic Periodicals in the United States, Origins to 1960: A Brief History and Comprehensive Bibliography*. Houston, TX: Arte Público Press, 2000.

———. "An Overview of Hispanic Literatures of the United States." In *Herencia: The Anthology of Hispanic Literature of the United States*, edited by Nicolás Kanellos et al., 1–32. New York: Oxford University Press, 2003.

Keller, Gary. "About Clásicos Chicanos / Chicano Classics." In *The Fifth Horseman*, by José Antonio Villarreal, v. Binghamton, NY: Bilingual Press, 1984.

———. "The Image of the Chicano in Mexican, United States, and Chicano Cinema: An Overview." In *Chicano Cinema: Research, Reviews, and Resources*, edited by Gary Keller, 13–58. Binghamton, NY: Bilingual Press, 1985.

———. "On Contemporary Chicana and Chicano Art: A Project Designed to Meet Las Alturas de las Circunstancias." In *Contemporary Chicana and Chicano Art: Artists, Works, Culture, and Education*, vols. 1 and 2, edited by Gary Keller et al., 13–18. Tempe, AZ: Bilingual Press, 2002.

Leal, Luis. *Decade of Chicano Literature, 1970–1979: Critical Essays and Bibliography*. Santa Barbara, CA: Editorial La Causa, 1982.

———. *Aztlán México: Perfiles literarios e históricos*. Binghamton, NY: Bilingual Press, 1985.

Lomelí, Francisco, and Julio Martínez, eds. *Chicano Literature: A Reference Guide*. Westport, CT: Greenwood Press, 1985.

Lomelí, Francisco, and Donaldo W. Urioste. Introduction to *Chicano Perspectives in Literature: A Critical and Annotated Bibliography*, 9–13. Albuquerque, NM: Pajarito Publications, 1976.

———, eds. *De Colores: Journal of Chicano Expression and Thought: Chicano Literature and Criticism* 3, no. 4. Albuquerque, NM: Pajarito Publications, 1977.

Méndez, Miguel. *Peregrinos de Aztlán*. Tempe, AZ: Bilingual Press/Editorial Bilingüe, 1991.

Ortego y Gasca, Felipe de. "Backgrounds of Mexican American Literature." PhD diss., University of New Mexico, 1971.

———, ed. *We Are Chicanos: An Anthology of Mexican-American Literature*. New York: Washington Square Press, 1973.

Otero, Miguel Antonio. *My Life on the Frontier, 1864–1882*. New York: Press of the Pioneers, 1935.

———. *The Real Billy the Kid: With New Light on the Lincoln County War*. New York: R. F. Wilson, 1936.

———. *My Life on the Frontier, 1882–1897*. Albuquerque: University of New Mexico Press, 1939.

Padilla, Genaro. *My History, Not Yours: The Formation of Mexican American Autobiography*. Madison: The University of Wisconsin Press, 1993.

Paredes, Américo. "The Folk Base of Chicano Literature." In *Modern Chicano Writers: A Collection of Critical Essays*, edited by Joseph Sommers and Tomás Ybarra-Frausto, 4–17. Englewood Cliffs, NJ: Prentice Hall, Inc., 1979.

Paz, Octavio. *El laberinto de la soledad*. México: Fondo de Cultura Económica, 1959.

Rebolledo, Tey D. *Women Singing in the Snow: A Cultural Analysis of Chicana Literature*. Tucson: University of Arizona Press, 1995.

Rebolledo, Tey D., and Eliana S. Rivero, eds. *Infinite Divisions: An Anthology of Chicana Literature*. Tucson: University of Arizona Press, 1993.

Rivera, Tomás. *. . . y no se lo tragó la tierra*. Berkeley: Quinto Sol, 1971.

Rodríguez, Juan. "Notes on the Evolution of Chicano Prose Fiction." In *Modern Chicano Writers: A Collection of Critical Essays*, edited by Joseph Sommers and Tomás Ybarra-Frausto, 67–85. Englewood Cliffs, NJ: Prentice Hall, Inc., 1979.

Saldívar, José. *The Dialectics of Our America: Genealogy, Cultural Critique, and Literary Theory*. Durham, NC: Duke University Press, 1991.

Sánchez, Marta E. *"Shakin' Up" Race and Gender: Intercultural Connections in Puerto Rican, African American, and Chicano Narratives and Culture (1965–1995)*. Austin: University of Texas Press, 2005.

Sánchez, Rosaura. *Chicano Discourse: Socio-Historic Perspectives*. Rowley, MA: Newbury House Publishers, Inc., 1983. Reprinted, Houston, TX: Arte Público Press, 1994.

Sánchez, Rosaura, and Beatrice Pita. Introduction to *The Squatter and the Don*, by María Amparo Ruiz de Burton. Edited by Rosaura Sánchez and Beatrice Pita, 5–51. Houston, TX: Arte Público Press, 1992.

Sommers, Joseph, and Tomás Ybarra-Frausto, eds. *Modern Chicano Writers: A Collection of Critical Essays*. Englewood Cliffs, NJ: Prentice Hall, Inc., 1979.

Sommers, Joseph, Tomás Ybarra-Frausto, and Antonia Castañeda Shular. Preface to *Literatura Chicana: Texto y contexto / Chicano Literature: Text and Context*, edited by Joseph Sommers, Tomás Ybarra-Frausto, and Antonia Castañeda Shular, xxi–xxii. Englewood Cliffs, NJ: Prentice Hall, Inc., 1972.

Stavans, Ilan. *Bandido: Oscar "Zeta" Acosta and the Chicano Experience*. New York: HarperCollins, 1995.

Thomas, Piri. *Down These Mean Streets*. New York: Knopf, 1967.

Torres, Hector A. *Conversations with Contemporary Chicana and Chicano Writers*. Albuquerque: University of New Mexico Press, 2007.

Trambley, Estela Portillo. *Rain of Scorpions and Other Stories*. Tempe, AZ: Bilingual Press/Editorial Bilingüe, 1993.

Urioste, Donaldo W., and Francisco A. Lomelí, eds. "Hacer crítica o ser criticado." In *De Colores: Journal of Chicano Expression and Thought: Chicano Literature and Criticism,* vol. 3, no. 4. Albuquerque, NM: Pajarito Publications, 1977.

Venegas, Daniel. *Las aventuras de don Chipote o cuando los pericos mamen*. México: Secretaría de Educación Pública, 1984.

Villanueva, Tino. *Shaking off the Dark*. Tempe, AZ: Bilingual Press/Editorial Bilingüe, 1998.

About the Author

Jesús Rosales was born in Durango, Mexico, and raised in Santa Barbara, California. He received his BA from the University of California, Los Angeles (UCLA), and his MA and PhD from Stanford University. Rosales's main research interests deal with Chicana/o literary history and Chicana/o literature written in Spanish. He has written *Alejandro Morales: Encuentro, historia y compromiso social* (Peter Lang, 1999) and is the founder and editor of *Puentes: Revista méxico-chicana de literatura, cultura y arte*. Rosales is currently an associate professor of Chicana/o literature at Arizona State University.